Tales of Texas Cooking

Tales of Texas Cooking:
Stories and Recipes from the Trans Pecos to the Piney Woods and High Plains to the Gulf Prairies

Edited by Frances B. Vick

Publications of the Texas Folklore Society LXX

Kenneth L. Untiedt, General Series Editor

University of North Texas Press

Denton, Texas

Permissions:
University of North Texas Press
1155 Union Circle #311336
Denton, TX 76203-5017

The paper used in this book meets the minimum requirements of the American National
Standard for Permanence of Paper for Printed Library Materials, z39.48.1984.
Binding materials have been chosen for durability.

Library of Congress Cataloging-in-Publication Data

Tales of Texas cooking : stories and recipes from the Trans Pecos to the Piney Woods and
    High Plains to the Gulf prairies / edited by Frances Brannen Vick. -- Edition: first.
    pages cm. -- (Publications of the Texas Folklore Society ; LXX) includes index.
    ISBN 978-1-57441-618-3 (cloth : alk. paper) -- ISBN 978-1-57441-628-2 (ebook)
1. Cooking--Texas. 2. Tales--Texas. 3. Texas--Social life and customs. I. Vick, Frances
Brannen, 1935– editor. II. Series: Publications of the Texas Folklore Society ; no. 70.
            TX715.2.S69T35 2015
            641.59764--dc23
            2015031823

*Tales of Texas Cooking: Stories and Recipes from the Trans Pecos to the Piney Woods
and High Plains to the Gulf Prairies* is Number LXX in the Publications
of the Texas Folklore Society

The electronic edition of this book was made possible by the support
of the Vick Family Foundation.

Dedicated

to

Francis Edward Abernethy

who brought so much to the Society that it cannot be measured.
He became editor of publications in 1971, taking over from
Dobie, Boatright, Hudson and others, becoming a giant among
giants for the 33 years he reigned.

He wrote, "The purpose of the Texas Folklore Society is . . . to
let that light so shine among men that all the world, but Lord,
most especially Texans may see the richness of the land and its
people and its continuity. In this land and its history
and its people Texans must realize the place of their belonging, a
mother land to moisten with their sweat, and finally
to nourish with their bones."

Rest in Peace, Ab Abernethy.
You will be sorely missed and always remembered by
the Texas Folklore Society you so loved.

CONTENTS

Stories and Recipes from the Blackland Prairies

Stories and Recipes from the Cross Timbers and Prairies

Stories and Recipes from the Edwards Plateau

PREFACE

This Publication of the Texas Folklore Society (#70) was several years in the making, gathering all the ingredients and carefully mixing them together to get this final product. Okay, that was as close to a pun as I'll come when describing what it took to create the book that you hold in your hands. As you can tell, it contains a lot of recipes; however, I trust that you'll come to find that it's much more than a mere cookbook that features the many diverse foods that people from Texas enjoy cooking and eating. This volume contains the lore that explains what is significant about those foods, and why they mean so much to us as a culture. Food is essential to everyone's existence, of course, but the rituals, recipes, and events behind what and how we eat are what bring us together and identify us as a group. Many cultural groups exist in Texas and the Southwest, but by examining the ways those groups celebrate their foods and the customs associated with them proves that the way we process and consume the nutrients vital to our survival is about much more than merely sustaining life . . . it's what binds us together.

In addition to a brief Preface, this PTFS includes an Introduction; this first chapter was written by Fran Vick, and it takes a deeper look at the reasoning behind doing an entire publication on this topic. She explains that these recipes—and especially the stories behind them—provide insight into intimate memories of family gatherings and loved ones who are no longer with us. The stories also commemorate the customs, rituals, foods, and methods passed down from one generation to another. Many of these works reveal the private feelings and experiences of the contributors, but in the end the food lore represented in this book is something that we can all relate to, in some way or another.

I'm grateful for Fran's efforts, to say the least. As much as I wanted to see this book done, I just couldn't seem to get the types of contributions necessary; Fran asked to take it over, and I gladly accepted her offer. She had apparently been interested in the project from the time I first announced my intentions, and she wanted to take on the role as "guest-editor." I turned over the files we had collected, Fran added what she had already, and then she began calling individually on others she knew had something to contribute. You'll find that some of the pieces have been printed elsewhere, either exactly as you see them here, or in another form, with some variation to make them more completely fit our purpose with this publication.

I thank Fran for her hard work on putting this volume together. I also give thanks to all of the contributors who wrote articles for this book. As always, I thank my colleagues and administrators at Stephen F. Austin State University who support the Society's efforts: Mark Sanders, Chair of the Department of English, and Brian Murphy, Dean of the College of Liberal and Applied Arts. I again thank the folks at the UNT Press for their dedication to the Texas Folklore Society and our long tradition of preserving and presenting the lore of Texas and the Southwest.

Although I usually provide some sort of dedication for each PTFS, this time Fran is doing that specifically.

Kenneth L. Untiedt
Stephen F. Austin State University
Nacogdoches, Texas
May 25, 2015

INTRODUCTION

by Frances B. Vick

When Ken Untiedt announced the topic of a Texas Folklore Society cookbook publication, my mind went off in several different directions. One of the first was remembering what that Renaissance woman—Jean Andrews, The Pepper Lady—had written about food: "Although food is eaten as a response to hunger, it is much more than filling one's stomach to satisfy nutritional requirements; it is also a premeditated selection and consumption process providing emotional fulfillment. The way in which food is altered reveals the function of food in society and the values that society supports."[1] So, the members of the Texas Folklore Society would not only be giving the recipe(s) of a particular food eaten in their family, they would also be telling the story of their people who ate it and defining them as well.

Another interesting comment of Jean's was her surprise at the lack of study of foodways. And indeed, the study of foodways was for a long time neglected, which is peculiar since all of us have to partake of food to survive. Some have felt that the reason it was not studied was that food preparation was basically a duty of the female, but that doesn't hold water when you think of the cowboys on the trail, the buffalo hunters, the army, the Texas Rangers, and other men who have wandered the trails of Texas. See, for example, Riley Froh's piece on Government Packer Grub or Robert Wilson's journal. However, Jean would be surprised today to see that the lack of study has come to a halt. She could watch a whole television channel devoted to food, with its popularity gaining daily. Furthermore, there are very popular food shows on the major networks, all of them producing foodways stars. Indeed, "foodways" has become a burgeoning industry. The food stars are turning out books. Blogs and Facebook pages on the Internet are full of recipes and stories of food. Many of us are entertained by the chefs—male and female—who have their own shows and are as famous as Rock stars.

However, the greatest joy for many of us is still to get in the kitchen and, inspired by the foodways stars, devise our own recipes around the likes and dislikes of our family. Of course, there can be some differences of opinion, as in the great chili fight between Jean and David Schnitz. However, by and large the family generally agrees on what it will and will not eat. For many families the fun is for the whole group to get in the kitchen and cook together, each one having his or her own duty to perform in putting the meal together and getting it on the table.

In reading about the history of foodways, I was surprised to learn that when the first colonists landed in Virginia and discovered the new food of the Indians, a number of the families were sent to live with the Indians and learn about these new strange foods that sustained the natives. If they were to survive, they needed to be able to recognize edible roots and learn how to cook them. They soon learned that corn would be a staple for them in making bread, ash cakes and hoecakes, so called because they were baked on a hoe held close to the fire. From hoecakes the recipes went to corn pones to corn sticks to Johnny cake to hush puppies. One of the wonders they discovered was that the squaws built fires by the cornfields to boil water, into which they tossed freshly picked and husked ears of corn. Then they ate it by moving the cobs across their mouths like harmonicas. The colonists accepted this, and also the mixing of corn with beans and meat. They observed the Indians using ashes and water to remove the skin from dried corn kernels, making them white and puffed. When this hominy was mixed with meat and wild greens, there was a new flavor altogether. As was noted, "Virginia cooks did more than accept the hulled dried corn called hominy; they made a sort of southern fetish of it."[2] And that fetish lives today as grits.

Virginia was also the home of the first regional cookbook for Americans, published in 1824—*The Virginia Housewife*, by Mary Randolph. There was less of the English tradition and more of other influences on foodways in the United States. She devoted an entire section to vegetables and featured some not used in England, such as sweet potatoes, pumpkins, squashes, and tomatoes. She was also the first to recommend boiling fresh young turnip tops with bacon.[3]

Other influences on our foodways are from Louisiana, with its French and Creole cooking. They, too, adapted the foods they found in the new land. The Louisianans saw and used the powdered sassafras leaves from the Choctaws for the modern version of gumbo filé. They picked up peppers from the Spanish, especially cayenne and Tabasco. Those combined with tomatoes were foundations of Creole cooking.[4]

Texas has a bountiful supply of ethnic groups influencing foodways. According to the Institute of Texan Cultures in San Antonio you will find African-American, Anglo-American, Belgian, Chinese, Czech, Danish, Dutch, English, Filipino, French, German, Greek, Hungarian, Irish, Italian, Japanese, Jewish, Lebanese and Syrian, Native-American, Norwegian, Polish, Scottish, Swedish, Swiss, Tejanos, Vietnamese, and Wendish.[5] There are no doubt more. So, the foods from all of those groups are to be found in Texas, sometimes blended with other groups, sometimes not. The Institute says: "Texas food is the perfect metaphor for the blending of diverse cultures and native resources. Food is comfort, yet at times, is political and contested because we are often what we eat—meaning, what is available and familiar and allowed. Food is a symbol of our success and our communion, and whenever possible, Texans tend to do food in a big way."[6]

Some of the observations I encountered along the way are surprising. According to John T. Edge in *The Southern Foodways Alliance: Community Cookbook*, gravy is something "born of privation"; that will be news to those of us who love it. However, what he writes makes sense: "When folks are poor, folks make do. Which means folks make gravy."[7] They "make do" with fat and flour and liquid. Obviously, we took that "make do" and made something good out of it to put on biscuits, chicken fried steaks and potatoes, to name just a few uses of gravy. Jean Schnitz's mother-in-law gave her a gravy recipe that Jean labels "Most Important Recipe!" And others have written that their mothers could make dinners expand to provide for surprise guests just by adding more flour to the gravy to make it stretch and by making the biscuits smaller.

Edge also tells us that we take comfort in our roots, that is, potatoes, rutabagas, turnips, sweet potatoes, beets, parsnips, radishes, onions, garlic and shallots.[8] He allows that an integral part if not the centerpiece of a southern meal could well be collards, turnips, kale, cabbage, dandelion, mustard greens—"simple, nutritious food that transcends race and class."[9] He says corn remains the major component of the region's culinary tradition, providing the basis of breads, grits, dumplings and fritters, and also being distilled as corn whiskey, "one of the most notable contributions of the Scotch-Irish to American culture."[10]

Fried chicken speaks to all of us. It brings back childhood memories of the "pulley bone" or "wish bone" and who would get to pull it, with the one who had the larger piece after the breaking having their wish come true. In the old days everyone had a couple of chickens in the yard, which kept the family in eggs. And there were usually enough to have a chicken to fry on Sunday.[11] This dish in particular is defined by place and memory for many of us.

The preservation of the bounty of the summer garden provided a time for the women with their daughters, sisters, and friends (and even the men in some instances) to gather to prepare the fruits and vegetables for sustenance in the winter. It was hard work, but the hard work was worth it for the "edible jewel-toned accomplishments" that came from those hands.[12] I, like most of you, took part in these events as a child and then later as an adult. When I was a child the family gathered on the porch with a bushel or two of peas to shell. There was nothing more satisfying than watching the peas mound up in the pan as the result of this activity. The great bounty, though, was that with the shelling came the stories of the family—where we came from, how we got here, the troubles and the adventures encountered along the way and after we got here. These pea-shelling times were full of laughter and camaraderie between the "elder" siblings and their offspring. So the preservation was not only of the harvest, but also of the family stories imbedded and passed down from mother and father to child, the honing of the stories with the siblings and the cementing of family ties.

As an adult I have had occasion to share this bounty with friends. When we lived in Waco, Sharon Allison, another one from the Piney Woods, called me to go pick muscadine grapes at a place she had discovered them growing. We brought them back to her house and proceeded to make jelly. I don't remember if it was good or not. That did not matter as much as a day with a good friend, both of us working together on a project that produced many laughs, a lot of exchanges of stories and, if we were lucky, some jelly we could put on our tables for our families.

Mary Etta Moreau and I have spent time picking blackberries at my family farm at Saron and turning them into jelly and cobblers. We also put up tomatoes and corn and anything else that we fancied from my father's garden and from hers. Again, it was the great joy of sharing that experience with a good friend and having the bonus of producing something for our family tables. It was a labor of love and great friendship.

My father always had a bountiful garden, full of the most delicious vegetables available anywhere. He did not care for gardening, but blessed with a green thumb and a wife who insisted on the garden and the freezing and canning that went with it, he acquiesced and planted and tended a garden each year she was alive. We took advantage of that mother lode whenever possible. We even started a small garden of our own, much to our neighbors' chagrin since it was in the side yard and visible to all who drove up our street. It did not look good to those in the neighborhood who were "climbing the ladder" of success to have a neighbor apparently reduced to planting a garden in order to eat. Our back yard was another problem because it had a thicket of wild plums I wouldn't allow to be cut. I could make plum jam to my heart's content from that thicket.

My father would go with one of his buddies out in a flat-bottom boat on one of the creeks and skim mayhaws off the surface and bring them to me. I loved making mayhaw jelly, which has to be the most beautiful color when it is done right. Both my father and his buddy are gone and no one knows where they went for the mayhaws. With clear cutting and changes in the topography, the trees may be gone, too.

I first fell in love with mayhaw jelly at my grandmother's knee at Alabama Creek. Every morning she made the most marvelous light, flaky biscuits that melted in your mouth when slathered with the butter she had churned and the mayhaw jelly she had made. All of her cooking was done on a cast iron stove. I have no idea how she regulated the heat to produce the wonderful things that came from that stove. I feel about Little Mother's kitchen the way Edward Harris Heth did about his mother's: ". . . It was a kind of holy place from which she ministered lavishly to her family via stove and sink and cupboards and flour bins. There were rag rugs on the floor... and almost always a rolling pin or flour sifter or earthenware mixing bowl in sight . . . Good cooking was a way of life and enjoyment."[13] Little Mother's biscuit bowl was wooden and it has a place on the bottom where it had been mended. It resides in my kitchen today, but it holds fruits and vegetables. I cannot make her biscuits because we can't find the recipe. I lament that loss.

It has been pointed out that our heritage can't be separated from its agrarian heritage. My father's garden is proof of that for me. My visits to the farmers' markets whenever possible are other proof. I want as close to the garden as I can get, and Safeway and H.E.B. or even Whole Foods don't cut it when it comes to that. Good though their produce may be, it is too many steps away from the garden to fill a need to find once again that heritage.

We all have what we call community cookbooks that came from churches or women's groups with recipes identified by the person who gave it. Some of them have stories with them, a line or two about where it came from or about the person who gave it. These are the *real* treasures in our kitchens. They convey a strong sense of place and each page delivers a strong sense of community—with family and friends. The contributions are from real people with real names, and the food is good. These cookbooks are dog-eared and splattered with remnants of the mixing, notes written in margins, newspaper recipes torn out and inserted along with index cards with recipes from visits to friends or family who served a particularly tantalizing dish and were eager to share. The notes bring back instantly the time when it was given, and for a moment, you are back in that kitchen with that person. I read these cookbooks the way most people read novels or short stories. And I read them over and over when I am looking for a particular recipe I remember and want to find. And like a good novel or short story, I get lost in them and read and read, often forgetting the recipe for which I was searching. This particularly goes on around holidays and celebrations.

There are some things I dare *not* serve. Mother's cornbread dressing for Thanksgiving and Christmas and Little Mother's oyster dressing, although my daughter is now making the oyster dressing. For festive occasions, Dorothy Lay's mother's cheesecake, although one son has now taken over the making of the cheesecake. For all birthdays, MeeMaw's chocolate cake, which was used in her family always so we are on a third and fourth generation of this cake recipe. This cake is made by all three children. These recipes are really an informal history of my family and the ones who came before me and also the friends who shared their food with me. Sharon's Mexican Cookies, which were always served with barbecue for Eastern buyers in town who wanted a taste of Texas; Mary Etta's Rice Casserole, which could feed an army as a side dish; Aunt Bess's Banana Bread with her note "this can be doubled because it's so good," and it is; and Mother's Chocolate Pie when comfort food is needed. These are just a start.

In trying to decide how to divide the recipes and stories in this cookbook, I looked at the publication of my good, dear friend, Joyce Gibson Roach—extraordinary folklorist—and her co-author, Ernestine Sewell, the award-winning *Eats: A Folk History of Texas Foods*. They divided Texas foodways into Northeast Texas, Deep East Texas, Central Texas, South Texas and West Texas. I thought to do the same, as that seemed to be the way the stories and recipes that I had were divided. Then I remembered Joyce always speaking of being from the Cross Timbers. I am from the Piney Woods. So I decided to divide the recipes according to these Vegetational Areas, as shown in the *Texas Almanac*. I also used the descriptions of those areas from the *Almanac* because it gives a sense of the area and because it helps show the diversity of Texas. I appreciate more than I can say the generosity of the Texas State Historical Association in allowing me to do this. Besides, our foods don't divide so easily into areas any more. Mexican food is all over the state, as is barbecue, southern cooking and Cajun cooking, to say nothing of Vietnamese, Chinese and you name it. Besides, there is something quite folkloric and descriptive to me about those designations, so that is what was used. Many of the counties have more than one designation, so I picked the one I thought closest to the recipe. Sometimes I used where the writer currently resides to place the recipe. As you can see, this was not scientific or maybe even logical, but the process certainly adds to the folklore!

One other thing I have done with this cookbook is use recipes from some of the Texas folklorists who have gone on before us. I could not leave out J. Frank Dobie, Archie McDonald, Hazel Abernethy, Martha Emmons, Jean Flynn, or Elmer Kelton, to name a few. They were all too important to the Society and to all of us to not include them—so I did.

What a treat—literally and figuratively—it has been to work on this Texas Folklore Society Publication. It was an inspired topic by Ken Untiedt and his kindness in allowing me to take on the project is greatly appreciated. Two of my great joys in life have been publishing their books and being a member of the Texas Folklore Society these many years. I published the first book in 1979 through E-Heart Press and was a member, of course, before that, or Ab Abernethy would have never let me publish that first book— *Built in Texas*. So, this cookbook is another in a long line of Texas Folklore Society Publications that I have enjoyed working on. The bounty never stops.

ENDNOTES

1. Jean Andrews, *The Pepper Trail: History & Recipes from Around the World* (Denton: University of North Texas Press, 1999), x.

2. Evan Jones, *The Gastronomic Story* (New York: E. P. Dutton & Co., Inc., 1975), 5.

3. Ibid., 27.

4. Ibid.

5. See listing at http://www.texanculures.com/educator_center/immigration/. Accessed December 3, 2013.

6. "Narrative Texts," http://www.utexas.edu/gtc/assets/pdf's/GTC_food.pdf. Accessed December 3, 2013.

7. Sarah Roahen & John T. Edge, editors, *The Southern Foodways Alliance Community Cookbook* (Athens: University of Georgia Press, 2010), 15.

8. Ibid., 53.

9. Ibid., 67.

10. Ibid., 83.

11. Ibid., 123.

12. Ibid., 209.

13. Ibid., 97.

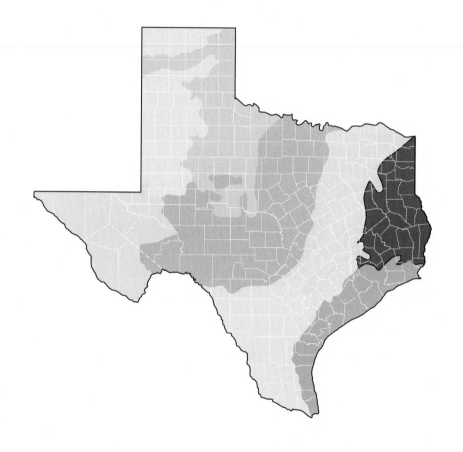

Stories and Recipes from The Piney Woods*

Most of this area of some 16 million acres, ranges from about 50 to 780 feet above sea level and receives 40 to 56 inches of rain yearly. Many rivers, creeks, and bayous drain the region. Nearly all of Texas' commercial timber comes from this area. There are three native species of pine, the principal timber: longleaf, shortleaf, and loblolly. Hardwoods include oaks, elm, hickory, magnolia, sweet and black gum, tupelo, and others.

The area is interspersed with native and improved grasslands. Cattle are the primary grazing animals. Deer and quail are abundant in properly managed habitats. Primary forage plants, under proper grazing management, include species of bluestems, rossettegrass, panicums, paspaiums, blackseed needlegrass, Canada and Virginia wildryes, purpletop, broadleaf and spike woodoats, switchcane, lovegrasses, indiangrass, and numerous legume species.

Highly disturbed areas have understory and overstory of undesirable woody plants that suppress growth of pine and desirable grasses. . . .Grasslands have been invaded by threeawns, annual grasses, weeds, broomsedge bluestem, red lovegrass, and shrubby woody species.

*Stephan L. Hatch, *Texas Almanac, 2014–2015*, Elizabeth Cruce Alvarez, editor (Austin: Texas State Historical Association, 2014), 114. Used with permission of Texas State Historical Association.

Senator Kay Bailey Hutchison

FAMILY RECIPE FROM CHARLES S. TAYLOR

by Senator Kay Bailey Hutchison

Charles Stanfield Taylor was born in 1808 in England, orphaned at an early age, and raised and educated in law by his uncle. When he came of age, he took his inheritance and came to America, landing in New York and sailing shortly thereafter to Louisiana. In 1828 he bought a horse in Natchitoches to ride to Nacogdoches, a journey of about one hundred miles. The horse died on the journey and he walked into Nacogdoches carrying his bags. He stayed at the Adolphus Sterne boarding house and began exploring opportunities in this new territory that was still part of Mexico. In June of that year, Eva Sterne's sister, Anna Mary, visited from Louisiana and met Charles at the Sterne home. Two years later, Charles and Anna Mary were married in the Sternes' parlor. . . . He joined Thomas Rusk, Sam Houston and many other Texans to protest heavy taxes by the Mexican government. When delegates were elected to the Texas Convention at Washington-on-the-Brazos to write a declaration of independence, Rusk and Charles S. Taylor were elected from Nacogdoches. . . .[1]

During the Runaway Scrape, while Charles and Thomas Rusk were at the convention, Anna Mary packed up her three living children and fought the elements with her friend Polly Rusk and her children and many others hoping to reach Louisiana. All three Taylor girls died within days of each other and were buried in Natchitoches. . . .[2]

Anna Mary and Charles later reunited in Nacogdoches to rebuild their family and bolster their young country. . . .[3] The Taylors had nine more children between 1837 and 1853, when the last, my great-grandmother Anna Mary Taylor, was born. After the tragedy of 1836, when they lost all their children, their indomitable spirit was rewarded. Each of the nine later children lived to adulthood.[4]

Julia Curl, daughter of Charles S. Taylor, handed down the following recipe to her descendants. With it came her eyewitness account of festive occasions in their family home in Nacogdoches. The state's first Senators, General Sam Houston and Thomas Rusk, were often guests, as well as others who arrived by wagon and buggy from miles away. Writing to Robert Irion in 1838, Taylor described the informal get-togethers, called "drop ins," where a few friends would meet: "a fiddle is sent for—the dance commences and is kept up for 3 or 4 hours—hilarity prevails, Judge Jeff tells some of his amusing stories, a cold snack is provided, with plenty of the requisite to wash it down."[5] Charles S. Taylor and Thomas Rusk, whose seat in the Senate I held from 1993–2013, were friends and business partners.

My aunt Lucette Sharp, our family historian, passed this recipe on to me.

Charles S. Taylor Family Cake

¾ cup shortening (I add extra shortening for
  moisture)
1½ cups sugar
3 eggs beaten
1¾ cups sifted flour (I use unbleached flour)
½ teaspoon baking powder
1½ teaspoon soda
½ teaspoon salt (optional)
2 teaspoons nutmeg
1 teaspoon cinnamon
¾ cup sour milk (add 1 teaspoon lemon juice
  to fresh milk)
2 teaspoons vanilla (or 1 teaspoon vanilla and
  1 teaspoon lemon extract)
1 cup coarsely cut roasted nuts

Cream shortening and sugar together until fluffy. Add eggs and beat thoroughly. Sift dry ingredients together and add alternately with sour milk. Add vanilla extract. Fold in nuts.

(To roast chopped nuts, place in a shallow pan and heat in a slow oven, 325 degrees, about 20 minutes or until lightly browned.)

Stir mixture frequently. Pour batter into a square or round greased pan or into a cupcake pan. Bake at 325 degrees about 30–35 minutes.

This is an old-fashioned tea cake. Though the original recipe does not call for icing, I add cream cheese frosting.

ENDNOTES

1. Senator Kay Bailey Hutchison, *Unflinching Courage: Pioneering Women Who Shaped Texas* (New York: Harper Collins Publisher, 2013), 19–21.
2. Ibid., 21.
3. Ibid.
4. Ibid.
5. Ibid., 22.

Jane Monday

RECIPES FROM SAM HOUSTON

by Jane Monday

——

Often when General Sam Houston was home, his Indian friends would visit the Woodlands. The Cherokees, in particular, liked to camp on the grounds of the Houston farm when they were traveling. Sometimes before leaving Washington, Houston would send word to the Indians giving them his arrival date and inviting them for a visit. At the same time, he would write and tell Margaret to expect them, and she would send Joshua to town to get extra supplies. Joshua was never surprised by the Indians' arrival if the wind was blowing from the north, because the old gray mule in the corral would snort and jump and nearly tear up the place about an hour before they arrived. When that happened, Joshua would tell Margaret so she could have Eliza and the other servants already cooking by the time the Indians would ride up. Then everyone would be seated on the back lawn, with the General and the Chief in the center of the circle. Eliza and the others would serve the feast, with baked beef ribs often being the main dish. The stripped bones were placed in a dishpan in the center of the circle after each person finished eating.*

* Patricia Smith and Jane Monday, *From Slave to Statesman: The Legacy of Joshua Houston, Servant to Sam Houston* (Denton: University of North Texas Press, 1993), 42. Used with permission of the University of North Texas Press.

The recipes are from Dr. Kristie Lynn and Robert W. Pelton. *The Early American Cookbook.* McCauley Publications; and are also found on the Sam Houston Memorial Museum in Huntsville website at http:// samhoustonmemorialmuseum.com/fun-stuff/recipes/.

Sam's Famous Barbecue Sauce

3 tablespoons cooking oil

¼ cup onion, grated

1 garlic clove, crushed

1 cup catsup

¼ cup Worcestershire sauce

¼ cup lemon juice

2 tablespoons white vinegar

1 teaspoon hot pepper sauce

¾ teaspoon salt

2 tablespoons sugar

2 teaspoons paprika

1½ teaspoons chili powder

1 tablespoon dry mustard

2 teaspoons water

Heat the cooking oil in a large heavy cast iron skillet. Add the onions and the garlic. Sauté this lightly. Stir in the catsup, Worcestershire sauce, lemon juice, white vinegar, hot pepper sauce, sugar, paprika, chili powder and salt. Blend together thoroughly the dry mustard and the water until smooth. Then stir this into the sauce. Slowly bring this mixture to a boil. Cover and let simmer for 20 minutes. Makes 2 cups. Sam used this spicy concoction both as a marinade and a basting sauce for his barbecued steaks, chops and chicken.

KOO WES KOO WE'S BREAD AND BUTTER MOLASSES PUDDING

Koo Wes Koo We was the Indian name of John Ross, a Cherokee chief born in Georgia in 1790, who fought with Sam Houston at Horseshoe Bend. He became principal chief of the Cherokee nation in 1828, and from the very beginning was an efficient champion of their rights against the encroachments and cupidity of the white man. When the Civil War broke out, the Cherokees joined the Confederacy over the protests of Ross.

8 slices stale bread cubed
1 cup seedless raisins
2 eggs
½ teaspoons salt
3 tablespoons molasses
3 teaspoons sugar
2 tablespoons butter
2½ cups milk

Cover the bottom of a well-buttered baking pan with all of the stale bread cubes. Then stir in the raisins. Beat the eggs, salt, molasses and sugar together. Melt the butter in the scalded milk. Stir this into the egg mixture and blend thoroughly. Pour over the stale bread cubes. Place the baking pan in another pan of hot water and bake in a moderate oven (350°) for one hour, or until the pudding is firm to the touch. This pudding should be served with whipped cream. It will feed 6 people.

Wanda Landrey

RECIPES FROM *BOARDIN' IN THE THICKET**

by Wanda Landrey

KOUNTZE: THE COMMERCIAL HOTEL

RED-EYE GRAVY

According to George Leonard and Bertha E. Herter's Bull Cook and Authentic Historical Recipes, red-eye gravy, an old Southern favorite, got its name from General Andrew Jackson, the seventh President of the United States. One day, while Old Hickory was still a general, he sat down to have his noon meal and called his cook over to tell him what to prepare. The cook had been drinking white mule (Southern moonshine corn whiskey) the night before, and his eyes were as red as fire. General Jackson, never a man to mince words, told the cook to bring him some country ham with gravy as red as his eyes. Some men nearby heard the general, and ham gravy became red-eye gravy from that day on.

> Take a large frying pan, put a heaping tablespoon of lard into the pan, and melt it. When melted, put in slices of ham and fry them until well done. Add 1 cup of water and 1 crushed clove. Bring to a boil and simmer for 5 minutes. Remove the ham and serve some gravy with the ham.

BEEF TEA

Grandma Bradley was well-known for her kindness to scores of down-and-out folks who came her way. She had a special recipe for

---

* Wanda Landrey, *Boardin' in the Thicket* (Denton: University of North Texas Press, 1990). Used with permission of the University of North Texas Press.

beef tea, or extracta, that was guaranteed to help anybody feel better, no matter how serious the ailment. In fact, if she got there in time, even death-bed confessions sometimes had to be postponed because of the miraculous recovery of the sick. Ruby Herrington, who gave me Grandma's recipe, told me that her father had actually been saved by Grandma Bradley's beef tea.

She would select a good lean piece of beef, put it into a jar without water, and seal the jar. She would then place the sealed container in a pot of boiling water and cook the meat until most of the juice had been extracted.

I tried this using a shank cross-cut of beef and observed that it does taste a lot better than the beef bouillon available today.

SOUR LAKE: THE SPRINGS HOTEL RESORT

Sour Lake resident Jessie Lea Mowbray told me that her father, Preston Mowbray, was an avid hunter in the late 1800s and supplied the Springs with most of its wild game. "Once," said Jessie, "my father killed enough ducks and geese to make five feather mattresses. At that time a lot of people in a small community cooked alike," Jessie continued. "It was the way one was taught—by word of mouth."

Since wild game hunters are often the best wild game cooks, the following recipes, which were Preston Mowbray's favorites, may have been used at the Springs.

Pan-Fried Venison

1 venison backstrap
minced garlic to taste
salt and pepper to taste
egg, milk and flour batter
¾ cup shortening

Slice the backstrap thin and rub each slice with minced garlic. Beat on both sides to tenderize. Season generously with salt and pepper. Dip in well-beaten egg and milk batter, then flour. Melt the shortening in an iron skillet and fry floured meat rapidly over high heat, turning once, until browned on both sides. Make gravy from the pan drippings.

DRIED VENISON

Cut venison into chunks. Mix 2 cups coarse salt, ½ cup coarse ground pepper, and 2 teaspoons saltpeter. Rub chunks with seasonings and put in a crock bowl. Let stand at least 24 hours. String each chunk and dip in boiling water until meat turns white. Hang up and smoke. When dry, venison is ready to serve.

BEAR MEAT

Bear meat from the Thicket, especially from an old bruin, was tough and required special treatment in its preparation. To tenderize the meat before cooking, it had to be well-seasoned with salt and pepper and boiled in water or soaked in a marinade for at least 24 hours.

Marinade (for a 6 lb. roast):
2 cups water
1 cup vinegar
½ cup olive oil
2 bay leaves
½ teaspoon sage
¼ teaspoon allspice
6 cloves
¼ teaspoon nutmeg
½ teaspoon red pepper
½ teaspoon garlic, minced
2 tablespoons chopped onions

Boil all ingredients 3 minutes then cool to room temperature before placing meat in the marinade.

Remove meat from marinade. Season with salt and pepper. Place meat in roaster and cover with 2 sliced

onions. Cover roasting pan and bake in a slow oven
(30 minutes per lb). Add water if necessary.

SOUTHEAST TEXAS: THE HARVEY HOUSES

No matter how unpredictable the schedules or how uncomfortable
the ride might have been on the Santa Fe, one thing that was always
good was the dining car. As part of the Fred Harvey Company,
the dining cars were operated under a contract agreement with the
Santa Fe and were often able to afford the traveler with a bright
spot in an otherwise dismal journey.

Traveling from Houston to Dallas, the highlight of the trip was
eating lunch in the diner. It was expensive fare, but the pleasure
from feeling sophisticated in posh surroundings made it worth
every penny. Attentive waiters attired in crisp white dinner jackets
served delicious food on lovely china plates. In addition, the spot-
less tablecloths and napkins, the silver flatware, the serving pieces,
along with the crystal glasses, inspired the traveler to display his
best table manners. . . .

From the late 1800s to the early 1900s, in addition to operating
the diners, the Fred Harvey Company also ran the Harvey Houses,
which were located approximately every 100 miles along the railroad line. These included lunchrooms and restaurants, news and
concession stands, hotel rooms, and other accommodations. Everything portable belonged to the company, including dishes, cooking
utensils, linens, and furniture. No matter what size an individual
Harvey House was, each had the reputation for consistently providing unusually good food and good service. And if those were not
enough to lift the spirits of even the weariest traveler, the neat and
attractive young Harvey House waitresses were. Although some
people considered them to be bold and risqué, the girls were generally well-bred, well-educated, and personable—the forerunners of
today's airline stewardesses. Working for Fred Harvey gave these
adventuresome young ladies the opportunity to see the country
at the railroad's expense because they were issued free passes and
given free meal tickets when traveling.

I was surprised to learn that there had once been a very large and elaborate Harvey House in Silsbee. Of course, during the early 1900s Silsbee was a busy railroad terminal on the Santa Fe Line. The business was completely equipped with a lunchroom, a restaurant, and a basement with a barbershop and a poolroom. After it burned in 1920, it was replaced by a smaller lunchroom, which provided service until it closed in 1926. . . .

According to Mr. Otis Thomas, who was manager of the Galveston Harvey House from 1929 to 1936, the food throughout the system was consistently good because the officials at the main office in Kansas City, Missouri, controlled its operation by a centralized form of strict management. It was there that all final decisions were made, all the choice meats were selected and shipped in ice, and all the managers and chefs were trained. Managers were issued a manual of recipes and instructions that explained every detail of food preparation, from the heating of the serving plates to the garnishing of special dishes. By frequently visiting each establishment along the line, Fred Harvey officials kept watch over the whole operation.

I couldn't believe my good fortune when I discovered that Mr. Thomas had saved his instruction book from Galveston and graciously agreed to allow me to use it. After checking several other sources, I decided this may be the only book of original Harvey House recipes around today, and therefore, a real treasure. I have tried many of the recipes, and so far I haven't found a bad one in the lot.

MAYONNAISE

Harvey House restaurants were known for making their own delicious salad dressings. After trying several of the ones listed in the chef's manual, I selected this tart mayonnaise recipe. It's easy to prepare and its distinct flavor makes it different from anything you can buy.

> 2 eggs
> 1 tablespoon dry mustard
> ¾ teaspoon salt

½ teaspoon white pepper
¼ teaspoon red pepper
1 tablespoon flour
2 cups salad oil
3 tablespoons boiling water
2 tablespoons fresh lemon juice

Put eggs into mixing bowl. Add the next 5 ingredients. Mix until thoroughly blended. Slowly add salad oil. When mayonnaise thickens, add boiling water and lemon juice. Mix thoroughly.

Corned Beef Hash and Eggs

Many recipes in the chef's cooking manual contained additional instructions and comments from the central office, such as the following:

This is a nice dish, not only for breakfast but very appropriate for the noonday bill. In fact, not objectionable for service throughout the twenty-four hours of the day.

We have had this on trial at two or three of the houses with very favorable reports, and if you see that it is made according to above, it should be very good. Do not permit any guessing. As a matter of fact, our cooks do too much guessing as to quantities, and, in my opinion, there is no reason why our cooks should not be as careful in compounding foods as a druggist is in compounding his medicine. I say this with all respect for the discriminating taste which we all recognize as being also most important, but I am giving you the exact amounts for the benefit of those who are lacking in tastes.

For a good breakfast dish put corned beef hash into individual serving dishes and hollow out the center. Place 2 raw eggs in the hollowed area and bake at 375° until eggs are cooked to desired firmness.

BESSMAY: THE BESSMAY HOTEL

Lumberman John Henry Kirby created Bessmay, another sawmill town, on the eastern edge of the Thicket. The sawmill there was the largest of the early Kirby mills and seemed to have John Henry Kirby's personal stamp all over it, even to being named for his only child. According to Mr. Homer Holland, Bessmay's last mill foreman, the mill produced around 160,000 board feet of lumber a day and was the first mill to start up again after the Depression. Also, it was in the Bessmay Hotel that a toddler who was to become a celebrity long after she left Bessmay, first attracted attention. . . .

In 1913, it was very unusual for a car to be seen in Bessmay, so it would have been strange for anyone in the neighborhood not to have observed a long, black automobile rolling slowly past the rows of company houses. It slowed to a stop in front of the house where a beautiful golden-haired toddler played quietly by herself. Getting out of the car, an attractive woman ran up to the porch where the child sat preoccupied in her world of make-believe and said, "Come on, Virginia, let's go for a ride." The little girl looked at the woman. Puzzled at first, her expression of surprise rapidly turned into a smile as she ran to the woman with outstretched arms calling, "Mackie, Mackie!" Although the little girl was grimy and disheveled, the woman excitedly embraced her before carrying her back to the car. Until the week before, the child, Virginia Katherine McMath, and her father had been residents of the Bessmay Hotel. Her mother Lela McMath, had separated from her husband and was pursuing a career in north Texas, so Virginia had remained behind with her father and her nurse, May Phillips. Because Miss Phllips loved the child and took exceptionally good care of her, Lela McMath agreed to the arrangement provided the child did not live with her paternal grandmother.

The time Virginia had lived in the hotel was well spent and actually served as a first training ground for her future. While she and her father resided there, the other boarders had come to love the little child who entertained them tirelessly. Her father often took her to the old lodge hall for Saturday night get-togethers, where she picked up the dance steps better and quicker than any of the adults. Every night, the boarders would look forward to Virginia's renditions of the latest dances. They were delighted by the child's antics and were sorry to see her move to a private house to be cared for by her grandmother. When the mother discovered that Virginia was living with her grandmother, she went to Bessmay and "kidnapped" her daughter. Soon afterward, Lela McMath married a Mr. Rogers. Years later people in Bessmay were thrilled to learn that Virginia McMath, the golden-haired girl who had tapped her way into their hearts, then been taken away, had grown into the famous dancer, Ginger Rogers, and was now dancing in the hearts of all America.

FRESH SHELLED PEAS

My roommate wouldn't eat peas on Sundays at all—cabbage or turnip greens or anything like that. He said, "I'll eat that six days a week, so I'm not going to eat it on Sunday." He would eat chicken and dumplings and fried chicken and stuff like that. Sunday meals he called them. Pervis Walton was his name. We called him "Spot."

—Homer Holland

4 cups shelled peas
water
salt to taste
bacon drippings, sliced bacon, or salt pork

Wash peas, place them in a pot, and cover them with water. Add salt and meat seasoning. Bring peas to a boil, reduce heat, cover pot, and boil gently until peas are tender.

VANILLA CUSTARD ICE CREAM

7 eggs well beaten
2 cups sugar
pinch of salt
4 cups milk
1 can sweetened condensed milk
1 large can evaporated milk
2 teaspoons vanilla

Put eggs, sugar, salt, and milk in large pot and cook over low heat until scalded well, stirring frequently. Add the 2 cans of milk and vanilla. Mix well. Freeze in a freezer for approximately 45 minutes, using 5 cups of ice to each ¼ cup of ice cream salt. Pour off the salt water, remove the excess ice, and wipe top before removing any ice cream.

To harden ice cream, replace top with cork, cover with ice, sprinkle with ice cream salt, and let it set.

JELLY CAKE

Pervis wasn't the only one who looked forward to Mrs. Collins's Sunday meals. Homer and Irene did, too. According to them, the old-fashioned jelly cakes, chocolate pies, and vanilla ice cream just couldn't be beat.

Jelly cake was baked in thin layers which were iced with an ample amount of jelly. Blackberry jelly was used most often, but other jellies such as mayhaw were sometimes substituted. The cake was always better after it would "set" a day for the layers to absorb the jelly.

2 cups sugar
1 cup butter
4 eggs
1 cup milk
3 cups flour
2 teaspoons baking power
pinch of salt
jelly

Cream sugar and butter. Beat in eggs. Add milk, flour, baking powder, and salt. Stir. Grease and flour five cake pans. Pour equal amounts of batter into pans for thin layers. Bake at 375° for approximately 20 to 25 minutes. Cool, remove from pans, and spread jelly between layers and on top of cake.

TRINITY: THE SCOTT HOTEL

While there were numerous hotels throughout the Big Thicket during the early part of the century for the convenience of white travelers, accommodations for blacks were almost nonexistent. Of course, the prevailing attitude of southern whites toward blacks hadn't progressed much since the years of slavery, so with the possible single exception of servants, blacks were excluded from the privilege of dining, much less residing, in any of the white establishments. Since I was perplexed about the available provisions for the blacks, I began to ask questions which were usually answered rather nonchalantly. "Oh, I guess they made out somehow. . . . They must've stayed in people's houses," were remarks that I heard. . . . My first clue that a hotel for blacks existed came while I was browsing in an antique store in Trinity, a small town on the northwestern edge of the Big Thicket. As I stood admiring a lovely old chandelier, I was told that the fixture had once hung in the dining room of the Scott Hotel, an establishment for blacks which had been in operation years earlier. . . . I wanted to know more.

. . . The son of a wealthy former slave-owner and an impoverished former slave, Walter Scott began his career as a mail rider between Trinity and Moscow. By the 1890s he realized that Trinity would offer many financial opportunities associated with the railroad, so it was there that he decided to build his future.

With little money but a big desire to succeed, Scott . . . bought an old mule and wagon and went into the draying business, but it wasn't long before he had so much work that the mule wore out and the wagon fell apart. Fortunately, he had already earned enough to invest in other things. He bought two new mules and two new wagons, a jitney for transporting people to other towns, a truck for making deliveries, and a fine hotel to accommodate all those blacks who had to stay in Trinity overnight before catching an early morning train.

Walter and Mattie Scott were proud of the advanced accommodations they offered their guests . . . excellent meals were always served on beautiful china and cut-glass crystal, embroidered napkins, and napkin rings . . . they had the ultimate in modern luxury, running water. . . . Long before most hotels had indoor plumbing, his was a landmark achievement.

PAN-FRIED STEAK

In the days before refrigeration, beef was not eaten as often as it is today. When a cow was butchered, the meat had to be eaten quickly, so it was usually sold or traded among neighbors. Most rural folks like the Scotts had a milk cow or two, but it was a lot cheaper and faster to fatten chickens and hogs than cattle.

When beef was available, this dish was popular.

> 2 lbs. thickly-sliced round steak
> salt and pepper
> flour
> 1 cup buttermilk
> 1 egg, beaten
> 1 cup flour
> 1 teaspoon baking powder
> bacon drippings

> Cut meat into serving pieces and season with salt and pepper. Pound (to tenderize) at least ½ cup flour into meat with edge of heavy plate. Mix buttermilk and beaten egg together in one bowl. Mix 1 cup flour and baking powder together in another. Dip meat into egg mixture and then dredge in flour mixture. Heat bacon drippings in skillet until hot and brown meat on both sides. Serve with cream gravy.

CREAM GRAVY

Pour approximately 4 tablespoons of bacon drippings into a skillet and heat. Add 4 tablespoons of flour, stirring until slightly brown. Gradually add 2 cups of milk and stir until mixture thickens. Salt and pepper to taste.

LYE SOAP

It was always my job to make our lye soap because everyone else pretended that they didn't know how. It was done outside in our big old cast iron wash pot and would take you a good half a day to make. I had to make it quite often especially during hog killing time.

—Hortense Green

You don't have to own a wash pot to make lye soap. It can be made in your kitchen in a big pot. Start by saving fat drippings in glass quart jars. (I asked a manager of a big meat market to save me the fat and then I rendered it.) When 4 jars have been filled, remove the grease from the jars and put into a pot (not aluminum or glass). Clean the grease by boiling it with an equal amount of water. Remove from heat and slowly stir in 1 quart of cold water. Remove fat when top gets firm. Dissolve one 3-ounce can of lye in 2½ pints cold water by slowly adding the lye to the water. (Protect your hands with rubber gloves and stand as far as possible from the pot to avoid breathing fumes.) Stir with a wooden spoon. Melt fat and let it cool gradually, stirring occasionally. Pour lye solution very slowly into the melted fat, stirring carefully. Continue stirring for approximately 15 minutes until it becomes the consistency of thick honey. Pour into a long pan. Set aside, let cool, cut into bars and let dry out.

COLMESNEIL: THE EAST TEXAS HOTEL

In the northern part of the Big Thicket on Highway 69 lies the small town of Colmesneil. Named after W. T. Colmesneil, a well-liked passenger train conductor, the town was the junction for the Waco, Beaumont, Trinity, and Sabine Railroad and the Texas and New Orleans railroad. Long-time resident Easter Matthews Mann, daughter of the last owners of the East Texas Hotel, recalled that her parents awaited a T&NO telegram every morning telling them how many people wanted to eat lunch and what time to have it ready because the train only stopped for a few minutes. The other train, the WBTS, was affectionately known by the locals as the "Wobble, Bobble, Turn Around and Stop," an obvious nickname in view of the train's slow, precarious manner of shuffling down the tracks. In fact, according to Easter, the train was so slow that the passengers often had time to get off and pick flowers.

COUNTRY-STYLE HOMINY

Few people around today know how to make hominy, so it is quickly becoming a lost art. But on the old-time farm, hominy making was a common practice.

In making hominy, hardwood ashes were saved in an ash hopper, which was actually a barrel or keg. The container, having a drain at the bottom, was placed on a low platform and tilted slightly. A pan was placed under the drain. After the ashes were packed into the container water was added. The water would seep through the ashes and drain through the hole and into the pan. The liquid, called potash, was a strong solution of lye and was a deep red in color.

The liquid was poured into a wash pot, large-grain corn was added, a fire was built, and the corn was cooked until the skin came off. The corn was then removed from the pot and washed until all the husks came off and all the lye was removed. Finally, the corn kernels, which were bleached white and fluffy, were stored in large containers until they were cooked.

Archie P. McDonald

RECIPES FROM *HELPFUL COOKING HINTS FOR HOUSEHUSBANDS OF UPPITY WOMEN**

by Archie P. McDonald

THE MAKING OF A HOUSEHUSBAND

It all started appropriately, by the dawn's early light. Eve prepared the first meal for Adam by serving him a forbidden apple. Husbands have been snake-bitten ever since when it comes to getting food on the table. For ages after Adam enjoyed that first forbidden meal, men toiled to provide their bread, women baked it, and the family shared the result of their joint labors. Things began to change.

In the middle of the nineteenth century feminists such as Susan B. Anthony and Amelia Bloomer spread the new gospel that women had rights, among them the prerogative to vote, wear funny clothes, and avoid the kitchen. In other words, they became Uppity. Then was born the New Man, the *homo sapius domesticus*, or, as he is better known in modern society, the HouseHusband.

DRAMATIS PERSONAE

Uppity Woman

Homo sapien famaleius uppitus. The girl you married who promised to love, honor, and obey, an implicit pledge to sew, cook, clean, look after kids, wash the car, keep the firewood cut, and scratch your back. These things are now forgotten in the Liberated Phase of Life. Aprons are traded for briefcases and someone else is hired or intimidated to keep the house cleaned and do the cooking. And it's high heels every day, baby.

---

* Archie P. McDonald, *Helpful Cooking Hints for Househusbands of Uppity Women* (Denton: University of North Texas Press, 2001). Used with permission of the University of North Texas Press.

HouseHusband
Homo sapius domesticus. The Bread Winner and Lord and Master who formerly came home to a meal he did not prepare, who now has been Liberated.

The Kids
They are the same, only bigger, and what they want to know most is, "When's supper?"

Hazel's Venison Roast

Hazel is the former Hazel Shelton, who somehow got mixed up with that Abernethy boy. They've stayed married until now, raised five kids, and are both accomplished in their chosen fields. One of Ab's interests is hunting, especially deer, as is often the case with Southern men. Since Ab is such a good provider of game, Hazel has to devise ways to use it all. Her recipe for venison roast is so good you will think it tastes like beef. If you want the gamey taste, you are out of luck. You must provide your own venison. At current costs for guns, ammunition, hunting license, and other items, venison costs about $50 a pound. But there is no greater thrill for a HouseHusband than cooking the produce of his garden or his hunting trip.

> Ingredients:
> 1 venison roast
> 1 package dry Lipton Onion Soup Mix
> 1 can Cream of Mushroom Soup (no water)
> Worcestershire sauce to taste
> 1 cup or so of red wine
> Meat tenderizer

> Preparation:
> 1. Line pan generously with foil, leaving enough to seal meat later.
> 2. Sprinkle meat tenderizer on roast.

3. Spread Cream of Mushroom Soup on roast.
4. Spread Lipton Dry Onion Soup Mix on roast.
5. Add red wine and ½ to 1 cup of water to keep meat from tasting "dry."
6. Fold over foil and seal.
7. Bake at 350° for about 2 hours.

Fresh Garden Greens

Now here is where I show my Southern-ness. I did not intend this book to have a narrow regional appeal. After all, some Yankee women are Uppity, and some Yankee men are HouseHusbands. However, this dish probably will appeal most to southerners. For a while, greens were known as "soul food." I can't think of a better description. Growing them, and then cooking and eating what you have grown, is truly good for the soul.

Ingredients:
1 to 2 bunches of greens (mustard, turnip, collard, chard, or beet tops)
1 tablespoon bacon drippings or 2 slices bacon or 1 package ButterBuds
1 teaspoon salt

Preparation:
1. Wash greens thoroughly. Be sure to check the underside of each leaf, to make sure it is clean.
2. If tender and fresh, whole leaves may be put into pot. You may want to remove center stems from mustard greens
3. Add enough water to prevent sticking on bottom.
4. Add bacon drippings, bacon slices or butterbuds.
5. Add salt, sprinkling it over the top of the greens.
6. Cover and cook on high until boiling.
7. Reduce heat and cook about 30 minutes, or until greens are a dark green.

8. Turn them at least once during cooking to insure they all cook evenly.
9. Taste to determine when done.

Martha's Peach Cobbler

Martha Emmons is one of my youngest friends. Martha started teaching high school students in the early 1920s, then moved on to the Baptist Vatican at Waco known as Baylor University. Whatever her age—and I won't ask—she has a twinkle in her eye that would dim a locomotive headlight, and a sense of adventure to match. Bless her, she wanted you to share her peach cobbler recipe.

Ingredients:
¼ stick margarine
1 No. 2 can sliced peaches
¾ cup milk
¾ cup Bisquick
¾ cup sugar

Preparation:
1. Melt butter in a Pyrex baking dish.
2. Pour in the sliced peaches.
3. Pour milk over peaches.
4. Mix together: Bisquick, sugar.
5. Pour over peaches.
6. Bake in a 350 degrees oven for 45 minutes, or until brown.

Ab and Hazel Abernethy with Archie

The Temple family at Boggy Slough
Front: Susie, Helen, Buddy, Ellen, Mary Ellen, Robert, Hannah
Back: Walter, Lilly, Bob, John, Whitney, Maggie, Chris and 2 lizards

BOGGY SLOUGH CHILI—50 YEARS OF CHILI MAKIN' IN EAST TEXAS

by Ellen Temple

The Neches is an ancient river that flows from springs in Van Zandt County 380 miles to Sabine Lake on the Gulf of Mexico. It is the ecological and cultural heart of the Pineywoods of East Texas. Primitive people such as the Clovis tribes, then the Caddo Indians, and then the Spanish, French and Anglo settlers lived along its shores. Until the 20th century the people lived off the land—harvesting deer, bear, fish, waterfowl—to sustain them.

The Neches River Valley in East Texas is home for 3,402 species of plants, including the rare Neches River Rose mallow (*Hibiscus Desycalyx*), more than two-thirds of the approximately 5,100 species known for Texas. It is a stop on the flyway for thousands of North American migrating birds. In the middle and late 20th century, people began to recognize its richness, preserving bottomlands and uplands along the river with the recent Neches River Wildlife Refuge, the Davy Crockett and Angelina National Forests, the Pineywoods Mitigation Bank, the Big Thicket National Preserve, and many conservation easements along its course.

Boggy Slough is one of those efforts to preserve this rich ecosystem. When T. L. L. Temple from Texarkana acquired 7500 acres from Mr. Diboll in 1893 to establish his family's Southern Pine Lumber Company, he continued to acquire land along the Neches River, harvesting timber for the business. In the early 1900s, one of his land acquisitions included what is known as Boggy Slough in Houston County between highways 94 and 103. Its 19,000 acres front the Neches River for eighteen miles.

Hunting pressure had pretty well wiped out the white tailed deer population in East Texas and under the leadership of T. L. L. Temple, Arthur Temple, Sr. and Arthur Temple, Jr., the family company began protecting the Boggy Slough lands, leasing the lands to the state of Texas as a game preserve in 1926. When Southern Pine Lumber Company went public in 1969, Boggy Slough began its history of company ownership under Temple Industries, Temple-Eastex and Temple Inland, and finally International Paper Company for two years. Those company leaders continued the policy of protecting Boggy Slough. Deer that found a safe haven there are said to be the beginning of the revival of the white tailed deer population in East Texas.

In December 2013, under the leadership of chairman Arthur "Buddy" Temple III, the T.L.L. Temple Foundation acquired Boggy Slough from International Paper Company, and the conservation of the unique heritage of Boggy Slough will continue for future generations—including the chili makin' tradition!

The Southern Pine Lumber Company had built a famous lodge where they hosted governors and other politicians, fenced the land, and managed it for the white tailed deer. They were so successful that the deer population outgrew the ability of that stretch of forest to sustain it. By the 1960s the company was getting game management advice. Each hunter was required to harvest a specified number of does, not just trophy bucks, which led to excess venison.

The hunters started the annual chili makin' to use up the excess venison. The first chili cooking goes back to 1963, with records of the event dating from 1968. Arthur Temple, Jr. put Arch Hollingsworth in charge of the cooking with John Booker to assist. Originally there was one central fire with several out-fires that were actually used to cook chili. After the company lodge burned in the 1960s, Mr. Temple began inviting hunters to join him on the land and formed the Sportsmen of Boggy Slough Hunting Club, which carried on the chili makin' tradition. This became a big social affair during the period when Temple Industries and Time, Inc. were merged, with executives from Time, Inc. joining folks in East Texas for the annual chili makin' at a company lodge in Newton County known as Scrappin' Valley. Lady Bird Johnson and Liz Carpenter came, too!

When we compiled the Temple Ranch Cookbook in 2013, we knew that we had to include Boggy Slough Chili—the recipe with the longest history in the book. Here's the story.

Fifty or so years ago, Gene Shotwell of Lufkin created a simple venison chili recipe with meat, garlic powder, cumin, salt, cayenne, paprika and chili powder, all cooked in suet (beef fat used for frying) in big black chili pots over gas burners. He served it to Arthur Temple and some other deer hunters, who loved it and adopted the recipe for their annual chili makin' in February after a season of deer hunting. A battle raged for years between those who were for using suet and those who preferred "sissy" cooking oil. Arch Hollingsworth and John Booker, the Great Chili Makers, perfected the recipe after years of experiments. John Booker reports: "This basic recipe has satisfied a lot of people through the years. From 1968 to 2012 we made 58,201 pounds of chili using basically the same recipe."

John Booker, the Great Chili maker, just gave us the Arch Hollingsworth's Chili Pot for Boggy Slough. Here's John's story:

> "This is the original Chili Pot we used making Boggy Slough chili. The pot is quite old. Arch told me it was his grandmother's, and she brought it with her when they moved to the Oklahoma Indian Territory. It is well over 100 years old, and we used it in all the chili makings. I no longer make large quantities of chili so my little pot will do me."

We share the Boggy Slough recipe that Patrick Heiger has reduced to a smaller, manageable version here with a tribute to all who cooked it and enjoyed it all those years.

BOGGY SLOUGH CHILI

The Boggy Slough cooks have made more than 50,000 pounds of this chili in the last fifty years. That's quite a pedigree! The club makes it in much larger batches, but this smaller recipe will work just fine for folks at home.

> 1 cup canola oil
> 2 pounds venison, diced into ½-1 inch cubes
> 1 tablespoon chili powder
> 1 teaspoon cumin
> 1 teaspoon garlic powder
> 1 teaspoon paprika
> 1 teaspoon salt
> 1 clove garlic chopped
> 1 8-ounce can tomato paste
> water

1. In a broad, 10-quart pot or rondo, warm the canola oil over medium-high heat until it flows freely. Once the oil is hot, add the diced venison. Cook until meat has been browned on all sides.
2. Add the spices and garlic to the browned meat. Cook 2 minutes, until the aroma of the spices is strong. Add the tomato paste and cook 1 minute.
3. Pour enough water into the pot to cover the meat and to achieve desired consistency. (For a thicker chili, add only enough water so the meat doesn't burn. For a thinner consistency, add more water during the cooking process.) Let the liquid come to a boil, then reduce to a simmer over medium heat. Cook until the meat is tender, approximately 2 to 3 hours.
4. Serve over cooked rice or spaghetti. Garnish with diced onions and shredded American or cheddar cheese. Serve hot.

Enjoy this special chili from East Texas!

RESOURCES

Abernethy, Francis Edward, with photography by Adrian F. Van Dellen. *Let the River Run Wild! Saving the Neches.* Stephen F. Austin State University Press, Nacogdoches, Texas, 2013.

Temple, Ellen and Patrick Hieger. *Temple Ranch Cookbook: A Tradition of Texas Conservation and Cuisine.* The Temple Ranch keepsake edition. 2013.

Ab Abnernethy's grandson, Jack Duffin with his first deer. He is now a Combat Medic, Specialist, in a cavalry squadron.

Craig Stripling

HANGING THE MEAT, AND RECIPES FOR MUSHROOMS AND POTATOES

by Craig Stripling

It is not always in every circle today that discussions can be had about the joys of hunting, harvesting, preparing, cooking, and eating wild game. Anyone reading this, however, is curious about the typical meat I slather in the mushroom and butter/cream sherry sauce recipe included herewith. When I was growing up in East Texas the main game to hunt was squirrel because there weren't in the 1950s many deer in this locale—you didn't count on a carpenter or painter or plumber or anyone else who didn't work in an office showing up on October 1st—opening day! Now there are more deer here than ever, and they provide for about as good bounty as can be had for the fan of red meat.

I remember as a lad getting to see some of the local men each November, usually around Thanksgiving, return from the Hill Country beyond Austin or from South Texas with hide-on deer strapped to the hoods of their vehicles. Always my neighbor, Mr. Cox, would offer to my parents and my grandparents a haunch, or ham. I thought the meat was a bit funky (they called it "gamey'), and that indeed I wasn't cut out for partaking in venison as table fare.

Only when I was grown and began the pursuit of meat on the hoof and after eating some outstanding wild game dinners prepared by hunter friends (especially Mike Rose, the provider of the mushroom recipe) did I realize that the meat I ate some sixty years ago was basically spoiled. It had traveled from the Hill Country to Nacogdoches after hanging in a tree—hide still attached—for two or three days in 70 to 80-degree weather on the hot hood of a car. Indeed, it was "ripe"—borderline rotten. Thus, the funk. I realized soon after having the decades-later good meals, that prompt removal of skin, quartering the carcass, and cooling the cuts of meat in a cooler of ice resulted in jam-up outstanding meat, which, unless chicken fried, is best hot coal grilled just past rare—way this side of pink and never to the shade of brown or grey.

The wonderful mushroom dish—so simple and so good—was given to me about forty-five years ago by my still good friend and extraordinary cook, deer, goose and duck hunter, Mike Rose, of Houston, Texas. I've since given it to dozens who have craved it after eating the mushrooms. It's a necessity with red meat.

These two recipes are simple and good. I use them both very regularly.

Mushrooms and Sauce/Gravy

Mushrooms go very well with red meat—beefsteaks and venison roasts especially. An old hunter friend of mine gave me his oh-so-easy recipe for cooked mushrooms and sauce. He primarily used it for deer and wild duck and goose recipes, but I use it for grilled steaks and grilled venison roasts. I like to have the local plant process deer hams into boneless roasts of about two pounds each.

> After marinating them overnight in a chopped onion, salt, pepper, Worcestershire sauce, peanut or olive oil, red wine vinegar and a can of beer, I cook them rather rare over hot coals. I slice them thin with an electric knife and serve the pieces covered in the mushrooms and sauce/gravy. Ditto thick red cooked beefsteaks.
>
> Wash and put one pound of fresh whole raw mushrooms in a sauce pan. Place a stick of butter in the pan, add ¾ cup cheap jug type cream (has to be cream) sherry. Turn on the fire medium low and cook until the butter and sherry become a medium-thick sauce or gravy. The mushrooms will cook and be sort of candied, and are, along with the sauce, absolutely delicious on the meat.

Skillet Potatoes and Onions

You've got to have potatoes to eat with the red meat. One of the easiest and best recipes for good skillet potatoes and onions is as follows:

> Peel 8 potatoes (big new potatoes, medium large Idaho potatoes or Yukon Golds or whatever you like). Peel 6 medium-large onions—preferably a sweet type such as Vidalias, Noondays, Texas 1015's, or Walla Wallas. Drizzle olive or peanut oil over the potatoes and onions after you've set them in a covered or foil sealed baking pan. Bake them an hour and 45 minutes in a 375 degree oven.
>
> Put ⅛" olive oil or peanut oil in a cast iron skillet. Once the potatoes and onions cool, coarsely chop them and put into the skillet. Heavily salt with sea salt and generously shake on finely ground black pepper. Turn skillet on medium high. When the potato and onion mixture starts browning and sticking a bit, turn it over with a spatula. Drizzle more oil if necessary. When it starts to brown again you're ready. Best potatoes dish ever.

R. G. Dean

MY DAGWOOD BUMSTEAD SANDWICH

by R. G. Dean

When I was growing up in San Augustine, Texas during the 1930s and early 1940s, the social life of my family was limited—to say the least. As well as I can remember, the most likely social event in our annual calendar was the Homecoming and Dinner on the Ground at the Attoyac Cemetery in lower San Augustine County. Why the event was held in August—not the most pleasant time of the year to be spending several hours outside in the heat—is something no one has ever been able to explain to me.

Also, when my family often did not have money to buy new clothes or shoes or many things most families considered necessities, from my earliest memories, some of them when I was barely three years old, we always took one or two daily newspapers. Both my father who had not completed five years of formal education and my mother who had completed only eight years of school, read the papers religiously. I can remember my mother reading the "funnies" to me before I was four.

One of my favorite comic strips was *Blondie*, about the Bumsteads. I was captivated by the sandwiches the impetuous father of the family, Dogwood, liked to construct for midnight snacks, sandwiches which usually appeared to be about eighteen inches tall—they would make the McDonald's Triple-Decker look like a morsel!

One year when I was about six or seven, although it must have wrecked our budget, Dad came home on a Saturday with a couple of loaves of store-bought light bread, a couple of types of sliced cheese, sliced ham, sliced baloney, sliced pickle loaf, and probably a head of lettuce and jars of salad dressing and prepared mustard—all things I had never seen in our house before. Seeing all that was like an answer to an unspoken prayer—there was all I needed to build a Dagwood Sandwich. I began asking, and eventually begging to be allowed to make for myself my dream sandwich to take for my lunch at the Attoyac Cemetery Homecoming and Dinner on the Ground, which was to be the next day. Finally, my parents agreed to my pleas—on one condition—that I eat all of my sandwich before I ate anything else at the Homecoming. I agreed!

My sandwich wasn't as tall as Dagwood's: my parents saw to it that my sandwich did not measure up to the dimensions of Dagwood's masterpieces. They allowed me only enough ingredients to construct a puny approximation, which was only five or six inches high. On Sunday, when everyone spread their contributions to the dinner-on-the-ground, there was fried chicken, baked chicken, chicken dressing, chicken dumplings, baked and fried ham, baked and fried pork, baked beef roast, home-stuffed sausage, black-eyed peas, crowder peas, cream peas, snapped beans, pinto beans, butterbeans, turnips and turnip greens, boiled cabbage, fresh tomatoes, corn on the cob, corn off the cob, squash, potato salad, cucumber pickles, vegetable salads, fruit salads, chocolate cakes, coconut cakes, white layer cakes, apple pies, peach pies, syrup pies, chocolate pies with meringue topping, peach cobbler, berry cobbler, several kinds of puddings, and several flavors of ice cream in freezers, including vanilla, my favorite. And I couldn't have any of it until I ate my Dagwood Sandwich! Needless to say, by the time I ate my sandwich, I was too sick to want anything else to eat—ever. It was not the happy day I had envisioned—but, at least it was an educational one.

Ice Water Pickles

Six lbs med size cucumbers
each cut in 4 to 8 pieces
according to size of cucumbers
Soak in ice water 3 hrs - drain
pack into sterilized Kerr jars
add 6 pickling onions. 1 piece
Celery. 1 teaspoon mustard seed
to each jar Solution

   3 qts white vinegar
1 cup salt. 3 cups sugar
bring to boil. pour over
cucumbers and seal jars.

Janell Croley Chesnut

HERSHEL PUDDING

by Janell Croley Chesnut

This is a recipe that was popular with older women, including my grandmother, Jessie Chandler Croley (Mama). She prepared this for many years in Gilmer, in northeast Texas. There was a "Book Club" which met each month to visit and have a social time for the older women residents. Contrary to the name, this was a club whose main activity was to play 42 (played with dominos). They did exchange books, as well as the latest gossip or local news.

The famous dessert served was Hershel Pudding. I do not know where the name originated. My father always asked my grandmother what she was serving when her turn came to have the Book Club. The answer was the same, Hershel Pudding. This recipe is noted in only one recipe book I found published by the Twentieth Century Club 1965, a women's club in Gilmer, Texas. My copy of the recipe is on a hand written-note on a faded piece of paper. We were also treated to this dessert at Christmas. Mama Croley was not known for many of her recipes, except this one and fig preserves.

The measurements are as noted in the original recipe. Enjoy!

HERSHEL PUDDING

1 small jar cherries (chopped)
1 tablespoon gelatin
6 eggs, separated
6 tablespoons sugar
1 teaspoon vanilla extract
1 cup nuts, chopped
1 cup water
1 small box vanilla wafers, rolled

Dissolve gelatin in one cup of cherry juice or water. (You can use the juice from the cherries plus enough water to make one cup.)

Cook egg yolks, sugar, and gelatin mixture until it thickens, add vanilla wafers, cherries, and nuts. Then add stiffly beaten egg whites.

Chill and add whipped cream if desired when serving. Serves 8.

Cherry Pie Cake

Serves:

1 #3 Can cherry pie filling
½ pkg. white cake mix
¼ st. butter melted

1 C. chopped pecans
1½ C. Whipping cream
2 Tbs. powdered sugar
1-2 Tbs. Kirsch

Spread cherry pie filling evenly over bottom of 9 inch square baking dish. Sprinkle dry cake mix evenly over the cherries. Dribble melted butter over cake mix. Cover with pecans. Bake at 350° for 1 hr. Cover with foil loosely if cake browns too quickly. Whip cream then whip in sugar + Kirsch. Serve cake hot or cold, cut in square with generous topping of cream. Serves 8 to 12.

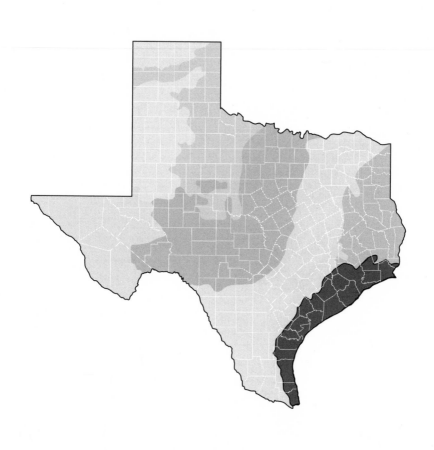

Stories and Recipes from the Gulf Prairies and Marshes*

The Gulf Prairies and Marshes cover approximately 10 million acres. There are two subunits: (a) the marsh and salt grasses immediately at tidewater, and (b) a little farther inland, a strip of bluestems, and tall grasses, with some gramas in the western part. Many of these grasses make excellent grazing. Oaks, elm, and other hardwoods grow to some extent especially along streams, and the area has some post oak and brushy extensions along its borders. Much of the Gulf Prairies is fertile farmland, and the area is well suited for cattle.

Principal grasses of the Gulf Prairies are tall bunch grasses, including big bluestem, little bluestem, seacoast bluestem, indiangrass, eastern gamagrass, Texas wintergrass, switchgrass, and gulf cordgrass. Saltgrass occurs on moist saline sites.

Heavy grazing has changed the native vegetation in many cases so the predominant grasses are the less desirable broomsedge bluestem, smutgrass, threeawns, tumblegrass, and many other inferior grasses. Other plants that have invaded the productive grasslands include oak underbrush, Macartney rose, huisache, mesquite, prickly pear, ragweed, bitter sneezeweed, broomweed, and others.

*Stephan L. Hatch, *Texas Almanac, 2014–2015*, Elizabeth Cruce Alvarez, editor (Austin: Texas State Historical Association), 114. Used with permission of Texas State Historical Association.

Mary Margaret Dougherty Campbell

MARIA'S MOM

by Mary Margaret Dougherty Campbell

John wanted to learn how to make tamales. One day in the faculty lounge at St. Joseph High School, he just happened to mention this desire. Without hesitating, Maria said, "My mom makes the best tamales I've ever eaten. She's going to be visiting in a couple of weeks. Maybe I can talk her into a tamale-making lesson while she's here."

By the time Mrs. Apac arrived for her visit in Victoria, plans were set for the tamale lesson. We would gather at Maria and Paul's home early Saturday morning. Because John was the one who wanted to learn, he would fully participate in the process. Maria would assist her mother as necessary. John had appointed me the Recipe Recorder and Debbie the Observer, both of us helping out as needed. A cozy kitchen turned into a crowded kitchen with five people and the intrusion of the oversized table necessary for the tamale process. But with the warmth and welcoming atmosphere, no one even noticed.

Mrs. Apac had prepared the pork roast and hog's head on Friday because, according to her, each meat must cook "until a fork can be easily poked through to the bottom of it." Anyone who has cooked a roast knows for meat to be that tender, it must cook a very long time. Even with the meat already prepared, a full day's work lay ahead of us. Poised with a note pad and pen, I was ready to document the tamale-making process.

What I hadn't fully comprehended was that Mrs. Apac spoke little-to-no English, even though Maria had already warned us. Born Maria Aurora Acosta in Mexico, she had immigrated to the United States as an adult with her husband and children. Adhering to tradition, she had worked in their home as a homemaker rather than outside of it. The Catholic church she attended in Corpus Christi had Masses in Spanish, and her children learned English in school and could interpret for her. Thus, her learning to speak English was never a necessity. Oh, she understood more than she let on, but she spoke Spanish, with an occasional word in English thrown in with a grin. So, every instruction and bit of advice from Mrs. Apac that Saturday passed through Maria. Likewise, every question from John and clarification sought from me passed through Maria. For instance, when adding the tomatillos to the mixture, the conversation went something like this:

Mary Margaret: "How many tomatillos?"

Maria: "Mama, cuantos tomatillos?"

Mrs. Apac: "Pues, seis estan bien."

Maria: "She says six will be good."

Even Maria slipped in and out of Spanish as she spoke to us gringos in the presence of her mother. While preparing the shucks, she said to me, "First, we have to clean out all of the pelitos from the shucks."

"The what?" I laughed.

"The pelitos, the little hairs."

"I know what pelitos are, but I've never heard corn silks called pelitos!"

At first, I thought about the adult hairs one shudders to find in food at a restaurant, or anywhere else for that matter. But as I cleaned the pelitos from the shucks, I realized they are like babies' hair—soft and fine and shiny.

Through Maria, Mrs. Apac also schooled us on different kinds of chiles. For example, chiles anchos are wrinkled and small like raisins, adding color to a dish. Cascabels are hotter and add flavor. Chiles de arbol are really small and really hot. Prior to the lesson, I had seen the varieties in the grocery store but had no idea of the differences nor the courage to experiment. We also learned about using a molcajete properly to grind spices. Mrs. Apac explained as she demonstrated that after the spices have been removed from the molcajete, if you add a little water to the molcajete and swish it around with your finger, you can pour the spicy water into your dish, thus not wasting any spices and not mixing in unwanted spices later.

She was patient with us, enjoying the opportunity, I think, to teach us about something dear to her heart—cooking. Plus, she met and got a chance to know some of her daughter's friends.

Like so many cooks from her generation and culture, Mrs. Apac cooked with her senses rather than a recipe and strict measurements. We watched her smell and taste the chiles and meat mixture, measuring in her hand—or John's hand so he could feel and see the necessary amount. When I asked for measurements for the recipe I was noting, she'd wrinkle her nose and think for a minute before giving Maria an estimate. She'd used measuring spoons and cups before; she just had to stop and think about it, making the comparison in her mind before speaking. The next spring, I readily accepted a dinner invitation to Maria's home while Mrs. Apac was visiting. That evening, I watched her make a chicken and rice dish, which she also prepared predominately using her senses. I never saw her refer to a recipe or use measuring spoons or cups. I doubt she even owned a cookbook.

After about ten hours that December Saturday, uncooked tamales sat by the dozen in Ziplock bags on the table. Mrs. Apac only cooked a couple of dozen for us to taste and enjoy that evening, saying that she preferred to package her tamales uncooked because they taste fresher from the freezer if they haven't been cooked before freezing. We feasted on the delicious fruits of our all-day labor, washing the tamales down with beer. Even Mrs. Apac washed hers down with Budweiser from a small glass, which reminded me of my grandmother who would drink beer when she ate enchiladas or pizza, always drinking it from a small glass.

We used all of the meat mixture but had some masa and cleaned shucks left over. The next morning, I went back to Maria's and helped spread a refried bean mixture on the masa in the shucks, making bean tamales, a novelty to me. After we had spread all of the mixture, I borrowed pen and paper so I could add the bean mixture to the tamale recipe notes from the previous day. Since then, I have eaten other cooks' bean tamales, but none as sabroso as Mrs. Apac's.

When I commented on the bean tamales' delicious taste, Mrs. Apac said she thought cooking beans in a clay bean pot makes the difference. I had noticed the bean pot on the stove. Looking at it took me back to my childhood when most Mexican people I knew cooked beans in a similar pot rather than a metal one. That morning, I commented that I would like to cook beans in a bean pot, that my beans taste okay but I'd like to improve their taste. One morning not long after that, Maria came to me at school, grinning. She said, "Mom went to Nuevo Laredo and brought back a bean pot for you!"

"For me? She bought a bean pot *for me*?" I felt very special, almost blessed.

"Yes, she did! Next time she comes, she'll bring it with her"—and she did.

That was the evening of the chicken and rice dish. But, she wouldn't let me take the pot home. Mrs. Apac said that she wanted to cook the first pot of beans in it because often those pots will have a crack that is hard to detect, and if it has a crack, cooking in it will make a big mess (spoken in Spanish, translated through Maria, of course). She only wanted me to have the pot if it were perfect. But for some reason, I never got the pot. I moved away from Victoria shortly thereafter and never got it from Maria.

The reason I went back to Maria's that Sunday morning after the tamale lesson was to take Mrs. Apac some flowers. She had been so kind to us the previous day that I thought I'd say "thank you" with flowers. I chose Shasta daisies, my favorite. When I arrived, Maria exclaimed, "Margaritas!"

My name translates into Spanish as Maria Margarita, and I'm accustomed to having it shortened to Margarita, so I said, "Yes! I'm back!"

Maria said, "No, margaritas" pointing to the daisies I carried. Still confused, I was thinking, "It's too early in the morning to drink margaritas—and it's a Sunday morning, at that!" To my astonishment, I learned my favorite flower is my name in Spanish. As Maria would say, "Go figure!"

Eight years have passed since the tamale lesson. Last night I attended Mrs. Apac's rosary in Corpus Christi. Maria emailed me a few days ago with the news of her mom's passing. In the past couple of weeks, Mrs. Apac had undergone two heart surgeries. Three days from her 82nd birthday, her tired body gave up. Debbie called me with arrangements.

After signing the book, I spied Debbie but not Maria. Debbie told me that Maria was inside the chapel, so that's where I went. As soon as I stepped inside the door, Maria swept me into her arms and hugged me long and hard. While we stood at the back of the chapel talking, one of Maria's nieces, Pat, approached us. Apparently, when I walked in, I interrupted a conversation. Maria asked Pat to drive to Mrs. Apac's house to pick up a cassette tape that Maria had inadvertently laid down and neglected to pick back up. I heard her tell Pat, "They're supposed to start playing it at six." Pat left, and Maria resumed telling me about her mother's recent illness. After a few minutes, she asked, "Have you seen her? Of course not! I stopped you as you entered!"

So, we walked up the aisle to the front of the chapel, where the casket lay among the customary flowers and plants, so I could view her mother. As we neared the casket, someone stopped Maria, so I knelt down and said a "Hail Mary." Before I knew it, Maria was standing beside me, so I rose. I commented on how nice her mother looked. That's when she told me about the makeup. The funeral directors had asked for her mother's clothes and makeup. Maria and one of her sisters had difficulty trying to figure out which among her mother's cosmetics to take, that they couldn't seem to find an appropriate shade of foundation. To solve the problem, Maria offered her own makeup bag and proudly told me, "All of the makeup on Mom tonight is from my bag. Mother was always envious of my foundation; now she's wearing it." She smiled at her mother's face.

Mrs. Apac was wearing a chiffon dress, a light shade of olive, with a lace mantilla on her head. You don't see mantillas much anymore. There's only one woman where I attend Mass who still wears one. Actually, there may be more wearing them at the 7:30 a.m. Mass, but I'll probably never know firsthand if anyone wears a mantilla at that Mass or not. Anyway, Mrs. Apac's mantilla was long and beautiful.

I noticed butterflies made of some kind of material—perhaps silk—in various colors sitting here and there inside the casket; one even rested on Mrs. Apac's dress. Reading my mind, Maria simply said, "Mother loved butterflies." Later, I noticed a young woman, who turned out to be a great-granddaughter, attaching wire to similar butterflies for family members to wear on their lapels. Rather than mere ornaments, the butterflies were angels surrounding Maria's mom, telling her loved ones that she was already in Heaven with them. Mrs. Apac also had a rhinestone "J-e-s-u-s" pinned to her dress and a small broach at her throat that I couldn't quite make out. It may have had a pearl in the center. Of course, she had a rosary, which is standard Catholic. Atop the closed half of the casket, between the floral spray and the opening, sat a candle that had "AURORA" lettered in gold.

Later, in the lobby, I sat on a sofa visiting with Debbie when Maria finally made it out of the chapel and onto the adjoining sofa. Her cell phone rang; it was one of the priests wanting to discuss funeral details. I overheard her say she would be singing at the funeral. I turned to Debbie, "Did she just say she's *singing* tomorrow?"

"Yes, and I don't know how." Me neither.

When I taught with Maria at St. Joseph's in Victoria, I had listened to her sing and play her guitar at Mass each month, as well as on other occasions. She has an absolutely beautiful voice. But beautiful voice or not, I found it hard to believe she could pull it off at her own mother's funeral. For my father's funeral, I wrote a eulogy that never was read. I was afraid I couldn't do it, so I asked someone else to give the eulogy, and he spoke his own thoughts rather than mine. Before my grandmother died, I had written a poem about her and had read it to her. She asked that it be read at her funeral. Again, someone else did it for me because I was afraid. Maria, however, is more courageous than I.

Debbie and her group left just before the rosary due to the long drive back to Victoria. I told Maria that I was staying for the rosary. She smiled her sweet smile and said, "Oh! I'm so glad! Knowing you are here will give me strength to sing for Mom." Tonight, too?

Shortly before 7:00 p.m., the specified time for the service to begin, I returned to the chapel and took a seat in the last pew on the left-hand side, an aisle seat. I wanted to make sure I could lean out into the aisle so I wouldn't miss anything. As I sat there and watched the PowerPoint show with photos spanning Mrs. Apac's life, I noticed music sung in soft, sweet Spanish filling the chapel. A gentleman standing behind me said, "That's Maria singing." Of course! The cassette tape! Realization hit me like a rush: The tape Maria had sent Pat to retrieve was a studio recording of Maria singing. In the lobby before I reentered, Al King and I happened to be standing by a stereo system talking. One of the funeral directors walked past us and put a cassette tape in to play. Neither of us really paid much attention, but I did pick it up to read the jacket. On what is the equivalent of its spine, the cover read "Canciones de Maria Apac." Al and I assumed it to be a collection of songs Mrs. Apac liked, probably belonging to our friend Maria. Were we wrong.

The prayer service was bilingual. The priest presented his opening remarks first in Spanish, followed by English. Maria's daughter Marissa read a passage from the Bible in English after the opening prayer. From time to time, the priest referred to the "leaflet," as he called the program, to guide the audience through the service. Before the recitation of the rosary, the priest gave a eulogy in Spanish, which disappointed me because he had the audience laughing most of the time. I could only imagine what he was saying, knowing what a character Mrs. Apac had been. She loved to laugh and joke with others.

He began the rosary and recited the first decade in Spanish: "Dios te salve, Maria, llena eres de gradia, el Senor es contigo . . ." ten times. I know the rosary and enough Spanish to keep up. I listened for " . . .y bendito es el fruto de tu vientra, Jesus" but followed with "Holy Mary, Mother of God, pray for us, sinners, now and at the hour of our death. Amen" while the rest of the group recited, "Santa Maria, Madre de Dios, ruega por nosotros, pecadores, ahora y en la hora de nuetra muerte." To my relief and surprise, the second and fourth decades he recited in English. Most of what followed the rosary recitation he spoke in Spanish. I tried to keep up using the "leaflet," but he didn't follow it much as far as I could tell.

As I had surmised, not only would Maria sing at the funeral the next day, but also at the rosary prayer service that evening. She and another lady, whom I did not recognize, sang four songs in all, interspersed throughout the rosary and the prayers afterward. First, they sang between the first and second decades of the rosary. Although they sang in Spanish, I could tell it was a song to Holy Mary. After they finished, Maria explained, in both languages, that she had composed the song while "living in the Community" in 1978 in honor of her parents' special anniversary. When she speaks of her days in the religious life, she says "living in the Community" or "with the Sisters."

The second song, between the third and fourth decades, she explained before singing it, was a prayer composed by one of the Sisters in the Community. She said the prayer reminded her of her mother, so she shared it with her. Maria thought the prayer so beautiful that she "put a melody to it." After the service, she told me that she'd explained the prayer in English just for me, that she wanted to make sure I knew what the words were saying so I could enjoy it more than on its melodic level. She wanted to ensure I experienced it completely. Again, I knew Maria sang and played the guitar, but that night I learned more about my friend, that she composed music, lovely music that fills one's heart with joy, while "living in the Community."

After the priest's final prayer and dismissal, I made my way up the center aisle through the throng of people to say goodbye to my friend. Waiting my turn in line to speak with Maria, I took the opportunity to compliment the lady who had accompanied Maria. She was putting musical equipment away behind Maria. I introduced myself and told her I formerly worked with Maria at

St. Joseph, hoping she would tell me who she was. I was thinking she was, perhaps, a relative. All she told me was her name, Teresa Koehler, and thanked me, actually trying to give Maria all the credit. Later, I learned that Teresa is Maria's friend, a friendship that goes back to high school. Maria explained, "We have pretty much sung together a lot for over twenty years now. She was in the religious life when I was there." Their voices blend as though God created them to sing together.

When my turn in line came to speak with Maria, I told her how much I enjoyed the music, for it truly was spiritually peaceful and uplifting, and that it was time for me to head home. She gave me one last hug and said what I was thinking: that we needed to keep in touch with each other better. She invited me to their new home in San Antonio and enticed me further with, "And I still have your bean pot!"

"I *know* you do!"

From the mortuary, I drove to Taco Cabana because I felt compelled to eat Mexican food and sip a margarita in honor of Maria Aurora Acosta Apac. Of course, the food couldn't begin to compare with Mrs. Apac's cooking, but it was the best I could do at 8:50 p.m. on a Sunday night in Corpus Christi by myself.

I don't know if John ever attempted to use the recipe I typed up after our tamale lesson with Mrs. Apac. What I do know is that because of his curiosity about making tamales, I met a woman who taught me about her culture and cooking and appreciation for life.

TAMALES

3½ lb. lard (Manteca)

10 packages shucks

15 lbs. masa (5 lb. = 10 dozen tamales, more or less)

1½–2 teaspoons per 5 lb. of masa baking powder

salt to taste for masa (about a palmful per 5 lb.—should taste a little salty)

AND 2 tablespoons for cooking meat

6 whole balls Pimienta Dulce

1 pork roast (5 lbs.)

1 hog's head

1 lb. shortening (Crisco) can (serves as a seal; holds the lard in)

8 chiles ancho, dried & cleaned out—these chiles are really wrinkled and smell like raisins (if you want tamales hotter, use 6 chiles cascabel, also dried & cleaned out; cascabels add flavor; anchos add color; OR chile de arbol = really small & really hot)

1 sliced onion

6 sliced tomatillos

2 med. or 1 large, sliced red tomatoes

2 whole heads, peeled garlic

1 tablespoon (or a John-handful of real pepper balls)*ground pepper

1 tablespoon (or a John-handful of comino seed)*comino

1 fried corn tortilla

1 slice, fried [if you don't have bread or tortilla, can use 2 tablespoon masa] bread

*If you use the balls and seeds, grind them in a molcajete before using them.

Preparing the meat:

Fill a large pot with water and add the spices—one head of garlic, 2 tablespoons salt, and 6 whole balls of Pimienta Dulce; bring to a boil. Put the ROAST in the boiling water and spices; the water should always cover the roast. The meat is ready when a fork can be easily poked to the bottom of the roast. Cool and shred the meat. RESERVE THE BROTH!

Cool the water and skim the fat before cooking the hog's head; RESERVE THE FAT.

In the same broth as you cooked the roast, cook the HOG'S HEAD. You will have to add more water. Follow the same process as with the roast. Cook the head until the meat falls off the bone. Debone and chop up the meat. Again, RESERVE THE BROTH.

Preparing the shucks:

Spread open the shuck and clean out all silks, etc. Soak the shucks in warm water until softened. When ready to spread, pull them out and rinse them—pass under water. Pat dry.

Preparing the chiles:

Open the chiles and take out the seeds and veins. Fry the chiles in lard—really hot; make a pass; mash with spatula while frying. Fry all varieties of chiles in this manner. Put the chiles in a pot and add warm water to soften them.

Preparing the tamale filling:

In a skillet, melt some lard to fry the vegetables and bread. It must be really hot but only enough to fry the ingredients (just to pass them through it). Fry in the hot lard: onion, tomatillos, tomatoes, and one whole head of garlic. Cut up or tear the tortilla and bread; then fry them—just a pass! (The tortilla and bread are for thickness.)

Then, blend the fried vegetables with the chiles in a blender, alternating the vegetables, chiles, and water. (It won't all fit at once). Add warm water a little at a time while blending. Place the bread and tortilla on top of the last mixture. The ground pepper and comino should be added in the last blending. Blending speeds: chop first, then blend. Pour the mixture into a pot and continue the process until all of the vegetables and chiles are blended. Put a little water in the blender to clean it out; pour it into the pot with the rest of the mixture.

In a REALLY BIG pot, melt 2 tablespoons lard (enough to cover the bottom of the pan). Pour the chile mixture slowly into

HOT lard. Rinse the small pot and pour into the big pot. While stirring, add 2 tablespoons salt (salt to taste, but should be a little salty). Cook, while stirring, until the mixture comes to a boil. As it thickens, add the meat a little at a time while continuing to stir. You may add cayenne pepper if it's not hot enough, but it's better to roast some chile de arbol (canned cayenne will give it a bitter taste). [After roasting the chile de arbol, put it in the blender with water and garlic (4 cloves to about 15 chiles).] If you choose to add more chiles, you will need to add more salt because the chile takes away the salt. When the mixture comes to a boil, turn it off.

Preparing the masa:

In a small pot, melt 1 tablespoon Crisco with 1 tablespoon skimmed fat from the roast and about 1 ½ cups broth. Mix melted fat, masa, powder, and salt. Mix five pounds of masa at a time. Break up the masa; add the melted fat and masa a little at a time. (to taste and for texture).

Dump onto the table and knead (play with it); fold into center and mash. Once masa does not stick to your hand when you pat it, it's ready. If it sticks to your hand, it needs more lard. Put extra lard in the next batch. (it can be tested while mixing in machine.)

Melt the remainder of fat with Crisco and broth—a little of all of it together.

Assembling the tamales:

Spread a small amount of masa onto the shucks—about the bottom half to ⅔ of the shuck (the top part is for folding over). Spoon a small amount of the meat mixture onto the middle of the masa. Fold the right side over; then fold the left side on top of the right; finally, fold the top of the shuck over the front folds/crease; cover the crease with the top fold.

BEAN TAMALES

If you are making bean tamales, with a gallon of refried beans, 2 tablespoons lard, and 2 tablespoons all-purpose flour, put chiles cascabel or ancho. Use the same process as for meat tamales when frying in lard: chiles, onion, garlic, flour. Then blend after frying. Add beans, and bring to a boil. Spread and fold as above.

Jean Schnitz looking at her three favorite cookbooks: Better Homes and Gardens, Our Lady of Refuge, and Nueces County Legal Secretaries.

MY FAVORITE STORIES AND RECIPES

by Jean Granberry Schnitz

Many years ago, I decided to compile a cookbook filled with recipes that were quick, easy, and economical. Originally, one of the purposes of the cookbook was to help my college-bound sons think of things to eat that they could cook without lots of ingredients or equipment. The book progressed very slowly for more than thirty years while I found other things to do besides work on a cookbook. I actually began the cookbook before we had a computer. I typed the first recipes on a small, portable typewriter. When we got an XT computer, I first used an ancient program called First Choice. The cookbook progressed through about ten editions of WordPerfect. Each time we bought a new computer I would run across this cookbook and make small additions and revisions. It always quickly got pushed back to the bottom of the list. Despite many years of hibernation, it kept growing, and probably will continue to grow because when it comes to food, there is no end of ways to prepare things.

Many of the main dishes I cook start out the same way. That is, I sauté onions and green pepper, and add tomatoes. Sometimes things go in another direction by adding fruit instead of tomatoes. Sometimes I use flour to thicken things, and maybe I put in milk. I do not make things using a full-fledged roux like Lew does because it takes too long. I'm kind of a "slap dash" cook like Daddy was! Lew's roux dishes are great, but they don't fit my formula of fixing good things that are fast. Actually, I have included some of Lew's favorite recipes here—because they are too good to leave out.

People who have had little experience in the kitchen are often amazed at how simple it is to prepare a meal. Actually, anyone who can read can cook—and, maybe a few people who can cook cannot read. It helps to understand why things are done and to prepare foods with an eye to ease of cleanup afterward. Few people like to wash dishes. Another priority has been to find things that are economical to prepare and fun to eat. Most of the things in my cookbook are easy and fast to prepare!

When I began, my cookbook included only meat and main dishes, but now it has grown to include vegetables, salads, breads, and desserts, and even my favorite appetizers, beverages, snacks, and Mexican food dishes.

When I taught Home Economics at Refugio High School in 1956–1957 and again in 1960–1961, Mrs. Mayme Day was the "Senior" teacher, and I generally taught the Freshman girls. (I also taught General Science.) Mrs. Day was a wonderful person, a wonderful teacher, and a fine mentor. It was one of the duties of the Home Economics Department to be in charge of entertaining just about anybody who visited the Refugio High School. This included serving meals to the School Board and others. What we did the most, however, was to serve refreshments for numerous occasions. That way our girls gained experience in baking cookies and in serving punch and cookies—and complete meals—to various groups of people.

Mrs. Day was one of the first home economics teachers to have some boys in her classes. Most were Seniors. I have forgotten what it was called at the time, but it was a consumer education class, more or less, and they talked about various subjects related to preparing for marriage, including cooking and sewing. Nowadays, the schools not only focus on this aspect, but the name has been changed from "Home Economics" to "Consumer Education." In the late 1950s and early 1960s it was very innovative. I have included some of the recipes from some of these special occasions, including Mrs. Day's favorite punch recipe, which she called F.H.A. Punch (Future Homemakers of America Punch).

F.H.A. PUNCH

2 packages strawberry jello
2 packages strawberry kool-aid

Mix each of above ingredients as directed on the box.
Add ½ cup freshly squeezed lemon juice and 1 tall can
pineapple juice.
Freeze in washed half-gallon cardboard milk cartons.
About an hour before serving, peel away the cardboard
and place about two frozen cartons in a punch bowl and
add a can of canned fruit cocktail or a package of frozen
strawberries and 2 bottles of ginger ale.
Add more fruit and ginger ale as frozen containers of
punch are added.
Serves 75
Note: This tasted "good to the last drop" because no ice
was added to melt and dilute the punch.

SPANISH HAMBURGER CASSEROLE

½ pkg. macaroni
1 lb. ground beef
⅓ cup chopped green pepper
1 chopped onion
2 tablespoons salad oil or olive oil
1 teaspoon salt
⅛ teaspoon pepper
⅔ cup grated Cheddar cheese (½ in sauce,
    ½ on top)
2 tablespoons flour
½ cup canned diced tomatoes
1 cup milk

Cook the macaroni. Drain. While macaroni is cooking,
sauté onion and green pepper in oil until tender. Add
meat and cook until red color is lost. Add flour to the
meat mixture in skillet, and stir in milk. Add ½ of the
cheese and stir until melted. Add tomatoes. Put alternate layers of macaroni and meat-cheese sauce in a baking dish. (OR—you can stir it all together in a skillet or

an electric skillet.) Top with grated Cheddar cheese. Bake uncovered in 350 degree oven about 20–30 minutes, or until cheese melts and sauce is bubbly.

(If there are any leftovers, heat in a skillet with a little bit of milk to keep it from being dry.)

I got the above recipe when I was studying "Foods" when I majored in Home Economics at Texas College of Arts and Indus-tries, later Texas A&I University, and still later Texas A&M University at Kingsville. It was one of Aline McKenzie's favorite recipes. The way I now make it, however, is different from the original recipe, which made a white sauce separately from the meat mixture. It had the same ingredients—just put together differently. One day in 2009 I got a phone call from my grandson, recently married. He used the above recipe, and complained that it didn't taste like he remembered it. When I took another look at the original recipe versus the way I actually cook it now, I realized why it had changed. Here is my version of Spanish Hamburger Casserole—as in 2010— quoted from the e-mail I wrote my grandson:

Okay, John Wayne, let's see if I can help get this recipe to turn out right. Sometimes when we have made a recipe for more than fifty years, it gets changed somewhat and I don't even realize I am making it different. I see something already. I cook the macaroni as stated, and I like to use "large el-bow macaroni." When I say "½ package," that, of course, depends on the size of the package you are using. Sometimes I go ahead and boil the whole package of macaroni because if any is leftover, it can be made into a tasty salad—or something else. Re-member, though, that you end up with a lot more than you started with because it "swells up" in the boiling water. ALSO, be sure to put salt in the boil-ing water—at least a teaspoon or maybe a teaspoon and a half. This adds some taste to the pasta itself.

The recipe calls for a pound of hamburger meat. I usually don't use the expensive "low fat" kinds for several reasons—but mostly because having some fat in the ground meat gives it more flavor. Usually, that means using a pound of meat that is somewhere between "low fat" and "high fat."

The other thing I do different from this "official recipe" that I got when I was in school is to start off with the hamburger meat in the skillet with a little bit of oil to keep it from sticking. (The recipe starts off with the veggies and not the meat.) When it loses its red color, that's really when I add the onion and green pepper.

Aha! Now I know what is missing from this recipe! A clove of garlic! A "clove" is one of the little pieces of a "pod" of garlic. If they are small, use two. If they are large, one is enough. Mince that up and add to the meat in the skillet along with the onion and green pepper. The recipe says "1 chopped onion" which to me says one small or medium onion. It IS possible to get too much onion if you use a very large onion, but I usually use about the same amount of onion as green pepper, and chop them both up. I put onion, green pepper AND garlic in just about everything I cook.

SO, you are going to use 1 SMALL chopped onion, and ⅓ or ½ cup chopped green pepper AND at least one large minced garlic clove in with the meat and cook it on medium heat until the veggies get somewhat softer than they were when they were raw.

THEN, I pour off any excess hamburger grease. You don't want it dry, but you sure don't want it to be "swimming in grease." To the meat and veggies in the skillet, I add maybe ⅓ or ½ cup of flour and stir it all up with the meat and veggies. Then, add some milk—about a cup or more—enough to make it have a gravy-like consistency. Add ½ of the grated cheese to that so now you have meat and veggies in a cheese sauce.

Now, here is a "chemistry thing:" Always add the tomatoes last and stir them quickly into the milk and cheese and everything else. If you did it the other way around and poured the tomatoes into the veggies and flour before adding the milk, the milk would curdle and you wouldn't like it! So that's why you add the tomatoes last. Not only that, but too much tomato isn't good. So, to everything else in the skillet, add about half of a No. 2 can of diced tomatoes (or instead, I like to use one small can of Rotel tomatoes with green chiles to make it a bit "hotter.")

Aha! Again. The original recipe doesn't call for "cominos." I stir in about 1 teaspoon of whole ones OR about 1 teaspoon of ground cumin. I like the whole ones better. If you can't get them where you are, let me know, and I'll mail you a package of them. When we were in Missouri in October, we were talking about Pa's recipe for "carne guisada" with some cousins, and they complained that they couldn't get cominos in Pennsylvania. We couldn't get them in Missouri, either, so I sent them some when we got home. "Ground cumin" is simply ground up cominos and it works fine, but I like the crunchy comino seeds. At some point about here, taste to see if it needs more salt.

No wonder it hasn't been coming out right—without BOTH garlic and cominos! That's my fault for not checking the original recipe and telling ex-actly how I make it. Actually, I thought I was doing good to put in the "original," but yep, you found out that is NOT how I make it.

Oh, yes—NOW you have the meat and sauce all in the skillet. SOOO, you then stir in the drained macaroni. You have control of that! If you want more or less macaroni, you can do it your way. (If I am serving several hungry people, I add more macaroni than when just a few of us are eating. That's called "stretching" the meat to make it go farther!) I had a classmate who had eight children, and she confessed to doing an awful lot of "stretching" on these recipes. You can then simmer the whole dish in the skillet and sprinkle additional grated cheese on top of the skillet and/or on your plate OR you can bake it like the recipe calls for. Sometimes when I'm running late or in a big hurry, I won't bother to bake it, but when I do that, I usually let it simmer together VERY CAREFULLY over low heat for five or ten minutes just to blend the flavors better.

In my opinion, it is better when it bakes as the recipe calls for BUT sometimes time doesn't allow the luxury of baking it. It's already cooked by the time everything is put together, so it can be eaten right away if you want to. Most of the time during the thirty years I was working and running late, we usually ate it right out of the skillet.

Another detail is the cheese you grate to put on top. I use what we call in Texas "rat cheese" or what can also be called "mild cheddar." I don't use "sharp cheddar" or other kinds of cheese like Velveeta for this casserole. If you bake it with cheese on top, don't bake too long or too hot because the cheese will get "rubbery."

If there are any leftovers, heat in a skillet with a little bit of milk to keep it from being dry. Or you can actually put a serving on a paper plate or in a microwaveable dish, and add a small amount of milk and/ or cheese, and micro-wave it a minute or so.

Nanny's Tomato Gravy (Most Important Recipe!)

My wonderful mother-in-law made the most fabulous sauce for meats of all kinds. We called it "Tomato Gravy." It is good on beef, chicken, pork, game, and just about everything else.

> First, fry the meat and set it aside. Sauté onions, green pepper and garlic. (How much onion, green pepper and garlic varies with the amount of gravy you intend to end up with. To serve four people, I usually use one onion, ½ green pepper, and 1 clove of garlic.) Pour out excess fat (anything more than about ¼ inch of fat in the pan) and add flour to make a paste. Add WATER (not milk) and a small can of diced tomatoes. Stir until it gets thicker and put the meat back in the gravy.
>
> This can be cooked on the top of the stove or in the oven, and is good with everything! Meat simmered slowly in tomato gravy will be very tender. Hint: Don't start out with the gravy too thick because it will thicken as it cooks. If it is too thick, add more water a small amount at a time. If it is too thin, you can stir in a tablespoon or two of flour mixed to a paste with water. Always taste to be sure it is "just right"—not too salty. You can always add more salt, but it is hard to remove too much salt.

You know, life was better before the scientists discovered what was causing hardening of the arteries. Years ago I rarely cooked round steak or beef cutlets any way other than frying. Now—it's sure to kill you! But do it anyway. Life is short.

Fried Chicken

Until I was grown, I didn't know there was another way to eat chicken. What we did was catch a couple of Grandpapa's chickens, and wring their necks or chop their heads off with a hatchet. I tried not to be the person who did the wringing or chopping of necks, and was usually successful in avoiding this duty. The poor, dying chickens would flop all over the yard or garage or wherever they were until they died in a few minutes. That's not the best part of this process. Then, when the water got to boiling, we'd pour it over the chickens in a big enameled dish pan. After it soaked a minute or two and the water got cooler, it was the job of the children to pull the feathers off the chickens. This was a messy job and it didn't smell good, but we got past that part by thinking of things to come.

After the feathers were gone, the ladies (Grandmama and Mama) took the chicken to the kitchen where they removed the innards, washed it thoroughly, and cut it up. Mama would put lots of flour into a paper sack, add salt and pepper, and then put the drained and/or dried off chicken into the sack. Meanwhile, bacon drippings were getting hot in a big skillet on the stove. When it got hot enough, the chicken was dropped piece at a time into the hot fat until the skillet was full. Chicken was cooked over a hot fire (so it wouldn't sit there and soak up fat) with a lid on, and it was turned over frequently so that it cooked evenly and didn't burn. After a while, the lid was removed so the chicken would get crisp.

After it got brown, the chicken was removed to a huge platter. Mama and Grandmama always fried the livers and gizzards, too— before making the gravy.

Fried Chicken Gravy

Fried Chicken Gravy is made almost exactly like Chicken Fried Steak Gravy. The only difference is the flavor of the bits and pieces of flour and whatever that are not strained out of the fat. Flour was added to the fat until it becomes a paste, and milk (which came from the cow in the back yard) was stirred in until the gravy got to be the right consistency. The milk used was likely to be pretty heavy with cream, which also helped make it taste good. The gravy was better because none of the "drippings" or pieces of skin and/or cooked flour was removed. It just made the gravy better.

Another good fried chicken meal could be had at Aunt Mary Granberry's house near Sinton. She could see us coming across the prairie. As soon as she could see the car, she went out and caught several big chickens, and followed the routine above to produce a wonderful meal, complete with big, fat biscuits, chicken, and gravy.

CARNE GUISADA (POR LEW SCHNITZ)

Olive Oil
2½ lb. pork (pork roast, pork loin)
2½ lb. beef (stew meat, chuck, etc.)
14–16 oz. tomato sauce
2 large onions
2 cloves garlic
½ teaspoon oregano
½ teaspoon cumin powder
2 dried poblano peppers (ancho, chili pods)
1 tablespoon chile powder
flour
salt and pepper

Cut up the meat in bite sized pieces—salt and pepper meat well and dredge in flour (a plastic bag or paper sack works well for this).

Cut up the onions, garlic, and peppers (de-seed and de-stem peppers and cut in thin strips).

Heat a small amount of olive oil in medium sized pot and brown the meat.

Add cumin, oregano, and chile powder to the meat and stir in.

Add onions, garlic and poblano peppers.

Add tomato sauce to cover meat. Stir in well and simmer about 5 minutes at low heat.

Add a quart of water and bring to a boil.

Add salt and pepper to taste.

Make a paste out of flour and add to the mixture to thicken (like stew).

Simmer the mixture for about an hour until meat is tender. Check for consistency. Additional flour and water paste may be added a little at a time if needed, simmering awhile after each addition. Add flour paste early to make the consistency desired. Serve with flour tortillas, along with sliced tomatoes, avocados, and peppers (Serrano or Jalapeño peppers).

This is good with a bowl of pinto beans on the side—No beans in the carne guisada, please.

It is even better the next day (if there is any left over).

Chicken Schnitz—Lew's Famous Recipe!

1 cut-up chicken (or several drumsticks, thighs
    and bosoms)
olive oil and flour
1 clove garlic, minced
1 medium onion, diced
1 can cream of mushroom soup
1 soup can of water
2 tablespoons Worcestershire sauce

Brown chicken in a heavy skillet. Remove the chicken from oil and put it in a sprayed baking dish. Stir in enough flour to make a paste with the olive oil, or you may have to add a little oil. Make a roux by stirring oil and flour until it browns. Patience is the key to making a good roux—make a paste and stir continuously over low to medium heat until the flour is dark brown. Add onions and garlic and simmer with roux until they are translucent. Add soup and water and season with salt and pepper. Add Worcestershire sauce. Bring to a boil. Pour over chicken, cover, and bake an hour at 350. Serve over rice or mashed potatoes.

HAM WHAT AM!

When I was growing up, there was some comic character who would say, "I want some ham what am!" I don't remember who it was, but at my house, it was not often that we said the word, "ham" without adding the rest of the expression—however silly. It was always good for a smile!

We didn't eat ham often because we didn't raise hogs and ham was pretty expensive, but when we did have ham, it was a whole ham and not just half a ham or a slice or two like can be found in supermarkets today. The hams were also uncooked, but they had been cured in a smokehouse with lots of salt. Mama didn't like it so salty, so she would usually boil it awhile in a big pot of water (sometimes outside in a big iron pot over a fire). That helped get some of the salt out. Then she would put the whole ham into a large pan and score the skin and fat on the top. To do this, she (or Daddy) would cut squares about 1 inch square. It was my job to stick whole cloves into the squares (unless the skin was too thick). There were always plenty of cloves in the top. Then Mama would put the ham into the oven to bake for several hours. For about the last hour of cooking, she would spread some brown sugar on the top of the ham. If brown sugar wasn't available, Daddy always had some sorghum molasses around and she might spread a thin layer of that on top of the ham. Sometimes she used honey. One way or another, there was some sort of sweet topping on a baked ham. (Brown sugar is my favorite.)

We ate sliced ham until there were only pieces left. Mama made ham and scrambled eggs with the pieces. Finally, when only the bone was left, we boiled the bone with lima beans for yet another meal.

CHILE A LA JEAN

Many Texans disagree about how to fix chili. Some (such as David Schnitz) say that it is terrible to add beans. Some (including David Schnitz) say it is terrible to use tomatoes. I use both. I like my chili and I stand by it—even if David won't eat it. Besides, this way I can have some left over for tomorrow!

2 pounds ground chili meat (ground more
   coarse than hamburger—venison chili
   meat is best)
1 medium onion, chopped
2 large cloves of garlic, minced
2 tablespoons chili powder (or more if you like
   lots of chili powder, but go easy)
1 tablespoon whole cominos
1 small can tomatoes with green chilis—or plain
   tomatoes plus a small can chopped chiles
2 cups or more of cooked pinto beans (I cook
   extra so I can have some for chili)
1 tablespoon salt
½ teaspoon pepper

In a large, heavy pot, brown the chili meat. When it is almost done, add the onion and garlic and saute a little while. Stir in chili powder (add more later if your taste calls for more) and cominos. Add tomatoes and green chilis, plus beans, salt and pepper. Add about two cups water. Mixture will be thin. Add a cover to the pot and bring to a boil. Simmer an hour or two, adding more water if necessary. At the end of the cooking time, if chili is too thin, mix a couple of tablespoons of flour with water and mix until there are no lumps. Dilute somewhat, and stir into the chili a little at a time. It will thicken quickly and might make the chili too thick if you add all the flour and water you mixed—so go slow! You can add more, if necessary. Serve with crackers OR tortilla chips or fritos.

"Fire in the Hole" Chili—David Schnitz' Recipe

1½ pounds venison—coarsely ground
1½ pounds beef stew meat—chopped
2 medium onions (sliced and quartered)
3 cloves garlic (crushed and chopped)

1 large red pepper

2 jalapeños (with seeds)

1 bell pepper (sliced and cut into 3-inch pieces)

3 serrano peppers with seeds

2 chili pods (without seeds—chopped)

2 8-oz. cans tomato sauce

2 cans Buckhorn beer

1 can water

1 teaspoon comino

1½ teaspoon oregano

2 teaspoons paprika

1 teaspoon pepper

2 teaspoons salt

2 teaspoons chili powder

2 teaspoons flour

1 quart ice cream (for the next day)

Brown meat, and then pour off most of the grease, but not all. This serves to coat the lining of the stomach. Dump all other ingredients into the pot. Bring to a boil, stirring often. Turn down to simmer and cook 2½ to 3 hours. Thicken with flour and water. It's better the second day. This is mild and good for general consumption. To conserve chili and weed out the wimps, double the jalapeños and serranos. If too many people are still eating, add more chili powder and go to the store for more ice cream.

GRANDMAMA SCUDDER'S POUND CAKE

The first cake recipe I thought of to put into this book is the one my Grandmother Dora Belle Lee Scudder used for what she called "Pound Cake." Grandmama was not known in my family as a great cook, but when she was in her '80s and '90s (in the 1960s and 1970s), her specialty was a "Pound Cake." She loved to tell that when there was an event at the church or elsewhere where people were asked to bring food, she would be specifically requested to bring her "Pound Cake." You will note that her recipe is heavy on eggs. She always said she developed this recipe because Grandpapa grew chickens, so they always had to figure out ways to use all those eggs. Grandpapa always told that he ate seven (7) eggs for breakfast every morning of the world—and he lived to be 85. He DID eventually develop what they called "hardening of the arteries," but it took him longer than you might believe if you consider his daily cholesterol intake.

> 1 cup shortening
> 6 eggs
> 1⅔ cups sugar
> 2 cups cake flour
> 1 teaspoon vanilla

> Sift cake flour only once. Cream shortening and sugar. Add eggs and beat well. Add vanilla. Stir in the cake flour. (Grandmama always cracked each egg in a saucer and added it only after she was sure it was "good.") Bake at 350 degrees for one hour in a greased and floured loaf pan. Put a pan of water in the oven with the cake while it is baking to keep it moist. Cool slightly and remove it from the pan onto the serving dish. Slice and serve. This is good plain or with whipped cream and strawberries.

Dewberry Cobbler

The next to the most fun is a dewberry picking expedition. Go in the late spring—around the last week in April or early May and pick the purple ones! Wear sunscreen and long pants. Avoid copperheads, rattlesnakes, vines with stickers, grass with stickers, prickly ash with stickers and mosquitos, and remember to wear rubber gloves to keep your hands from itching later. Keep berries in an air conditioned area or shade after picking. The MOST fun is the eating!

> Mix together in saucepan ¾ to 1 cup sugar and
> 1 tablespoon cornstarch.
> Stir in 1 cup water gradually

Bring to a boil. Boil 1 minute, then add 3 cups
of dewberries. Stir and let sit while you make
the crust.

Crust:
Make dough of 2 cups flour, 2 tablespoons
    sugar, 3 teaspoons baking powder, and 1
    teaspoon salt.
Cut in 6 tablespoons shortening.
Add ⅔ to ¾ cup milk to make a soft dough

Pat one-half of the dough into a well buttered or sprayed
10 × 2 inch baking dish.
    Pour the berry mixture onto dough. Dot with ½
tablespoon butter.
    Roll out the other half of the dough and place on
top of the berries (OR drop by tablespoons on top).
    Bake at 425 Degrees 15–20 minutes or until bubbly
and the crust is tan in color.
    Eat with vanilla ice cream while warm!

PINEAPPLE FILLED OATMEAL COOKIES

This was my brother Bill's favorite when he was one of the "Junction Boys" at Texas A&M in the 1950s. I made them and mailed them to him. I got this recipe from Aline McKenzie, head of the Home Economics Dept. at Texas College of Arts and Industries. I have changed some things, but it is basically the same as it was more than sixty years ago.

Melt in a large skillet: 1½ sticks oleo or butter.

Add to melted oleo in skillet:
2 cups quick cooking oatmeal

2 cups flour
1 cup brown sugar
1 teaspoon baking soda

Stir in 1 teaspoon vanilla.

This will be a very dry mixture. Work it with a wooden spoon (well-washed hands work better) and press one-half of the oatmeal mixture firmly into the bottom of a well-greased baking pan. Set aside until filling is prepared.

Filling:
Combine:
¾ cup of white granulated sugar
2 tablespoons flour and
¼ teaspoon salt.

Add 1 cup crushed, drained pineapple (one
      large can).
Beat two eggs and stir into the mixture.

Cook over very low heat, stirring constantly until thickened. Add vanilla. (I have better luck cooking the filling in the top of a double boiler because it scorches easily over direct heat. It takes longer, but doesn't result in a scorched filling.)

When the filling is thick, pour over a layer of the oatmeal mixture in baking pan and spread evenly. Pour remaining oatmeal mixture on top and pat it down to edges of the pan. Clean hands work best.

Bake at 375 degrees for 25–30 minutes. When cool, cut into pieces. (If it is cut while it is too warm, it will crumble pretty badly. I store in the refrigerator if any is left over.)

Marilyn Manning, age ten

OBSERVATIONS ON COOKING AND EATING

by Marilyn Manning

THE BAKER

When I was about eleven years old, my mother went to work at the post office in our little town. I was a very responsible kid and besides that, all the neighbors were watching my every move. If I had gone near to any trouble, my mother would have heard about it before I did it.

That summer I was bored and decided that I could bake a cake. After all, you just open the cookbook, do what it says, and you get a cake. So I found one of my mother's cookbooks and looked up the wonderful variety of cakes that we had never tried. There it was: Lady Baltimore Cake. Very impressive sounding. My strategy was to just get started. I couldn't reach everything in the cupboards, so I got a chair and found the shortening and a teacup. I needed ¾ of a cup. I found a mixing bowl and put the shortening into the bowl. It said, "Stir to soften," so I stirred it.

Next: 2 cups of sugar. I found the sugar canister and there was a little over 1 teacup full in there. I emptied the sugar bowl and had almost enough, so figured that would be okay. I mixed the shortening and sugar together. So far, so good.

Extracts. I found some vanilla and a spoon from the silverware drawer and put that in. Now, hmmm, there was no lemon extract. Oh, well, it only calls for ¼ of a teaspoon . . . how important could that be?

Next I was supposed to sift a bunch of stuff together: flour, baking powder and salt. I found the sifter, found the baking powder and salt, but the flour canister only had about a cup of flour in it. I needed 2½ cups. I looked at everything in the cupboard and finally decided that cocoa had about the same consistency as flour, so I put that together with the rest and thought Lady Baltimore will be chocolate this time.

Next: 6 egg whites! I was supposed to beat them. And suddenly the directions became a little scary with how all this stuff was supposed to come together. Milk and water and egg stuff and creamed stuff and dry stuff—so I just decided to dump it all in together and see what happened. I stirred it up, and poured it into a greased pan. It said to put paper at the bottom of the pan, but Momma never did that so I didn't either. Two round cake pans went into the oven and then I turned on the heat.

That afternoon when Mom came home there were two thin, round, hard dark things. I explained that it was supposed to be a Lady Baltimore Cake but I didn't have enough sugar to make the frosting. Everybody had a piece of my cake. Not much got eaten, but there was a general consensus that I was ready to learn something about baking.

The New Meat

Growing up, I spent a good deal of time at my friend Fran's house. Her momma always seemed to have something cooked on top of the stove for anyone who happened to be hungry. Like a "self-serve buffet," sort of. One afternoon we were hanging out and I was in the kitchen getting a drink of water and noticed a nice pile of corn meal-breaded meat on top of the stove. It didn't look familiar and I asked what it was. I was told and Bess, Fran's mom, said to have some if I wanted to. So I did.

It was really good! And I had never had any like that before. Yummy. So I made sure I knew the name of this meat so I could tell my mother.

When I went home I told my mother that I had had this great snack at Fran's and it was a new kind of meat and it was so good and I hoped she could find it at the store for us to have, too. She asked what kind of meat it was. And I told her, "It's called Tripe! Can you get us some Tripe, too?"

Her face went white. This Dutch woman from Michigan was not going to get us any tripe. I'm still sad about that.

Jello

You may or may not have had the experience of eating Jello in its original form: a powder—a sweet, sort of sticky powder with a strong flavor (that may have been the beginning of SweeTarts).

As it happens, in about 1950 my seven year-old younger brother was in some sort of stage where he believed his food needed to be protected from the touch of anyone other than himself. He had learned about GERMS! He seemed not to notice that food was touched in the kitchen, but when it was delivered to him on a plate the bearer's hands must not creep around the edge of the plate where the food was. His feelings were very strong about this. We all learned how to keep him from throwing a tantrum.

One evening when my parents were out, I was, as usual, his sitter. He decided that he needed a package of Jello powder for his dessert, so I let him have it in a small bowl. He preferred to eat it from his wet finger and he was very engrossed with this project when my friend, Fran, came over to visit. We talked for a while and then she became aware of Billy's project with the Jello. She loved to tease him anyway and this was too good to let go by, no matter how I pleaded with her.

"Well, there, Billy, what do you have there?" she asked.

"Jello. It's mine!"

"It is nice to share with others, don't you think?"

"NO!"

But she laughed and reached over his shoulder, put her fingers in the bowl, and said, "You can share with me, Billy . . ." as he yelled, "NOOO!" and let fly with the bowl and the Jello. It went across the room and landed on the piano keys.

I was held responsible.

Household Tip: It is virtually impossible to remove this mixture from piano keys.

Bess Brannen

C. A. "Baby" Brannen

Fran at 17

HOW I SAVED BABY'S LIFE WITH MY MOTHER'S CORNBREAD

by Frances B. Vick

When I was seventeen years old my mother sounded an alarm. It was not that she was going into the hospital for serious surgery, which she was. It was that if I didn't learn how to make cornbread the way she did and the way Little Mother (her mother) had before her, there was a good chance my father—she always called him "Baby"—could starve to death before she got back on her feet. I took this seriously because he did have rather peculiar eating habits. One of them was chewing his food thirty-two times, even soup, which meant we were all through with the meal a long time before he was. Another was that he was almost a vegetarian in a time before such things became the norm or were even heard of much. It was particularly peculiar for him since he raised cattle.

It wasn't that he was a health nut. His favorite dessert was often opening a can of Eagle Brand Condensed Milk and spooning two or three bites out. And once, when he and my brother were out working the cattle he introduced him to a salt sandwich. It seems that Mother had discovered that our father was taking my brother, Joe Pat, out to work cattle without providing any food until they returned late in the evening. She bawled him out for not feeding Joe Pat, so the next time they went out my father bought a loaf of sliced light bread, as they called it in those days. When lunchtime came he sat down on a log, took a slice of bread and gave my brother one. Then he reached over and got some salt off the salt block for the cattle and sprinkled it on his bread and ate it. My brother did the same. When they got home Mother asked Joe Pat what he had lunch and he responded that he had a salt sandwich, which of course got our father in more trouble with her.

In any case, it was imperative that I learn to make the cornbread because if all else failed, Baby could make a meal from either buttermilk or pot likker with cornbread crumbled in it, and my mother felt this would keep him alive for a while anyway. So here is how I learned to make cornbread.

MOTHER'S CORNBREAD RECIPE

Heat bacon grease in the cast-iron skillet. She said to use enough to make the cornbread, which was a rather nebulous direction. I think it must be about ¼ cup—maybe more. You will have to experiment as I did. (I now use vegetable oil, by the way.)

Mix together:
1 cup corn meal (The cup she used was the green one she got in a carton of food as a prize—Mother's Oats probably. It was not a measuring cup. I am not sure she had a measuring cup. I do not remember them being around much. Again, you will just have to guess and experiment. I use a measuring cup.)
1 cup flour (Use the same cup as for the corn meal.)
1 teaspoon sugar
1 teaspoon salt
3 teaspoons baking powder (I wonder why it was measured this way instead of saying 1 tablespoon? I don't know, but I have seen it used in other recipes like this. I religiously use 3 teaspoons. If you are brave you can use 1 tablespoon, I guess.)
2 eggs

Add enough milk to make it of a nice consistency. (I am assuming you will know what this means. I don't but, again, I experimented.) Add most of the oil and stir it in. Leave some oil in the skillet. If you want a dark, crusty and grainy consistency on the bottom, sprinkle corn meal in the hot grease for a bit before adding the cornbread batter. Do not leave too long or it will burn.

I bake this in a 375° oven. Mother did not give directions here. I think I was supposed to put it in the oven and check on it periodically until it was golden on top, at least that is what I did. Now I check it after 30 or 40 minutes.

Surprisingly, this came out to be very good cornbread, which Baby declared was "larrupin'." And he did not starve until Mother could once again take over cooking duties.

LITTLE MOTHER'S 1-2-3-4 CAKE

1 cup butter
2 cups sugar
3 cups flour
4 eggs
2 T. baking powder
1 Cup sweet milk

Phyllis Bridges

KING RANCH CHICKEN

by Phyllis Bridges

This recipe is believed to have been developed by Henrietta King, owner of the King Ranch in South Texas. Henrietta and Richard King employed hundreds of workers of Mexican descent in their vast ranching empire. Henrietta showed an interest in the culture of her workers and adapted this recipe from some of their folk cooking. There are many variations of this recipe. The recipe below was given to me by Dorothy Porter of Denton County. Dorothy had grown up with this recipe in her family treasury in East Texas. Some people use tortillas instead of Doritos in the dish. Henrietta King would have used tortillas. Dorothy Porter used Doritos. Either one makes a true Texas dish.

KING RANCH CHICKEN

3 pounds of chicken
1 small chopped onion
¼ pound of butter
1 can mushroom soup
1 can cream of chicken soup
1 can Rotel tomatoes
Jalapeno peppers to taste (or none if preferred)
¾ pound of grated cheddar cheese
1 package of Dorito chips (any flavor you prefer)

Cook chicken until tender. Reserve one cup of broth. Cut chicken into bite-sized pieces. Saute onion in butter. Add soups, cup of broth, and Rotel. Add jalapenos (if desired). Line greased pan with crushed Dorito chips. Alternate layers of chicken, soup, and cheese. Top with crushed Doritos and cheese.

Bake at 350 degrees for one hour.
Recipe serves 10–12 people.

Helen Corbitt makes the same sort of casserole the following way.*

CHICKEN AND GREEN CHILES CASSEROLE

1 4-pound chicken or 2 2½—pound frying chickens or 2 pounds boned canned chicken

For uncooked chicken, cover chicken with water plus 1 tablespoon salt. Simmer until tender. Cool, and remove chicken from bones. Cut in large pieces.

4 tablespoons butter
1 cup coarsely chopped onion
3 tablespoons flour
2 cups milk
1 cup chicken broth
1 4-ounce can green chiles, seeded and cut in strips
5 ounces canned Rotel tomatoes with green chiles (you may omit)
1½ teaspoons salt
10 or 12 tortillas
4 cups grated sharp Cheddar cheese

[Preheat oven to 375 degrees.] Melt the butter. Add the onion and sauté 1 minute. Add flour, cook until bubbly. Gradually pour in milk and broth and cook until thickened, stirring with a French whip. Mix green chiles with the sauce, add the Rotel tomatoes. Place a layer of chicken in the bottom of a buttered shallow 3-quart casserole, then a layer of tortillas torn into bite-sized pieces,

*Patty Vineyard MacDonald, editor, *The Best From Helen Corbitt's Kitchens* (Denton: University of North Texas Press, 2000), 139. Used with permission of the University of North Texas Press.

cheese, then sauce. Repeat, with cheese on top. Bake until bubbling. This may be prepared ahead and frozen. For myself I make individual casseroles and freeze to have when I crave a touch of Mexico.

If you like this recipe hotter, add 2 tablespoons slivered jalapeno peppers.

[Helen adds: If you are taking South of the Border seriously, you might serve a guacamole salad with this and some canned or frozen pineapple spears, some toasted pecans and a bit of candy as the ending.]

Leon Hale

NEW YORK CAFÉ BEEF ENCHILADAS*

by Leon Hale

I needed seven years to get a college diploma but it did help me find a job at Texas A&M in College Station. I was a sort of press agent there, and for a year I came close to starving. My salary was $200 a month and by the time they finished carving deductions out of it I had about $160 to put in the bank. I was paying thirty dollars to rent a room and eating out every meal and buying a used car and trying to chase girls and the pay check was a joke.

There were days when I thought about the Army again. When I came out as a tech sergeant I was making twice as much as the A&M job paid and maybe three times, considering that I got free room and board and medical care and clothing. But I was convinced in those days that we'd be having another war in a few years, this time with Russia, and I'd had enough of war.

That A&M job taught me how to eat cheap. I found boarding houses where you could get a decent breakfast for thirty-five cents, and a country-style supper of black-eyed peas and biscuits and maybe a pork chop, for a buck. But the greatest discovery I made was at the New York Café in downtown Bryan—a plate of three beef enchiladas for ninety cents. Not what you'd call a balanced meal but I ate those enchiladas for supper at least three times a week and never got tired of them.

They were served in the iron plate they were cooked in and when they came out of the kitchen the juice of the meat would be bubbling all around their edges and they were covered in a thick layer of cheese, the kind that would stretch into long strings when you lifted it with your fork. Pierce that cheese covering and lovely little streams of steam spurted out and you had to wait a while before you took the first bite or you'd blister your mouth.

* Leon Hale, "The Family Table," *Supper Time* (Houston: Winedale Publishing, 1999), 129, 157. Used with permission of Winedale Publishing.

The combination of flavors in a bite of those enchiladas—mainly beef, cheese, onion, tortilla, and cumin—became for me one of the most delicious of all tastes. On pay day I used to head for the New York Café and eat two plates of those babies and sleep like logs.

One night I was sitting at the café counter polishing off an enchilada plate and I felt somebody watching me. He was two stools down, a fellow of maybe sixty with a kind of gray complexion, watching my every bite. I looked back at him, so he could speak to me if I was violating any manners that offended him. He grinned and said, "I was just watching you eat because I would give $500 if I could have a plate of those enchiladas." Meaning that the condition of his stomach couldn't allow him to eat spicy chow.

Sometimes now, so many years later, when I see young people devouring great plates of Tex Mex food I think about that fellow with the bad stomach and I understand how he felt. Today I have to limit my own intake of Mexican food but it's not because of a bad stomach. It's because of all that cheese and grease that the doctor tells me I mustn't eat.

The New York Café was operated by a big broad Greek named John Miniatis. When he retired and the cafe closed I went into grief, and then began a search for enchiladas as good as those I lived on so long, for less than a dollar a plate. I've never found them. Over forty years, in my travels over Texas, I tested enchiladas in scores of Mexican restaurants, searching for the flavor I remember from the New York Café. Sometimes they came close. John Miniatis' enchiladas ranked ten on my scale, and I found others I graded as high as eight and I had evenings of weak judgment when I gave out a couple of nines. Probably I shouldn't have.

Tex Mex food has been a big thing in my life, almost as big as my mother's fried chicken Sunday dinner. I still eat it once a week, at a place that prepares a few Mexican dishes in health food style. I have an idea what John Miniatis would think about such dishes that don't even involve rat trap cheese or hot grease.

I've eaten so much Tex Mex that I've developed a sort of possessive attitude toward it. I do a lot of complaining about restaurants that do a bad job of preparation and serve food that has no more flavor than Johnson grass hay. Nobody pays me any attention, though.

. . . . .

A few years ago I mentioned those New York Café enchiladas in the column and I got a letter from Phyllis and Jim Miniatis who live in San Antonio.

Jim is John Miniatis' son, and worked in his father's restaurant when he was a high school boy. We corresponded and established the high likelihood that Jim served me a few plates of those enchiladas when I was living on them back in '46. He and Phyllis invited me to spend a night in their home, and Jim would make enchiladas exactly like those perfect ones I remembered, and I could have some Number Ten 'ladas at last.

So I went to San Antonio for the Great Test. We had a couple of cold ones and talked about the old days and then all went to the kitchen for the preparation of the enchiladas. Phyllis had the ingredients laid out beautifully. The ground beef and the shredded cheese and the onions and the corn tortillas. Jim rolled and cooked the enchiladas in the very same iron pans used in the New York Café when I was eating there.

They were, of course, delicious and I gave them a 9.7. I wanted desperately to give them a 10, since Jim and Phyllis had opened their home to me and gone to all that trouble, but I just couldn't do it in good conscience. They were the best enchiladas I'd had since the 1940s and yet, some vague element was missing. I couldn't quite detect the exact flavor and the texture that I remembered and expected.

Driving home I decided why Jim's enchiladas were not 10's. It was because 10's don't exist, or at least they exist only in my memory. For forty years I'd been searching for something that was not possible to find. That trip to San Antonio convinced me that it's probably folly to roam around in search of any food that tastes the way you remember it from decades ago. I had to confess to myself that even my mother's fried chicken, that she'd cooked that first night I was home from the Army, wasn't quite as good as I expected. I still classed that meal the best I ever had because of the circumstances but the chicken, well, it wasn't exactly what my tongue remembered back in the tent in Italy when we talked about favorite meals. In the years I'd been away I'd thought about that chicken dinner so many times I'd remembered it being better than it was, and I'd done the same thing with those enchiladas.

New York Café Beef Enchiladas

This recipe is from Phyllis and Jimmy Miniatis. Maybe one reason it didn't taste exactly like I remembered was because they used bacon grease when they cooked 'em for me, instead of lard. The comments on the chili part are from Phyllis; the directions on assembly are in Jimmy's words, told to Phyllis.

New York Café Chili

3 lbs coarsely ground meat
½ lb. lard
1 T. chili powder
4 T. paprika
2 crushed garlic cloves
2 T. ground cumin seed (comino)

Render the lard in a pan, add the meat and brown it.

Add the spices.

Cover with water and cook slowly, stirring occasionally.

In another pan, cook two cups of red (pinto) beans with ½ T. comino and 1 T. paprika. Cook one hour.

Put in blender or mixer and process ("like mashed potatoes").

Add mashed beans to chili ("Remember! No tomato sauce.")

Assembling the enchiladas:
Chili (as above)
Large skillet
Vegetable oil
Corn tortillas
Chopped onion
Rat trap cheese
Metal plates that can withstand broiler heat

Take a large skillet. Pour a thin layer of vegetable oil (about ¼ inch). Heat the oil until hot—not sizzling. Take corn tortillas and drop in the hot oil. Leave for a few seconds until tortillas are soft and pliable. Blot with paper towel.

Lay one tortilla on a flat surface. Spread a thin line of onions in center of tortilla. On top of onions place a tablespoon of hot chili and a thin layer of rat trap cheese.

Roll the tortilla around its contents into a tight roll. Place three of these tortillas side by side in a metal plate. (Three to an order.)

On top of these three enchiladas, spread more onions. Then cover with a liberal layer of chili and then top with rat trap cheese.

Place the metal plate of enchiladas under the broiler until all the cheese has melted and is bubbling.

Serve.

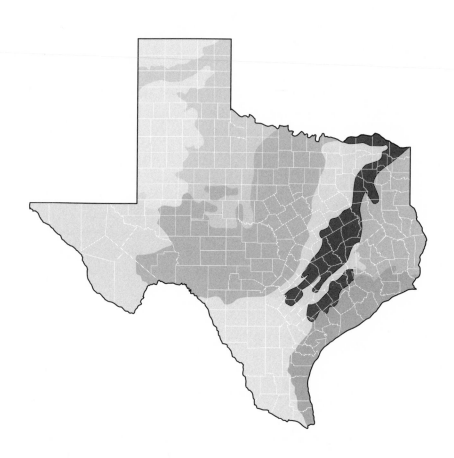

Stories and Recipes from the Post Oak Savannah*

The secondary forest area, also called the Post Oak Belt, covers some 7 million acres. It is immediately west of the primary forest region, with less annual rainfall and a little higher elevation. Principal trees are post oak, blackjack oak, and elm. Pecans, walnuts, and other kinds of water-demanding trees grow along streams. The southwestern extension of this belt is often poorly defined, with large areas of prairie. The upland soils are sandy and sandy loam, while the bottomlands are sandy loams and clays.

The original vegetation consisted mainly of little bluestem, big bluestem, indiangrass, switchgrass, purpletop, silver bluestem, Texas wintergrass, woodoats, narrowleaf, post oak, and blackjack oak. The area is still largely native or improved grasslands, with small farms located throughout. Intensive grazing has contributed to dense stands of a woody understory of yaupon, greenbriar, and oak brush.

*Stephan L. Hatch, *Texas Almanac, 2014–2015*, Elizabeth Cruce Alvarez, editor (Austin: Texas State Historical Association), 115. Used with permission of Texas State Historical Association.

Doris Clark Compton, ca. 1916

MY MOTHER WAS THE BEST COOK IN TOWN

by Robert Compton

That's what my dad used to say, and I sure didn't know a better one.

The Central Texas town where we lived was small in those days of the Great Depression (in that time, we didn't call it that; we just said that "times were bad"), and almost every mother in town cooked family meals, and that meant three a day, no vacations. So there was competition.

But Mother was the best. And she loved it, never wanted to be anything but a cook and a mother, which she started out to be after her wedding in 1916. Her main desire was to please the palate of my dad. Her first child—me—didn't arrive until ten years after her marriage.

She fixed every meal almost every day for every year I can remember, from grade school until I left for college. My younger brother and I ate every meal—breakfast, dinner, supper—at home because schools were nearby, and my dad always came home from work (the lumberyard he managed was only about a mile from home). In that time, "dinner" was at noon. "Lunch" hadn't been invented. Supper was at 6:00 p.m.

There were varied dishes, too—meat loaf was a favorite, and Mother cooked calves' liver usually once a week—"shouldn't eat liver more than once a week," she'd caution. Sweetbreads were not what you think they are—she broiled them in butter, put them on toast, and we thought they were fit for a king. In those days, hardly anyone ate sweetbreads and butchers almost gave them away; the same with liver. I didn't learn until many years later that sweetbreads were considered a delicacy, a food for gourmets.

She'd throw in something exotic from time to time, just so we wouldn't be bored—Hungarian Goulash (her own concoction of sort of a vegetable stew), and a dish she called "Talerine," a meat casserole with corn kernels, ripe olives, and noodles from a recipe exchange with a neighbor.

Most of the food came from our garden, where we planted corn, peas, carrots, tomatoes, lettuce, squash, okra, and a variety of peppers—all the good fresh stuff we needed.

Mother depended on the grocer for a few meats—whatever was cheap—and staples like sugar and flour. We got our cornmeal from a grist mill a few blocks from home. Mother would send me down to Mr. Tacker's mill and tell me to get 10 cents worth of yellow cornmeal, and I would stand there fascinated as he ground up the corn between two huge stones, weigh up a couple of pounds and pour it into a brown paper sack, then tie it with a string.

We had a cow, which I milked every morning from when I was ten or eleven until I graduated from high school. Lots of folks in town had cows. I think I could still mix up the morning feed—some bran, cotton seed hulls, yellow cotton meal—but maybe not the right proportions.

We also had a pen of chickens, so we ate lots of that, mostly fried. My dad was a hunter and a fisherman, and our home-grown food was supplemented, in season, with quail, dove, turkey, duck, wild goose, venison, and fish he hooked at the town lake—whatever he brought home.

Becoming the best cook in town hadn't been easy for my mother. She was eighteen when she and my dad married, and they set up housekeeping in a rented house. She used to tell us about the awful beginning of her home-cooking, how my dad came home one day for lunch that she had toiled over all morning. She didn't recall the menu, but my dad sat down at the table, filled his plate, and began to taste the offerings. After a moment, he pushed back his chair, announced, "I can't eat this stuff," suggested she ask his mother how to cook, and went back to work.

Mother vowed, "I'm not going to ask his mother a damn thing," and then collapsed at the table, in tears.

And she cooked every day for days, asking friends for suggestions, calling on the electric utility and gas company home economics advisors for recipes and instructions, and in a few weeks, she was ready to lay out another lunch for my dad. That one and every one after that brought only high compliments and dig-ins for second helpings. She never faltered again, and became so especially inventive at desserts that women in town of lesser cooking skills often called her to bake for them.

We loved her pies, cakes, cookies and other confections—preserves and jellies, many of them made of figs from two trees in the back yard and grapes from our summer excursions into the country where vines grew on fences—and she never failed to produce them for us.

One that I especially remember was what I regarded as a somewhat exotic dish she called Spanish Cream. I've never had it anywhere except at Mother's table, and few people I've mentioned it to have any clue to what it is. But it's delicious.

It takes a bit of patience, especially in the step where you have to stir "until somewhat thickened," because it's an instruction that has all kinds of interpretations.

Spanish Cream

1 tablespoon Knox gelatin (1 envelope)
3 cups milk
½ cup sugar, scant
3 eggs, separated
¼ teaspoon salt
1 teaspoon vanilla

Soak gelatin in milk about 5 minutes, then place in a double boiler over hot water.

Add sugar after gelatin has dissolved, and pour the mixture slowly over yolks of eggs, slightly beaten. Return to the double boiler. Cook until somewhat thickened, stirring constantly (this takes longer than you might expect). Remove from the stove, and add salt and vanilla. Add egg whites, beaten until stiff.

Turn into a casserole dish or individual dessert dishes, and put in the refrigerator until set, about half an hour.

Green Pastures Restaurant in Austin, Texas

CENTRAL TEXAS CZECH RECIPES*

by Mary Koock

I suppose I have catered for a thousand wedding receptions during my career. My friend Gina Mezzatti had the right idea about them. She said that the ceremony should be sweet and solemn and the reception fun and festive. "It is a time for great celebration—there should be music, champagne, dancing, food, and laughter!" Virginia Prasatik's was such a reception.

There is a sizable Czech population in Central Texas, and they have made great culinary contributions to these parts. Maybe one reason I like the Czech weddings so much is that they bring all the food! For Virginia's reception, we got Green Pastures all dolled up and baked some hams and beans. But then came her Uncle Henry from La Grange with one hundred pounds of hot Czech sausage; the Bartoshes came with large bowls of potato salad; Louis and Johnnie Struhall brought a gigantic bowl of the greatest cabbage salad (Selovy Salat), which Louis said his mother always took to picnics, weddings, and wakes; Martha Hill brought pans of apricot, prune, and poppy-seed Kolaches; and the bride's grandmother, Mrs. Wychopen, brought the strudel. Green Pastures made a tall, beautiful wedding cake, but really shouldn't have bothered because Aunt Octavia brought three, Mrs. Simmicek came with two, and Lillian Struhall brought her fabulous Banana Cake.

Selovy Salat (Cabbage Salad)

½ medium cabbage, cut as for slaw
3 tablespoons apple cider vinegar
2 scant teaspoon salt
3 (or more) tablespoons sugar

*Mary Faulk Koock, *The Texas Cookbook* (Denton: University of North Texas Press, 2001) 37–42. Printed with permission of University of North Texas Press.

½ teaspoon ground pepper
1 small chopped onion
2 tablespoons fresh bacon drippings

Having cut cabbage, place on fire in boiling water. Cook rapidly 5 minutes; drain. Take apple cider vinegar, salt, sugar, ground pepper and onions and bring to boiling point then add bacon drippings. Pour this juice over the cooked cabbage and mix. Season more if desired. Serves 6.

KOLACHES

Soft yeast
2 cups lukewarm milk
¾ cup and 1 teaspoon sugar
2 tablespoons salt
¾ cup shortening
2 eggs
3 cups flour, and some more

Prunes, apricots or poppy seeds

Dissolve soft yeast in milk. Add 1 teaspoon sugar and let stand long enough for yeast to rise. Cream ¾ cup sugar, salt and shortening. Add eggs and beat. Add dissolved yeast and about 3 cups flour and beat well. Keep adding flour little by little until the dough comes out smooth and has some blisters on it. Let rise until more than double in size. Roll on floured board. Cut in 3-inch squares. Make slight indention, and fill with cooled prune, apricot or poppy-seed filling.

Prune Filling:
1 lb. prunes
sugar
cinnamon
grated lemon peel
vanilla

Topping:
¾ cup sugar
½ cup flour
soft butter

Cook prunes, drain and pit them. Then chop and gradually add sugar, cinnamon, a little grated lemon peel and a little vanilla. Top this with mixture of sugar, flour and enough butter to form crumbles. Bake in 375° oven for about 12 to 15 minutes.

Besides all the cakes, there was an abundance of cookies. Mrs. Zvesper brought Listy.

LISTY (LEAVES)

3 eggs
¼ cup powdered sugar
½ cup cream
pinch salt
about 2 cups flour

Beat eggs separately, add sugar, cream, salt, and flour enough to make still enough dough to roll out very thin. Roll out a small piece at a time as thinly as possible on floured board, cut into pieces about 4 by 6 inches. Make 3 or 4 slits in them and fry light brown in hot deep fat. Sprinkle with powdered sugar. Makes 3 dozen.

Well I don't know why I said that food is number one—number one is actually beer. I remember the first wedding reception I planned for one of the charming Czech people. The bride-to-be, from a Czech settlement near La Grange, said that her uncle would bring the beer. "Beer?!" I exclaimed "But, dear, I don't have enough of the right kind of glasses for beer. We usually serve punch or champagne, and I have really never served beer at a wedding reception!"

"Well," she said firmly, "In La Grange, I have never been to a wedding reception where they didn't serve beer, and they just use paper cups!"

So, we set up a keg of cold beer under each of the two big oaks in the front yard, and a good time was had by all. Some of the old-timers brought along their dominoes and had a few games in the shade, while the dancing and merrymaking went on inside.

Easy Recipe for Dill Pickles

For 1/2 bushel cucumbers:

Wash and pack in jars. Place 4 pieces of garlic and 3 or 4 hot peppers to each quart. Add 1 dill head to each jar.

Boil 6 qts. water + 2 c. stock salt (or ice cream salt). When boiling, add 1 qt. vinegar. Pour over cucumbers in jars + seal while hot.

For a small amount use:

4 c. water	or	2 c. water
1/3 c. salt		2 2/3 tablespoons
2/3 c. vinegar		1/3 c. vinegar

Carolyn B. Edwards and the junkosaurus

YOU ARE WHAT YOU REMEMBER YOU ATE—

by Carolyn B. Edwards

Mom's Bread

I don't know how many loaves of bread Mom made in her lifetime of eighty some-odd years. When I was growing up as a baby boomer, she made at least three to six loaves every week, year after year. We did not buy "bought bread" except on very rare occasions.

If there were crops in the field to get in, Mom would start her dough in the early morning hours, so she could set it on the second rise at breakfast time. Then she'd go out and pick cotton for a couple of hours before walking back to the house to put the bread in the oven and fix lunch (or dinner, as we called the mid-day meal).

She made her bread with white flour she bought in 25-pound sacks made of printed cotton. She collected the sacks until she had enough to sew one of us a dress or a shirt, or make a set of new curtains for the kitchen. When the clothes wore out, she recycled the soft cotton fabric into kitchen towels and finally into cleaning rags.

Mom had a big, heavy crockery bowl she used almost exclusively for her bread making. It kept the temperature modified as the dough rose to yeasty goodness. She kneaded the big lump of dough on a square of canvas that had reached an amazing softness from years of use and multiple washings.

Mom put her whole self into her bread making. When she kneaded the dough, we could hear the old, round, oak pedestal table rhythmically hitting the kitchen wall—thump, thump, thump. She punched the dough down with her fist, gave it a push, folded it up, and turned it a quarter of a turn. She energetically repeated that motion until the dough was smooth and elastic, not sticky. "It should feel just like a baby's behind," she said.

After the thorough kneading, she plopped the dough ball into her bowl, covered it with a clean towel and let it rise until it was coming over the rim of the container. Then she punched it down again, pulled it out onto her cloth, cut it into three or four loaves, kneaded each one a bit more, and put them into her bread pans.

I think Mom inherited her three rectangular pans from her mother-in-law. They were made of heavy tin and encrusted with decades of burnt-on "stuff." As Mom was something of a "clean freak," I was always a little puzzled by those bread pans, which appeared to be the only items in her kitchen that were not sparkling. I've decided that that's how they looked when she got them and their thick black crust may have been the secret to Mom's delicious bread.

Since she only had the three pans, if company was coming she stirred up enough dough to make four loaves and put one in a round cake pan to bake. I was convinced those round loaves tasted better!

There is no better odor in the world than the smell of fresh bread baking in the oven. It would have been easy to devour an entire loaf of that freshly baked bread, but Mom in her wisdom always managed to bake the new loaves while she still had at least a half a loaf of older bread in the breadbox! That got eaten first.

Bread helped stretch the main dishes. None of us ever grabbed a piece of beef or sausage without being told, "Get a piece of bread to eat with that."

Mom's homemade bread was wonderful all by itself, but it was especially wonderful spread with fresh-made butter. A big treat was having big mugs of hot chocolate into which we dipped our slices of buttered bread. Ambrosia!

A freshly buttered thick slice of bread could be topped with a generous slice of onion from the garden, generously sprinkled with pepper and salt. Fresh tomatoes could substitute for the onion. Being of German background, we sometimes opted to sprinkle the tomato with sugar and cinnamon instead of salt and pepper.

Any kind of soup Mom made from scratch was always accompanied by a plate of sliced bread. Dip that slice into a bowl of hot chicken noodle soup and slurp it up!

For a sweet treat, I liked to spread the bread with fresh cream. I'd put the cream on in stages so that the bread could completely soak up every drop. Then I'd sprinkle sugar and cinnamon on top.

If we took a lunch to school, or needed one for a field trip, Mom would pack us up a couple of homemade bread and steak sandwiches smeared with butter, wrapped in wax paper and neatly tucked into a cardboard shoebox with a tomato and a fat home-canned dill pickle.

Eating this well was one of the bonuses of growing up poor on a farm in the '50s and '60s! Strangely enough, we so envied those "town kids" who had bought bread and baloney sandwiches in their boxes.

Bought bread. That's what we called that soft, sliced white stuff you got at the grocery store. A couple of times a year, Mom would buy about five pounds of market-made wieners from Patek's and two loaves of Butterkrust bought bread. She'd boil the wieners in her biggest pot, and we'd slather the sliced bread with mayo and mustard for our version of hot dogs. It seems odd now to remember how much we enjoyed those rosy-red skinny wieners, but they were such a change of pace from our usual diet of steak, roasts, pork chops, bacon, ham and sausage.

In the mid-'60s my older brother came home on leave and told Mom about pizza. We'd never heard of it. After questioning him closely, Mom headed to the kitchen and stirred up a batch of her bread dough, spread it across the bottom of an 8 × 13 pan, topped it with about a quarter of an inch layer of seasoned cooked ground beef, poured a cup of tomato sauce over it, and then generously covered the whole deal with good cheddar cheese. It looked like no pizza anyone has ever seen, but, boy, was it good! The bread was thick and crusty enough that you could take a square slice and walk around eating it. It was like having your meal on a plate you didn't have to wash up later.

If she wanted to make sweet rolls, she used milk and butter instead of water and lard in her basic dough. She also increased the amount of sugar to about a quarter of a cup and stirred in a couple of fresh yard eggs. This dough was used to make pigs in the blanket, cinnamon rolls, and rolls containing poppy seed filling.

She also made pans of what I now call "Mom's Giant Kolaches." She would just pat her sweet dough out in a round pan, forming edges. Then she filled the center with prune, cottage cheese, or poppy seed filling. The following recipe makes three loaves of bread.

Mom's Basic White Bread

In a large bowl, mix 1 package yeast and 1 tablespoon sugar with 4 cups of warm water. Stir until the yeast is dissolved.

Add a couple of cups of sifted flour gradually, stirring as you go, until you have a bubbly paste. Don't put in too much flour at this point.

Cover the bowl with a cloth and allow it to sit in a warm place for about two hours or until it has risen about halfway up the bowl.

Add 2 tablespoons of salt and 2 tablespoons of melted lard.

Add flour cup by cup, stirring thoroughly after each addition, until the dough is stiff enough to roll out of the bowl onto a floured cloth to knead.

You will need 6–10 cups of flour altogether, but the amount varies depending on your flour and the humidity.

Knead the dough until it is smooth and elastic. Lightly grease the bowl and put the dough back in it, flipping it so that it is oiled on all sides. Cover and let it rise until doubled in bulk. Test by poking it with your finger. If the hole stays, it's ready.

Turn the dough onto the cloth and cut into three equal parts. Knead each part and shape into a loaf, but don't handle the dough too much at this point.

If you don't want loaves, you can cut it into small pieces and shape into dinner rolls.

Place in greased loaf pans, cover, and let it rise again until doubled.

Bake in a hot 400° oven for 45 minutes, or until brown and hollow sounding when thumped.

Allow the loaves to cool a few minutes before removing from pans and placing on a rack to cool completely.

Making Ice Cream

In the 1950s, a hot summer afternoon provided the best excuse for making ice cream. Across the road, Sestak's hill shimmered with heat waves. The breeze that always wafted through the dining room windows of our little farmhouse felt dry. The high-pitched squeal of cicadas rose from the tall hackberry tree out by the garden. Dust devils appeared out of nowhere in the corn field, sending smoky towers of dirt and crackling dry corn leaves up into a sky where turkey vultures circled lazily.

Mom wiped the sweat off her forehead and said, "Why don't we make a batch of ice cream?"

No one ever answered, "No, thank you"

She got out the heavy pot and poured in the cold milk and thick, fresh cream, about half and half of each, and put the burner on medium and heated up the milk, stirring it constantly to keep it from sticking to the bottom and burning.

When the milk steamed, she set the pot aside to cool while she cracked about a dozen eggs, separated the yolks, and beat them into a frothy pool of gold in a separate bowl. She added sugar and a pinch of salt to the eggs as she beat them. When the milk had cooled to room temperature, she stirred it into the egg mixture. Then all of that good stuff went back into the pot and was returned to the stove. She kept stirring with her big wooden spoon until the mixture began to thicken, coating the spoon.

Once again, she allowed the mix to cool before adding a generous slosh of the good vanilla she had bought from the Watkins man, who sold such things from the trunk of his car to farm women on their doorsteps. The rich odor of cream, eggs, and vanilla filled the house as the pot cooled into a thick custard on the kitchen table. The anticipation of the frozen treat to come seemed to make the house feel cooler.

One of my brothers, Leroy or Willie, drove into town to the icehouse to pick up a foot-square block of clear ice, carried home wrapped in a clean canvas cotton-picking sack. We took a hammer to the block in a big pan and hit it hard, breaking off big chunks that we pounded or chipped with the ice pick until they were the right size to fit into the ice cream freezer.

Mom poured the custard into the shiny metal cylinder that went in the center of the freezer, filling it about two-thirds full. She inserted the metal and wood paddle and twisted the aluminum lid on to cover it. This container then went into the wooden ice cream freezer tub standing ready in a dishpan in the shade of the back porch steps. The turning mechanism slipped into a notch on one side of the top of the tub, closed over the square top of the paddle that stuck out of the lid, and locked down into a notch on the opposite side.

As soon as everything was locked down, we packed our chipped ice into the wooden tub around the sides of the metal cylinder. After an inch or so was packed in, a generous sprinkling of salt went on top. Someone would start to turn the crank so the ice would pack down nice and solid. The layering of ice and salt continued until we had the ice all the way up to the top of the cylinder and over it.

"Put this old sack on top and sit on it," the littlest kids in the family were told.

If it was my turn, I folded up the old cotton picking sack and used it to pad the top of the freezer. Then I perched on top as big brother sat on the back steps and began to crank the handle in earnest.

Our dogs, a couple of farm mutts named Tip and Randy, crawled out from under the house and lay panting in the shade, alternately watching and napping. If my Grandpa Hoerig was visiting, he made himself comfortable on the steps and told us stories about the old days while the cream thickened and froze.

The cold of the ice gradually worked its way up through the folds of the canvas sack and chilled my behind, which felt really good on such a hot day. As the ice melted, the salty cold water dripped out of a small hole drilled in the side of the wooden bucket and flowed down into the dishpan. I liked to reach down with my finger and catch some of the salt water to lick off my hand. If the ice level went down too much, we uncovered the freezer, added more chipped ice and salt, and cranked some more. I'd grab a piece of salted ice to suck on before resuming my seat on top of the freezer.

My big brothers always started off spinning that freezer handle really fast with their strong, well-muscled arms, but after about fifteen or twenty minutes, the cream began to freeze up and they had to slow down. The whole freezer moved around under me. Within thirty minutes, the cream froze so completely they could no longer turn the handle. Off I hopped and brother carefully tilted the freezer to the side to pour off most of the salty water. Then we repacked the wooden tub once more with salt and ice, covered it all up, and let it sit for an hour.

While we waited, we put a stack of spoons and soup plates (not bowls, but plates!) on the long dining table, along with a pot of chocolate syrup Mom had cooked, nutmeg and cinnamon, and maybe a bowl of home canned peaches or some chopped pecans. And, of course, a box of Saltine crackers.

When the ice cream had settled long enough, or we just couldn't wait a moment longer, we uncovered the freezer and drained the salty water again. The icy-cold cylinder was carefully removed and carried to the table where Mom had a thick towel ready to set it on. We all slid onto the long benches on both sides of the table and held our spoons in eager anticipation.

Mom carefully untwisted the lid off the cylinder and lifted it off. She dipped into the frozen concoction with a big spoon and began filling our soup plates and passing them around. We added whatever toppings we wanted and dug in. That first big spoonful always hit right between the eyes for the traditional "ice cream headache," but the richness of the pale yellow custard with its egginess and hint of vanilla slid coldly down the throat with sighs of delight and contentment.

I don't remember Mom ever making any flavor but vanilla. The flavorings were always "on the side." I guess that was just the easiest way for each member of our large family to have their favorite without arguments. I liked to start with a bowl of plain vanilla, then have one with chocolate mixed in, and maybe, if there was still room in the tummy, finish off with one more plain vanilla. We ate with our spoons, or dipped it up with Saltine crackers. When we finished a bowl, we slurped up the melted remains by lifting the bowl to our lips and drinking it down.

When we had eaten the cream down just past the halfway point, whoever had done the cranking got to remove the "ribs," that wood and metal paddle, from the center of the container. He held it up in his big bowl and enjoyed every last drop of goodness. We all believed that the ribs held the very best tasting cream, and therefore it was only right that it go to the person who did the heavy labor.

Chocolate Fudge
1 Tall Can Carnation Milk
2 cups sugar
2 sticks butter
Cook to a rolling boil 10 minutes, stir constantly.

1 jar marsh mellow creme (1 pint)
2 pkg (bag) Chocolate Chips
2 tea spoons Vanilla
2 cups pecans
d of in spoonfulls on fair or wax paper

Ida Grohman

IDA GROHMAN'S EGG NOODLES

by Nelda Vick

My mother was renowned for her egg noodles. They were great favorites at the food sales booths at the Sacred Heart Church in Rockne, Texas—at the Bazaar each fall and at the Spring Festival. They were made by Ida Goertz Grohman all through the lives of her children. The recipe probably came from Germany with the original settlers.

The first Catholic settlers in the present day Rockne area met for religious services in a pioneer log cabin on Walnut Creek. Philip Goertz built the cabin around 1860. This cabin was the center of the community's life at its inception. The Church still is. After the Philip Goertz cabin burned, a new church was completed in 1892. The third and present church was built mostly by the parishioners themselves just as the earlier structures had been. The new, imposing edifice was remodeled in 1976, in time for the Centennial Celebration of the parish.

The grandmothers, mothers, daughters, sisters and friends helped build a really vibrant Catholic community. "The Sacred Heart community is blessed to receive the tender loving care of these noble women. Vielen Dank!—Many Thanks! and Guten Appetit!" (From *Country Cooking: Saint Ann's Society of Sacred Heart Church*, Rockne, Texas, 1994.

EGG NOODLES, MRS. IDA GOERTZ GROHMAN

Start with 1 cup of flour and 1 teaspoon salt mixed together and put in the center of the kitchen table. Make a hole in the middle of the flour and add two eggs. Work until smooth and then work in another cup of flour to stiffen dough. (It should not be sticky at this point.)

Roll real thin, cut into strips and keep well floured. Hang the strips around the kitchen on the back of chairs, etc., to dry.

I recall this ritual from my earliest childhood, the flour in the middle of the table and the noodles hanging around the kitchen to dry.

Sacred Heart Catholic Church in Rockne, Texas, where Ida's egg noodles were favorites at the bazaars

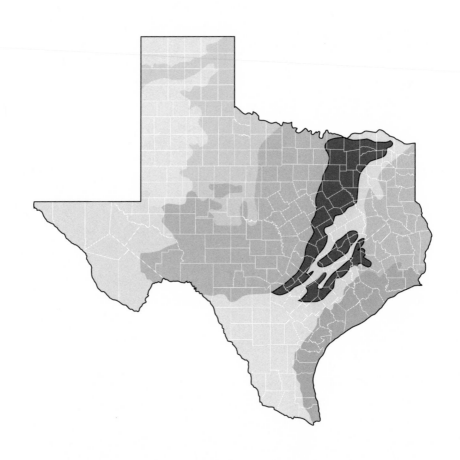

Stories and Recipes from the Blackland Prairies*

This area of about 12 million acres, while called a "prairie," has much timber along the streams, including a variety of oaks, pecan, elm, bois d'arc, and mesquite. In its native state, it was largely a grassy plain—the first native grassland in the westward extension of the Southern Forest region.

Most of this fertile area has been cultivated, and only small acreages of grassland remain in original vegetation. In heavily grazed pastures, the tall bunchgrass has been replaced by buffalograss, Texas grama, and other less productive grasses. Mesquite, lotebush, and other woody plants have invaded the grasslands.

The original grass vegetation includes big and little bluestem, indiangrass, switchgrass, sideoats grama, hairy grama, tall dropseed, Texas wintergrass, and buffalograss. Non-grass vegetation is largely legumes and composites.

*Stephan L. Hatch, *Texas Almanac, 2014–2015*, Elizabeth Cruce Alvarez, editor (Austin: Texas State Historical Association), 115. Used with permission of Texas State Historical Association.

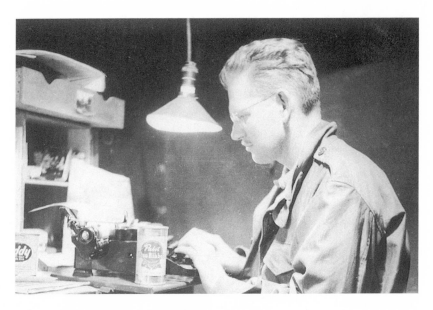

Marine Captain John W. Wilson in Korea in 1952

SLANG JANG: THE NATIONAL DISH OF HONEY GROVE

by John W. Wilson

Those among you who don't relish oysters—canned or raw—are free to leave the room. For those of you who choose to stay, I'll tell you a tale about the origins, the rise to popularity and fame, and the decline, almost to obsolescence, of a delicious, invigorating, summertime concoction known as "Slang Jang" and referred to by many as the national dish of Honey Grove.

Honey Grove is a town in the top of Texas, in Fannin County midway between Bonham and Paris, and how the town got its name is another story, well-based in legend and so often told that I won't bother with re-telling it here. Suffice it to say that Slang Jang originated in Honey Grove some fifty years or so after Davy Crockett camped in the area while on a hunting side-trip and he wrote a note about the several bee-trees his party found there. Had it been available, however, I'm sure Slang Jang would have been a welcome addition to their regular diet of branch water and buffalo hump.

The exact date is difficult, if not impossible, to pin down, but the origin of the dish appears to date to about 1888, although there is evidence that there might have been a predecessor, or at least a hint of what was to come, in a recipe from an earlier year.

In January 2003, the Newsletter of the American Dialect Society (NADS) carried an item requesting examples of usage of a list of words to be included in an upcoming volume of the *Dictionary of American Regional English*. "If you are familiar with any of the following words or expressions," the article requested, "please let us know." Leading the list was:

> slang-jang—a dish containing oysters, onions, pickles, peppers, etc. We have a single citation from Arkansas, but a Google search suggests that this is

still known, especially in the South and South Midland. Is this part of your culinary background?

You bet it was! I married a Honey Grove girl and, of course, Slang
Jang became a treasured part of my culinary background.

But a single citation from Arkansas? That could not be toler-
ated. It must have been due to a trickle-down effect from some
misguided North Texan who had happened to wander across the
state line. So, I fired off a response giving ample evidence of the
Honey Grove origin of the simple but delicious dish. I find that dia-
lecticians more experienced than I also responded, but since I have
not seen Volume V of the *Dictionary of American Regional English*,
I cannot tell you whether Slang Jang has been properly defined
therein, as anticipated that it might be in a much earlier publication.

For that definition we turn to the Honey Grove high school
annual for 1912. It was the school's first annual and the name chosen
for it was, proudly, *The Slang-Jang*, set in ornate, black-letter type.

"The word Slang-Jang is not found in the dictionaries," the
introduction to the annual notes, "but it will be given its proper
place when the lexicons are revised. We say this confidently, for
the makers of dictionaries are progressive and anxious to keep their
works up-to-date; therefore they will not fail to include in their next
editions the popular and widely-used word which forms the subject
of this sketch. When the word is given its place on the pages of the
lexicons, the paragraph will read about as follows:

> **Slang-Jang. n.** A delectable mixture of liquids and
> solids which originated in the city of Honey Grove,
> Texas, about the year 1888. A dish that everybody
> likes and nobody can get enough of. Never known
> to make any person sick, no matter how much of it
> was consumed. It is claimed that this dish can only
> be compounded correctly in Honey Grove, or by a
> native of Honey Grove.
>
> We are not permitted to print information re-
> garding the origin of Slang-Jang, neither can we
> make public the formula thereof; these are secrets

that have been sacredly guarded all these years. We must say, however, that it is both food and drink, a digestant, a stomachic and a condiment. It is a mixture that does everybody good and nobody harm.

This being true, we can find no good reason why our Annual should not be given the name of Slang-Jang. It is a Honey Grove publication, a mixture of beauty and homeliness, photography and fun, business and burlesque, which, we feel sure, will injure no one, but make those who partake of it feel better. Therefore, we christen our Annual "Slang-Jang," and send it forth with the hope that it will prove as delightful a mixture as the great dish from which it takes its name.[1]

The editors of the high school annual were a little coy in claiming that the recipe for Slang Jang was a secret, though even then the ingredients might vary somewhat from maker to maker, depending on what was conveniently at hand. And Slang Jang's origin may go back even earlier than 1888, according to recipes in a cookbook published for the ladies of the Kute Kooking Klub of Honey Grove.[2] The club had been organized October 29, 1886, and contained recipes that pre-dated that event. One, in particular, involved hollowing out a big block of ice and dumping in canned tomatoes, canned oysters, chopped-up pickles and onion, and salt and pepper seasoning to taste. When properly chilled, the mixture was ladled up, as from a punch bowl, and served in cups.

It should be noted that Slang Jang was principally a warm weather dish, often brought outside to serve from a picnic table in the back yard in the cool of the evening. And where, you might ask, did one get a block of ice in North Texas during the summer? It came from the town's ice-making machine, or, cut during the winter from a frozen lake, it came by train, packed in sawdust, from some northern state.[3]

As natives of Honey Grove prepared their gazpacho-like summer soup and served it to family and friends, its popularity grew, and legends of its origin began to arise. Probably the most popular tale has the invention occurring in Fritz Messerer's store sometime after the aforementioned high school annual was issued and forgotten. Why Messerer's store? Because, so the story goes, Fritz not only was a member of the band of inventors, but his store could furnish the essential equipment and ingredients. And, of course, he had the only ice-making machine in town at the time.

Evidence of the persistence of this legend is given by outdoorswriter Tom Lepere in a July 12, 1974, column in the *Dallas Times Herald*. On a break from fishing in Lake Crockett, a few miles north of Honey Grove, Tom was served Slang Jang for lunch by Shirley Ausburn of the Davy Crockett Lodge. "Every one around Honey Grove has his own idea about what goes into Slang Jang, but Shirley's is about the best formula I've sat at a table with," Tom wrote. He listened to her explanation of how the dish came to be.

"It seems," he wrote, "as though long ago there were three cronies in Honey Grove who fished and hunted together. They also were known to imbibe of the grape, sniff of the hops and luxuriate in the squeezings of the corn plant.

"They fished in the heat of the sun one day and naturally were forced to keep their innards cool by taking long pulls at icy brown bottles.

"They quaffed enough that they didn't realize they had failed to bring lunch with them. As darkness fell, they all decided they were beginning to get hungry. There wasn't any place around to eat, but one had a brilliant thought. He owned a grocery store so what would be a better place to get a mess of grub?

"They went to the store, got a dishpan, and started walking down the aisles, opening cans and dumping them into the pan as they went.

"Thus Slang Jang was born."[4]

(It is worthy of note here that the dishpan remained a key part of Slang Jang lore. Early in our domestic life, my beloved bride from Honey Grove had us invest heavily in a blue enamel dishpan and eight matching enamel cups for the proper brewing and serving of Slang Jang.)

Could Slang Jang have been invented more than once? Indeed it could, though it seems to owe its true origin to members of the

Kute Kooking Klub, and its popularity expanded rapidly enough to gain this notice in the August 23, 1901, issue of the *Commerce Journal*, published in a neighboring Northeast Texas town: "About fifteen couples enjoyed a 'slang jang' party at Iceland Monday night, where dancing and music was had until a late hour. All report a most pleasant time with the 'slang jang' as delicious."[5]

Not everyone had the same high opinion of Slang Jang, however. Preceding the story of the three beer-guzzling fishermen by many years is the origin-story attributed to J. H. Lowry, editor of the *Honey Grove Signal*. According to reports in both the *Dallas Morning News* and the *Galveston Daily News* issues of March 2, 1907, "Not long ago the editor of the *Honey Grove Signal* went to Austin, and while there he appears to have regaled his friends with a dish about which much has been said and little is known. The *Bonham Herald* mentions the matter in this way:

"The Honey Grove dish, their national dish, is slangjang. It is said to be made up of what generally gets in the receptacle for a pig's dinner, and it produces all sorts of things, including nightmares and new candidates. Editor Lowry introduced it at Austin the other night, when the effect was electrifying, we hear.

"There may be and there are people who are interested in this new culinary concoction, known in the locality of Honey Grove as 'slangjang'. Editor Lowry, once upon a time, sat down and told *State Press* all about the discovery of the dish, if such an expression is permissible, and also did the best he could do to introduce him into the mysteries of its making. Told in his way, a graven image would have become interested in it, and it is almost profane to attempt to repeat what he said, so despicable must be the attempt.

> He said that some years ago a party of well-fed Honey Grove men went into the Territory to hunt. They took with them much food, such as could be carried in tins. Moreover, they appear to have taken other things. The weather was beautiful and game scarce. The party remained in camp waiting for bad weather, having concluded that only when the deer

were so depressed by climatic influences that they would cease to run about and would finally lean against trees, they could be killed.

Lying around camp for several days, they became full of lassitude and other things, and the terrible condition was finally reached when each declined to cook. Starvation stared them in the face, though they reclined or were stretched in the midst of that plenty which the canned goods represented.

Thus flew one, two, even three days, when some one of them, less obstinate than the others, concluded to minister to his own appetite. He made a fire. He placed a kettle of water on it. He attacked the canned goods; he emptied them of their contents of tomatoes, corn, beans, pineapple, peaches, blackberries, ochre [*sic*], deviled ham, pickled pork, pickled beef and all the cove oysters into the pot. Then added pepper and salt ad libitum. He removed the pot when it began to boil.

His companions arose, every one of them, with such appetites as perhaps never man had before. They shook hands across the steaming agent of reconciliation. They drank deep drafts of branch water, and other things, to the eternal health of all. They crowned the genius who had conceived the great dish before them, and crowned him with oak leaves, one of the members having asserted that this is what they did with conquerors and public benefactors in the Roman days. Having eaten up everything they had brought with them, being physically unable to pursue even a squirrel, they pulled for home.

They brought back nothing but a reminiscence, and that was of the dish they had eaten. Confused in tongue, down and out in head, they stumbled on a name for the new conception, and "slangjang" was born. It is a great dish, so Editor Lowry assured

State Press; but a man must prepare himself for the enjoyment of it.

He must refrain from all other food for at least three days. During this time he must drink copiously of that which will make horseradish and sauerkraut indistinguishable to him. He must cultivate a sullen, obstinate and mean disposition. Then, when having undergone the ordeals mentioned, he will eat "slangjang" and call it something beside which the nectar of the gods is cold, stale and funky beer.[6]

From whence came the word "slangjang" is anybody's guess, but I suspect it was somehow related to "tanglefoot." Alcoholic beverages figure prominently in the creation stories and, indeed, in Shelby County of East Texas in 1914, "Slang Jang" meant "whiskey."[7]

Let's back off some from the boiling pot that nourished the starving hunters in the Indian Territory, for we have seen conclusively that Slang Jang is most palatable when well-chilled. The true recipe does not vary greatly from the original used with that hollowed-out block of ice in the 1880s. To me, the classic one is set forth in a 1922 cookbook.

Honey Grove Slang Jang

Mix together two 3-pound cans of tomatoes and three 2-pound cans of oysters, 1 large onion, 2 large pickles chopped, add vinegar, salt, red, and black pepper to taste, 1 large lump of ice to chill just before serving. Add crushed crackers to thicken.[8]

Years later, in her mastery of the kitchen, my wife and Honey Grove native added her variations on this theme in her:

Slang Jang

28 oz. can tomatoes, cut up; 8 oz. can oysters; 1 onion, chopped; 1 or 2 dill pickles, chopped; 1 or 2 tablespoons pickle juice; 3 gherkins; Tabasco, ½ teaspoon;

Worcestershire sauce, 1 teaspoon; salt and pepper. Mix. Chill. Serve with ice in bowl, with cheese and crackers.

Variations continued, and in the *Honey Grove Signal-Citizen* for Friday, March 15, 1991, we find mention of an entry by Mrs. George D. Carlock, Jr., of Honey Grove, that won Honorable Mention in August 1950 in a *Dallas Morning News* salmon recipe competition.

SLANG JANG

One can of salmon; 1 large can of tomatoes; 1 small can of oysters; 1 medium sized onion; 2 large pickles; salt, pepper and pepper sauce (to taste). Flake salmon and mix with tomatoes and oysters in a large bowl. Add chopped onion and pickles. Use salt, pepper and pepper sauce generously to taste. Add a few ice cubes to chill and keep cold. Serve with crackers.[9]

On the Honey Grove, Texas, Web site Mary Anne Thurman, an authority on the matter, comments as follows:

Slang Jang is a dish peculiar to Honey Grove. The legend says that a group of men in a grocery store concocted it for lunch one day. Its popularity grew until there were many people who had Slang Jang picnics at the City Lake. As a child, I can remember many weekends we spent at the lake playing and then eating the delicious chilled Slang Jang. I was a blue ribbon winner in the Slang Jang Contest during the Honey Grove Centennial in 1973.

SLANG JANG

Mix undrained canned tomatoes with chopped dill pickles and chopped onion to taste. Add a can of oysters, chopped. Add Tabasco, salt and pepper to taste. Add ice cubes to chill. Serve with saltine crackers.

Many people vary this recipe. Some add canned salmon or vienna sausage in place of the oysters, or in addition to the oysters.[10]

You can see the trend developing. While Mary Anne's recipe is classic, other cooks are following different pathways. Slang Jang is becoming thicker—more like a cold stew than a cold soup. With Shirley Ausburn's 1974 recipe, mentioned earlier, you see how it has become something resembling a seafood platter:

Diced dill pickle with a dash of the juice; a can of to-matoes chopped and dumped in with all the liquid; a diced onion; half pint of raw oysters; pound of boiled shrimp; and a quarter pound of boiled crab meat. Salt and pepper to taste.[11]

Sad to say, but by the 1980s Slang Jang has ceased to be a soup, or even a stew; it has become a relish.

I'll hit you with another recipe, this from an authoritative source: *Eats: A Folk History of Texas Foods.*

SLANG JANG

1 tomato, fresh from the garden, chopped; 1 sweet green pepper, chopped; 1 medium onion, chopped; 2 stalks of celery, sliced; about ½ pod of hot red pepper; a pinch of salt and sugar; ¾ cup vinegar; ½ cup water. Combine all ingredients. Add pepper and seasonings to taste.[12]

Today, or at least as of the time I write this, if you Google "Slang Jang" you will find more references to relish or salsa than you will to a cold soup. The noble, oyster-laden, national dish of Honey Grove and its folk-history roots are all but forgotten.

My personal, prejudiced, and completely unscientific theory is that the advent of home air conditioning and the ice-making refrigerator-freezer brought about the demise of the old Slang Jang. With ice no longer a rarity and the air inside the house much cooler than the air outside, who wanted a cup of something cold for lunch or supper?

But there is a glimmer of hope on the horizon. For the town's Davy Crockett Day celebration on October 4, 2008, the Honey Grove Chamber of Commerce sponsored a Slang Jang contest to re-focus attention on its honored dish. The prize-winner is far, far different from the namesake recipe, but, like earlier versions of Slang Jang, it comes with a story.

Winner of the blue ribbon was Phyllis Ryser of Honey Grove, who shared her story and winning recipe with me.

"My grandmother," she wrote, "used to make slang jang for the family every Christmas Eve. We liked it a lot but no one who married into the family would eat it. The usual response was YUK! Therefore her recipe is all but forgotten.

"Only ingredients that could be obtained from a small country store were available to Grandmother. She used Vienna sausage, canned tuna fish, canned tomatoes, dill pickles and onions. She mixed these ingredients with a large can of tomato juice. This mixture was served cold in soup bowl with crackers and Fritos.

"I tried to make a more palatable dish using the base foods. It seems slang jang is sometimes similar to seafood gumbo. In east Texas at the turn of the century the only seafood available was canned tuna fish, canned oysters, sardines, or other canned fish.

"Here is my recipe."

> 4 chicken thighs, skinned
> 3 tablespoons flour
> 1 medium onion, chopped
> 3 tablespoons salt
> 2 Italian sausages
> 1 bell pepper
> 1 stalk of celery
> 1 pound of shrimp
> 6 Roma tomatoes
> 1 large clove garlic

3 tablespoons olive oil
5–6 stems fresh parsley
pepper to taste

In a large, heavy saucepan, sauté the onion and crushed garlic in the olive oil until onion is transparent. Remove the onion and garlic from the pan and divide in half. Dredge the chicken thighs in flour and salt lightly. Brown in the pan where the onion was cooked. Remove from the pan and cut the meat off the bone. Cut the meat into small pieces. Boil the sausages and cut into circles, then cut the circles into ¼ pieces.

Boil the shrimp in salt (3 tbs) and water (1 qt) until it turns red. Shell and cut it into smaller pieces depending on the size of the shrimp.

Cut the tomatoes in half length ways. Place tomato halves in the saucepan and cook in the olive oil until outside is slightly tender.

In a blender place the tomatoes, bell pepper, parsley, celery, and ½ of the onion. Blend until smooth. Pour the mixture in the saucepan. Stir the mixture until it starts to boil, while scraping the browned bits of flour from the bottom of the pan. You should have a smooth, thick sauce. If it is too thick, thin with water or chicken broth.

Add the shrimp, sausage, chicken, and rest of the onion and garlic. Serve as a soup with chips or crackers or leave it thick and serve over rice.[13]

So here, since the 1880s we have run the gamut from thin to thick, from gazpacho to gumbo, from cold to hot to something to sprinkle over black-eyed peas, but still the dish retains its name and its connection with thirsty fisherman and hungry hunters. In whatever form it takes, long live Slang Jang, the national dish of Honey Grove! And who knows? With global warming looming and the outlook for Texas summers getting even hotter, maybe the true Slang Jang will rise again.

SOURCES

1. "The Slang Jang." Honey Grove High School Annual, 1912, p. 11.
2. Kute Kooking Klub of Honey Grove, Texas. *KKK Cookbook*. Robert Clarke Co., Cincinnati, 1894.
3. John H. Conrad and Otha C. Spencer, editors. *John Black's Pictorial History of Honey Grove, Texas, 1880–1925*. Hennington Publishing Company, Wolfe City, Texas, 1988, p.32.
4. 'Slang Jang—glutton maker' by Tom Lepere from *Dallas Times Herald*, Fri. July 17, 1974, p. 6-F.
5. Cited October 20, 2006, by Barry Popik at the following Web site http://www.barrypopik.com/index.php/new_york_city/entry/slang_jang/_
6. Ibid.
7. "Shelby County Rootsweb Facts, Week Ending December 12, 2003" at the following Web site: http://www.shelbycountytexashistory.org/Facts/wfacts12122003.htm
8. Honey Grove. *Cook Book of the Westminster Guild of the Presbyterian Church*. The Citizen Press. 1922. p 73.
9. "Slang Jang recipe and others from the past" by Honey Grove from *Signal Citizen*, Friday, March 15, 1991.
10. www.honeygrove.org
11. Lepere, *op. cit.*
12. Ernestine Sewell Linck and Joyce Gibson Roach. *Eats: A Folk History of Texas Foods*. Texas Christian University Press, Fort Worth, 1989, p. 63.
13. Letter, Phyllis Ryser to John W. Wilson, December 20, 2008.

Okra & tomato Gumbo

8 cups tomatoes
4 cups sliced Okra
2 cups chopped Onion
2 med sized bell peppers chopped
2 bay leaves
about 1 tablespoon salt

Brown Okra + Onions in
2 tablespoon Salad Oil or Butter
Add tomatoes. Season + Cook slowly about
~~tender~~ 1 hr.

Mountain Men with Pikes Peak in the Background. Back Row: Allen Manning, Jon Bauman, Steve Peek, Pat Vick, Ross Vick III. Front Row: Ross Vick, Jr., Manny Vidal, Ron Chamberlin, Tom Reeves, Dub Wood, Vic Manning

OLD SETTLERS BEANS

by Pat Vick

My wife Nelda and I were hosting a company party several years ago and needed the perfect complement to go with hamburgers and hot dogs. We could not think of anything so she called a good friend of hers who gave her this recipe for Old Settlers Beans. We liked this recipe so much that it has become a staple at family get-togethers. It is also made at an event my father hosts each summer—a men's retreat that has been dubbed the "Mountain Men Retreat" because we meet at the family place in Colorado at 9,000 feet with Pikes Peak for a view. We golf, play poker, sometimes go to Cripple Creek to try our hands at the slot machines or tables there, and in general have a fine time.

A couple of the men will usually fix dinner every night. The last couple of years, my brother Ross and I have taken the lead in planning the dinners. Old Settlers Beans have become a favorite and a regular at the retreat. I usually fix them twice during the week because you can eat them as a side with a main course or by itself. It also makes a good dip for chips.

OLD SETTLERS BEANS

½ lb. hamburger
½ lb. bacon, chopped (Tip: Freeze bacon for
    easier chopping)
½ tablespoon chopped onion

Combine and brown the above ingredients. Do not drain.

1 can pork & beans
1 can red kidney beans, drained
1 can butter beans, drained

Sauce:

¼ cup catsup

¼ cup hickory smoked BBQ sauce

⅓ cup sugar

⅓ cup brown sugar

1 tablespoon molasses

1 tablespoon mustard

Mix sauce with other ingredients. Cover and bake for 1 hour at 350 degrees.

Mmmmmmmmm, Mmmmmmmm. That's good eat'n!

Bizcochitos (cookies)

1 cup sugar	6 cups sifted flour
2 cups shortening	3 teaspoons baking powder
1 teaspoon anise seed	1 teaspoon salt
2 eggs	1/4 cup water

Cream shortening, add sugar and seed. Beat eggs and add to mixture. Blend until light and fluffy. Sift flour with baking powder and salt and add. Add water and knead until well mixed. Roll 1/2" thick and cut into fancy shapes. Roll top of each cookie into a mixture of sugar and cinnamon (1 t. cinnamon to 1/2 c sugar). Bake in moderate oven until slightly brown.

Kenneth W. Davis

CENTRAL TEXAS CANNING CUSTOMS IN THE THIRTIES AND FORTIES

by Kenneth W. Davis

—❦—

Two-bit and four-bit pieces served useful purposes in the canning of preserves and jams before the coin of the realm was debased by the addition of copper. In old Bell County where I grew up, housewives (with sporadic help from their husbands and children) cooked big kettles of peaches, plums, pears, and occasionally apricots to provide sweets for breakfasts and for snacks at other times of the day. The canning of black-eyed peas, green beans, potatoes, carrots, and tomatoes was also common. But silver coins of the realm were used only in the cooking of preserves and jams. Called "canning money," two-bit and four-bit pieces were treasured by housewives. Between canning seasons these coins were stored carefully in Ponds Facial Cream jars, in Kerr pint jars, and sometimes loose in the bottom drawers of cedar chests.

The coins were put in kettles containing sliced fruit, sugar, cinnamon, cloves, nutmeg, freshly squeezed lemon juice, a smidgeon of almond extract, and fruit pectin such as Sure Jell, a commercially prepared substance also used in the making of jellies. The purpose for putting coins in the fragrant mixtures was to keep them from sticking while they cooked slowly to just the right colors and consistencies. The coins moved slowly up and down during the cooking process. After many seasons of such use, the silver quarters and half-dollars became shiny and in time quite smooth because of their exposure to the acids in the fruits they kept from sticking. I don't know if the Environmental Protection Agency or the Department of Agriculture today would sanction the use of coins in canning fruits. Probably the residual silver would be considered a threat to health or sanity. But during the Great Depression of the Thirties and on to the Forties, Central Texas housewives didn't know about such possible health hazards, so they canned for their families and used silver coins with blissful abandon.

This facet of folk life, the preserving of foodstuffs, added a term to the patois of some residents of Central Texas. The use of canning money for any purpose other than as aids in the cooking of preserves or jams was forbidden whenever possible. In the late Thirties at the height of the Great Depression, farmers sitting under the tin awnings of storefronts in Holland and Bartlett, Texas, talked about their financial situations and would sometimes respond to a friendly question such as "Are you keeping afloat money-wise?" by saying, "Well, it's tough, but we're not down to the canning money yet." This reply meant, of course, that financial matters weren't quite desperate enough for spending the shiny quarters and half-dollars stored away for the next canning season.

The lore of home canning in the Thirties and Forties is extensive and treats the growing, picking, and preparing of the fruits and vegetables as well as the canning processes themselves. Many of the farms in Bell and Williamson counties had peach orchards, and some had at least a few pear trees. Wild plum trees and domesticated varieties were common, and there were a few apricot trees here and there. Farmers or their wives cared for these trees to keep them bearing the delicious fruits for preserving. One common treatment for trees was to paint the trunks to a height of three or four feet with a lime-based whitewash. This substance was supposed to keep the dreaded peach borers and other insects away. It was applied lavishly with large brushes of the sort sometimes used to sweep barns or filling station oil changing bays. Usually done by farm wives, this job was a somewhat messy one that required the carrying of large buckets of water and sacks of lime to the orchards that were far, far away from wells. Running water was almost non-existent. When the lime whitewashing was completed, the orchards literally gleamed on moonlit late spring and summer nights.

Another strategy to protect fruit trees from pests was to nail galvanized sheets of metal around the trunks of the trees to keep squirrels from climbing to steal the fruit before and after it ripened. In some orchards every tree would also have at least a few 12-penny nails driven randomly into its trunk to provide "iron." Many householders sincerely believed that in the black soil of old Bell County there were deficiencies in minerals, chief of which was iron.

And of course, thieving birds had to be dealt with. Or at least there had to be attempts to keep crows, jays, mockingbirds, and even some hawks from stealing fruit. Three methods were the ones most commonly used. First, shiny lids from syrup buckets were tied to the branches of the trees. The theory was that the reflections of the often relentless summer sun on the lids scared the birds so they wouldn't come close to trees thus protected. Second was the placing of homemade wooden owls in various parts of fruit trees. Brightly painted with really prominent eyes, beaks, and claws, these silent guardians certainly looked scary enough to me when I was about six years old. As best I recall, the owl sentinels were effective. Nowadays, a homemade owl from the first half of the twentieth century brings a good sum from collectors of authentic Americana.

The third method is one familiar to us all: the placement of scarecrows in the orchards. My maternal grandmother Laura Jane Perkins was a talented craftsperson as well as a world-class country cook. She delighted in making garishly elaborate scarecrows, complete sometimes with artificial spectacles and tobacco pipes. I know now that she made these colorful objects more to please and delight her grandchildren than to scare away marauding birds. She said a few months prior to her death in 1941 that often enough she found crows resting on the shoulders of the fearful replicas of humans she devised. She also used a method somewhat common among would-be fruit growers. When the gatherings of birds became particularly dense, she would take her trusty .410 shotgun out on the west porch and fire it into the air to frighten the birds away. When in a half an hour or so they returned, she would repeat this performance, one I am sure was also done to amuse the grandchildren.

In my family—as was the case with most other families in the neighborhood—there were rituals associated with canning season. On a typical rainy morning in June my father made the annual pilgrimage to our peach orchard that was situated in the deepest black soil found on our farm. He walked about looking wisely at the fat peaches—freestone and cling—stopping now and then to pick a few to take back to the house for my mother to examine to determine if they were sufficiently ripe. He usually gave my sister and me one peach to eat immediately. We always insisted that the peaches were ready, but the final judgment on that matter was left to my mother, the expert who had learned all about peaches and about canning from her mother who, of course, had learned from her mother back in dankest Alabama in the late 19th century. It is lore passed on by customary repetition.

When the three of us returned to the house with the samples for my mother to examine, she carefully peeled them, put a teaspoon of sugar on a few slices, and let them stand for at least half an hour. Then, she tasted them. If they had "the taste," we all went back to the orchard with bushel baskets to harvest the year's crop. When that chore was done and we were back on the front veranda, we sat around with paring knives, peeling and slicing peaches and putting them in large granite wash pans to soak overnight with a generous amount of sugar. By the next morning, this sugar had blended with the peach juices to make a liquid better than any nectar the gods might have concocted. To these large pans of fruit, nutmeg and cloves were added, as well as lemon juice, almond extract, and Sure Jell. And for a few more hours the mixture was left for all the flavors to meld, or as Huck Finn would have said, "to swap out."

While this second soaking went on, jars, lids, and rings were boiled to a fare-the-well. These now-sanitized containers and lids remained in the water until after the peaches were cooked—with the aid of shiny canning money—to the exactly right shade and consistency. Once the peaches were done, my sister and I had to get the jars out, dry them quickly, and line them up in neat rows. Then, with amazing quickness, my mother used an aluminum measuring cup to fill each jar to about a fourth of an inch from the top. While the jars of preserves cooled a bit, my mother melted Gulf paraffin to pour over the cooked fruit. And while the paraffin was "setting," my mother then boiled again the rings and lids. Just as the paraffin turned the proper shade of light gray, she rapidly put the lids and rings on and tightened them. The filled jars remained on the kitchen cabinet until from each one at varying times came the characteristic "ping" that indicated the sealing process was complete.

Essentially the same process was used for canning all fruits, whether the end result was to be preserves or jam. It was a folk activity with an honorable tradition. But the actual processes of growing, picking, and canning the fruits are not the only folkloric elements to be remembered.

Gender roles played a key part. Few men in the Thirties and Forties wanted to admit to helping out with so-called woman's work—even if almost all of them did sit out on verandas or galleries or porches to help with peeling of peaches or other fruit, or with the shelling of black-eyed peas or green beans or with the slicing of tomatoes, or the cutting of milky corn from cobs. This masculine reluctance to have it known that they did "women's work" at times is part of a folk tradition, vestigial remains of which are still with us. The same men who were so reluctant to admit to participating in canning fruits and vegetables did, nevertheless, delight in boasting in the barbershops, pool halls, and under those tin awnings of the amount of canned stuff accumulated during each season.

In many households, it was the custom to leave freshly canned fruits and/or vegetables out on counter tops in full display for visiting neighbors to see. The women who came by held up jars of peaches or pears to the light to inspect the colors of the fruit and to see if the fruit had been sliced and chopped into attractive, nearly uniform sizes. One lady in the Salado community became the object of quite a lot of gossip because her preserved peaches were cut into so many irregular sizes. My mother put a stop to the gossip with the comment that the odd-sized pieces had the best taste of any preserves she had ever eaten.

Those wonderful folk communal affairs—fall harvest festivals and county fairs—provided venues for good cooks and canners to have their talents recognized by a broad group of peers. Many housewives were also careful to keep the cardboard boxes in which Kerr or Ball canning jars came. They wanted to have them in neat condition for transporting canned goods to be judged at the festivals and fairs. Prior to packing the jars in these boxes, they were cleaned until they literally gleamed. My mother used a dish towel to handle her jars so that not one fingerprint could be found on them.

Because of the hard times of the Depression, few communal canning events were held on farms. Sometimes the women in Rogers, Little River, Sparks, Holland, and Bartlett banded together to buy gasoline to drive out to farms to pick black-eyed peas or fruits for canning or preserving. These activities became rare when gasoline and tire rationing set in during World War II.

Perhaps the very best part of the whole tradition of making preserves and jams was the eating of these splendid foods. If you have never had home-canned peach preserves on fresh biscuits slathered with butter from your own cows, you have missed one of the truly great glories of growing up in rural Texas. And if you haven't had in your tin lunch box a peanut butter and pear jam sandwich for your noon recess dessert—you need to consider turning the clock back to those days when folk life, folk foods, and customs and traditions were far more agrarian than they are now. If you can't grow your own apricots or peaches to do your own canning, go to a farmer's market and buy fruits fresh from the farms and orchards. If you can stir with a wooden stick the sliced, chopped peaches (or whatever) in a large granite enameled kettle, you don't have to lament that today's coin of the realm is too corrupted to use as canning money.

Cucumber Relish

Prepare 8 c. coarsely cut cucumbers, 1 c. coarse-ly cut onions, 2 c. seeded sweet red pepper, cut into strips. Blender chop in water. Drain & empty vegetables into large bowl..

Sprinkle with 1 tbsp. turmeric. Add ½ c. salt dissolved in 2 qts. cold water. Let stand 3 or 4 hrs. Drain. Cover again with cold water & let stand 1 hr. Drain. Tie in a bag 1 tbsp. mustard seed, 2 sticks cinnamon, 2 tsp. cloves & 2 tsp. allspice. Put spices into saucepan with 1½ c. brown sugar and 4 c. vinegar. Bring vinegar to boil, pour over vegetables & let stand overnight.

The next day bring vegetables & liquid to a boil. Pack into hot jars & seal at once. Makes 3 pts.

In Grandma's photo girls are from left to right: Rosa May, Fanny,
Jennie Hill

RECIPES WE BROUGHT WITH US

by Frances B. Vick

I received a handwritten journal of recipes from Ross Vick, Jr.'s grandmother, Jennie Claire Hill Vick, which came from her mother, Rosa Bell Ross Hill. Rosa was born in 1862 in Illinois, the daughter of Lewis Ross. Grandma had given the book to me because I seemed the only one in the family interested in family history. I eventually typed up the recipes and gave copies to everyone in the family for Christmas one year. In the book was the family recipe for Plum Pudding that had traveled, according to Grandma, from Rounds, England, with the family when they immigrated. I decided to make it one Christmas to see how it went over with the family. Here is the recipe.

PLUM PUDDING

½ cup of molasses
½ cup of sugar
½ cup of sweet milk
1½ cups of flour
½ cup of suet (a butcher can provide this)
1 egg
½ teaspoon soda
½ teaspoon nutmeg
½ teaspoon cloves
½ teaspoon cinnamon
1 cup raisins
1 cup currants

Steam for 2 hours.
(There were no directions with the recipe but after some researching this is how I did it.) Place the mixture in a pudding mold with a tight-fitting lid. In a heavy pan, put a trivet or something to hold the mold about an inch above boiling water. Cover the pan and let it steam.

There was not a recipe for hard sauce, but I knew it goes with this because I had been served it once on a trip to England when our English friends made sure we had their traditional plum pudding. I went to Helen Corbitt and used her Hard Sauce, which she says is her grandmother's, so it would be close enough to the same vintage.

HARD SAUCE

¼ cup butter
1 cup fine granulated sugar
2 tablespoons brandy
few grains of nutmeg

Cream butter in an electric mixer until soft and fluffy. Gradually add sugar, beating continually. Add brandy and continue beating until light. Remove to a glass bowl or jar, sprinkle with nutmeg, and keep in a cool place for several hours before serving. Serve on hot puddings and pies.

The family was not wild about the dessert, though I was, so I have not made it again. It got the same reception as my grandmother's fruit cake one year, which I also like, by the way. There is no point in even attempting the mincemeat pie she made that I loved.

Best Devil's Food

½ c. butter (or oleo) } creamed
1½ c. sugar

2 eggs

2 c. flour
½ tsp. salt } sifted
2 tsp. soda

½ c. buttermilk } add alternately
½ tsp. vanilla } with flour

⅓ c. cocoa dissolved in } added
½ c. hot water } last

Good Frosting

2 c. sugar
3 heaping tbsp. cocoa
1 tbsp. flour

1 c. sweet milk
vanilla
Butter "size of an egg"

Peggy A. Redshaw

THE CHRISTMAS "GOOSE"

by Peggy A. Redshaw

In the 1960s my father, Chick, worked as a Storekeeper for CIPS, a public utility company in Quincy, Illinois. His cousin, Les, owned Redshaw Freight Line and delivered material to his workplace. It was early December and Christmas was a couple of weeks away.

Les called my dad and talked about a freight delivery that was upcoming. As the conversation ended, Les said, "Well, Chick, what do you want for Christmas?" Chick replied, jokingly, "A Christmas goose."

Les said, "Really? I think I can deliver on that."

Dad told us about the conversation at supper that evening. I could not believe we would get a real goose, and Dad said, "Of course we won't. It is a joke."

I followed with, "What if we get a live goose?" My dad just chuckled again. He thought that it was the end of the "Christmas goose." But it wasn't.

A week later, the freight line delivered nearly a truckload of material and then the truck driver said, "Chick, there is one more parcel and it is addressed to you. Where should I put this coop?" Dad looked in disbelief at the driver.

You guessed it. There was my dad's "Christmas goose" in all of its feathers and glory. The driver chuckled, quickly closed the back of the truck, and was on his way. Dad just stood there staring at the goose, which seemed to get bigger every time he looked at it. As it was nearly noon, many of his co-workers were coming in from the field and all had a comment or two about Dad's goose and what to do with it.

During the afternoon, Dad made several phone calls and found a lady who would process the goose for him. So without bringing the goose home for us to see, he paid about $5.00 to have it prepared for the freezer.

A couple of days later, Dad brought the goose home for us to put in our freezer. It was so big that we had no room for any other food.

On one of our trips to Beardstown, Illinois, to visit my Mom's older sister, Beulah, we took the frozen goose with us and placed it in one of her freezers. Plans were finalized for the family gathering at Easter. Beulah said she would figure out a pan to roast the goose in, as well as the oven to hold it.

Beulah had an expansive basement, with one side holding a couple of freezers and a washer and dryer; the other side was finished into a room that was big enough to seat most of the family or play ping pong in. It was a perfect place for the family dinner that was being planned, and one of those big freezers was a perfect place to store the goose.

In late February, there was a frantic phone call from Mom's other sister, Mildred (Mil) to Beulah. It went something like this: "Beulah, how much freezer space do you have? We need it in ten minutes but we won't need it for long."

Beulah said come ahead, and went downstairs to rearrange the food in the freezers; she put some smaller packages in ice chests and took the goose out and placed it where she could see it.

In a few minutes, Mil showed up with her car trunk totally full of frozen ducks. Into the freezers they went. Ducks? My Uncle Jim, Mil's husband, hunted ducks along the Sangamon River. The game warden and he played "cat and mouse" all duck-season long with Jim ignoring the limit. Jim had gotten a tip that the game warden was on his way to the house. Their three freezers were unloaded into the car and off to town Mil came, passing the game warden as she drove nonchalantly to town. When Jim let the game warden into the house and the freezers were opened, there was absolutely nothing at all—in any of them! The game warden knew something was amiss.

An hour or so later, Jim drove into town and reclaimed the ducks and took them home, minus a dozen or so he left with Beulah for the Easter Dinner. Beulah unpacked her ice chests and carefully repacked the freezers. All the food fit back in so nicely she could not believe it!

About a week later, the basement began to smell, really smell, like a rat or mouse or maybe a cat had died down there. Reluctantly, she went downstairs to look around. She thought she might have to look under the washer or dryer to find the dead animal. As she reached that area, the smell was nearly overpowering. What in the world was it? She was mystified for a moment and then she cried out, "Chick is going to murder me! What am I going to do? How am I going to tell him?"

Everything had not been placed back in the freezer a week earlier. No wonder everything fit so easily back into the freezers. The biggest piece was left out, and it was Chick's goose.

Beulah got rid of the rotting, reeking carcass; it nearly filled her garbage can. Then she sat down and tried to figure out how to tell Chick about his goose. When she called, she talked to my mom a bit and then asked to talk to Dad. With great hesitation, she told him what happened and how sorry she was that his goose had unthawed, rotted, and was totally inedible. She knew how much he wanted his goose to be served at the Easter Dinner. I remember Dad started smiling and then said, "Thank you! For saving Easter for all of us."

For Easter Dinner, we ate in Beulah's basement and the odor was a distant memory. We had one of my favorite meals—Aunt Mil's duck and dressing dinner. We still had a problem, because Les believed we were going to have the goose for Easter. We decided if Les asked any member of our family about our dinner, we would reply, "It was the best goose we had ever eaten. It was too bad that you did not come eat with us."

THE BROWNS' RECIPE FOR WILD DUCK AND DRESSING

The recipe for baking wild ducks comes from Jim Brown's mother, Ruby Ethel (Dodds) Brown, who told Mil how to bake wild duck and dressing.

Preheat an oven to 350°. Roasting pan should be sprayed with Pam.

Wash and clean 4–6 ducks; salt and pepper the outside and the inside of the ducks. Stuff the inside of each duck with a small to medium sized peeled, whole onion. After you put the ducks in the pan, add about ½ inch or so of water or chicken broth. Cover the roasting pan with foil.

Bake the ducks until the legs turn easy when twisted. Each duck will be different and will usually require different baking times. This will vary from 1½ to 2 or more hours per duck.

After the ducks are done baking, debone, reserve the meat, and put it in a separate pan. Add a little water in the bottom of the pan and put it in a warm oven.

Save the duck broth; there should be at least 2 to 3 cups.

Duck Dressing

(from Jan Brown, daughter-in-law of Mil and Jim Brown)

2 stalks of celery, chopped
1 medium onion, chopped
15 slices of cheap white bread torn into pieces;
    dried overnight at room temperature
1½ teaspoon of sage
1 teaspoon salt
½ teaspoon pepper
2 eggs beaten
¾ cup duck broth

Place duck broth, celery, and onions in a small saucepan and cook until tender. Put torn bread pieces into a large bowl, and add onions, celery and broth mixture. Stir, then, add sage, salt, pepper, and beaten eggs. This mixture should be soupy. You may have to add more broth.

This mixture is placed in a 9 × 13 pan (sprayed with Pam) and baked at 350° for about one hour. The dressing should be lightly brown on top and set.

The duck and dressing dinner is not complete without cranberry sauce, mashed potatoes and duck gravy, wild rice and mushrooms, apple salad, and many desserts.

Nina M. Garrett

A BOUNTIFUL HARVEST

by Nina Lou Vansickle Marshall Garrett

In February 1938, our family returned to Oklahoma to visit Dad's younger brother Neal and his family. We had moved from Oklahoma to Chandler, Arizona, in 1934, seeking work for our family of seven. Dad and Mom, along with my two older brothers, had worked hard doing different jobs that would sustain us while living in Arizona. We left Oklahoma because of a drought, crop failure, and hard luck that follows such down times and the Depression of the '30s. When we arrived at our uncle's home, we had all of our possessions in a big truck with my older brother Julius's bicycle tied to the side.

We three younger children had cousins to play with that we had not seen in quite a while. Dad, Mom, Aunt Ollie, and Uncle Neal had lots of news to catch up on for several days. My younger brother Major and I visited school with our cousins, as they lived across the road from the school. It was our intention to return to Arizona after our visit, but the situation of Uncle Neal's farming was such that it made us want to make arrangements to rent land and once more become sharecroppers near the Red River, where the land was fertile and the rain came just at the right time to help a farmer be successful.

At the end of the month, we moved to a large, thirteen-room house that had once been a boarding house and one of a group of houses that had been a large plantation in the 1800s. The houses served the community farmers that had been set up with an overseer who took care of the renting of land and other duties for that kind of operation. Because Uncle Neal had a garden that he had started, he and Dad made a deal to share the garden together for that year, and they doubled the size of the garden. Dad purchased a team of mules and a cow. He made arrangements to use the community farming equipment he would need. He hired a single, long-time friend to help with the work, and furnished him room and board.

We started to school and our life began again to take some semblance of order and accomplishment. Of course, we children had no idea of how much money our family had; we knew it was limited, but our parents began to plan and work toward a new life. By April one could search the areas near the small branch that separated our home and Uncle Neal's, and find poke sallet, greens that, when handled right, became a good food. Mother made many trips that spring, picking the poke sallet to accompany the beans and other food she planned for our meals. Mom bought 100 baby chickens to feed and take care of, and we could have fryers for fried chicken. For the first few months we had lots of beans because Dad bought a 100-pound sack of dried pinto beans. He also bought a barrel of flour and lard in a large can.

Soon, we began to find berries and large yellow plums that grew in the woods between our house and the Red River. Mom and we three younger children would walk, with buckets in hand, to pick the fruit early in the morning before the sun was hot, and carry it back to our house to wash and can in jars. Of course, we had fresh fruit pies and cobblers, too. By that time we were enjoying the vegetables from the big garden. While the older men were working, Mom and we younger children were busily picking the bounty of the land that could be used for our food.

On rainy days when it was too wet for farming, the men cut wood and stacked it for winter. They also cut wood that was split and made into palings which they used by tying them together with wire and making a fence around a large area near our house to be used for a garden in the fall and coming year. Dad would spread the word that he would be taking his truck to town the following Saturday and would welcome anyone who wanted to ride there and back for 50 cents apiece. He made that trip many times that year and the next, which supplied money for our needs.

When the next spring and summer came we had an abundant harvest from our garden and the plums and berries we could find in the patches near the Red River. I remember I was about twelve years old, and I and the other friends my age were helping our mothers can as much as we could for the next winter and spring.

By the middle of summer we had preserved 500 quarts of food for our next winter.

Because the only method we had of canning the abundant harvest of tomatoes was by open-kettle method, Mother was very careful to be sanitarily safe and did everything she could to keep the tomatoes from spoiling after canning. She made sure the jars and lids were washed in warm soapy water, rinsed, and sterilized. After carefully filling the jars with tomatoes, she took a sterilized spoon and dipped off the bubbles that had collected on the top of the tomatoes before putting on the sterilized lid. It was her opinion this helped to keep them from spoiling. We checked them each morning to see if they were still all right, and occasionally one would be spoiled. If the contents were bubbling and had not exploded, she would carefully lift the jar out and take it outside to dispose of the spoiled tomatoes.

However, on one morning she found that several jars had spoiled and exploded, sending their contents onto the other jars that were close by. She asked me to dispose of the broken jars and to wash and clean the tomato-splattered jars and floor. Later that same day one of the bankers from Durant came to our house to see Dad. Because of his pride and exuberance, he invited the man to come inside our home to see how much food we had been able to preserve. After the visitor left Mother came hurrying to me and asked, "Nina, did you clean the room this morning where the tomatoes are?"

"Yes, Ma'am, I replied."

She said, "Your dad took that man in to see all the jars we had canned, and I do hope you cleaned it." We hurried into the room, and she was pleased that I had done such a good job. I learned a lot from my mother that helped me in later years to preserve food for my family.

By the next year, Mother had joined the local Home Demonstration Club. The club was a group of women from the community, and their leader was Miss Nina G. Craig, who was employed by the federal government to teach the women of the county. They would meet once a month, and she taught them how to use a steam canning cooker. She also gave a cooker to the club to be passed from one to another to use. At some of the meetings she used to teach them about cooking, meal planning, sewing, and general homemaking. One of the first cookbooks I had was one she had given to my mother, and I think I still have it. Later in the fall, Miss Craig spent several days in one of the big store buildings to teach the women to make mattresses from the cotton they had saved from their husband's cotton patch. They planted cotton for a money crop, but saved a small part of the cotton patch to use for their mattresses. Our family learned to love and respect Miss Craig, as she was educated and eager to help the families all around us in the community.

I remember when my two older brothers had enlisted in the Army after the Pearl Harbor bombing, and they both came home on furlough before going overseas. Mother and I fixed three young chickens to fry for our breakfast the next morning, along with biscuits and gravy and other breakfast food. By this time Dad was raising hogs, owned several cows, and had purchased another team of mules. These are examples of growing, harvesting, and preparing the kinds of food we had available for our family meals; but, we had to exert our energy and know how to make it real.

The stories are still with me and I think of them often. It amazes me to think of how many people it took, the cooperation, work, and planning of our parents to enjoy the good food that God provides for us. Thus, my older days are filled with memories of days gone by, but I am busily writing of the examples that passed my way while I was most aware and now that I have the time and thoughts to place it in these pages in hopes of entertaining those who are interested in a story of long ago.

Violets (Med.) Sour Pickles   Easy!

1 gal. cider vinegar   1 C. salt   1 pkg. pickling
½ gal. water   1 C. white sugar   spice

Mix and bring to boil. Pour over scrubbed, medium-size cucumbers in sterile jars. Wait 3 weeks to serve them. (Use white porcelain tops on lids over vinegar.)

Ambrosia bowl first owned by Carol Hanson's great-grandmother, and passed through the Worthy family

IS THIS YOUR AMBROSIA?

by Carol Hanson

Greek legend says that Ambrosia is the food of the gods. Of course, we're not talking about the same food that the Greek legends refer to, nor is this Ambrosia likely to grant immortality to anyone. However, the recipe for Ambrosia has been an old favorite among families in the Southern swath of the United States across several generations.

Encyclopedia of American Food & Drink describes it this way: "Ambrosia, a Christmas dinner dessert made by layering sliced oranges, sugar and grated coconut in a glass bowl, was a Southern dish with origins during the plantation era."[1] It later states that dried coconut meat was known to American cooks since at least 1830, reaching extreme popularity in the early part of the twentieth century.

Although the recipe originally consisted simply of oranges, sugar and grated coconut (sometimes spelled cocoanut in old cookbooks), the recipe has evolved since its beginnings in the mid-to late-nineteenth century. My family's recipe was very similar to what was described above. I was always torn between seeing it as a fruit salad or a unique dessert.

Here is a good descriptive Ambrosia recipe from *Harper's Bazaar* from 1879:

> Spread in a glass dish a layer of grated cocoa-nut and sugar, then a layer of peeled oranges sliced thin, and so on alternatively until the bowl is full. The top layer is of the cocoa-nut and sugar. Let it be made several hours before serving it up. The precise proportions are difficult to give, as the amount of sugar required must vary according to the flavor and sweetness of the oranges. A generous allowance of sugar, however, ought to be made—say, one pound

and a quarter to one dozen fine juicy oranges, and
the meat of one fair-sized cocoa-nut.[2]

I have seen many versions of that old recipe, some adding bananas
(like our family's recipe), others adding pineapple, and a few that
added both.

My mother's paternal side has deep roots in the old South
of the nineteenth century, like Ambrosia, before moving first to
Oklahoma and later to northern Texas in the early twentieth. So,
of course it makes sense that the recipe followed them here. After
more research, it has occurred to me that the Ambrosia recipe
may have really originated in Florida, and then moved into nearby
southern states.

In that state of tropical climates, the ingredients were at hand,
literally in everyone's backyard or along any roadside. Oranges have
grown in the wild for generations there. And coconut trees have
flourished since sometime in the early to mid-nineteenth century
in Florida. As stated previously, old versions of the recipe often
included either pineapple or bananas, and both have also long been
grown in the sunny climes of this old Southern state.

My grandfather was born in Vicksburg, Mississippi; later his
mother, Emma, adopted a young girl after the baby's mother (a
friend of Emma's) died as a result of a fire. However, the two families remained in contact, even when the baby's birth-family returned
to their old home in Florida. For many years, Emma took her own
two sons and the little girl to Florida by train around the Christmas
holidays to visit and maintain that family bond for the young girl.

Now, it's likely that my great-grandmother was already familiar
with this fruit dish called Ambrosia in Mississippi. Since she brought
her young family to Florida during the holidays, it seems probable
that Ambrosia was traditionally served at the Christmas dinner, possibly in a beautiful glass bowl as many families did.

My mother was born in Hickory, Oklahoma, in 1924, and by
that time Emma had died. But she left behind her Ambrosia bowl
for her daughter-in-law (my grandmother Nettie) to serve the
unique salad for the holidays. By 1930, my grandfather had moved

his family to Dallas, where his brother's family already lived. The two families shared a home on Simpson Street for a while. Mama recalled helping Nettie prepare Ambrosia for the holidays. Her job was grating the coconut.

You have to realize that coconut (or cocoa-nut) has not always come grated and packaged in the store. No, no, no! In those days it took some time and effort. The "meat" of the coconut had to be retrieved from a very tough, hard exterior.

A popular cooking columnist for the *Atlanta Journal* included a recipe in the 1941 edition of *Southern Cooking*, with instructions about retrieving the coconut's meat. "To get the cocoanut out easy, remove the milk and place in a hot oven until the shell is quite hot to the hand. With a hammer tap over the nut, then give a hard knock to crack the shell, which will break and come from the nut meat."[3] After those instructions, she says to remove the brown skin and put the coconut through the food chopper or grate. (Or hand your daughter a grater with the coconut meat as a chore while you take care of other food preparations, like my grandmother did.)

One day during a lunch break as librarian at Dallas Public, I was looking through some cookbooks and happened upon an old southern recipe for Ambrosia. My family's recipe calls for orange juice drizzled over each layer of oranges, coconut, and bananas. I was very familiar with that part of the recipe. I glanced over this one, just to see if there was anything different about it. There certainly was! My eyes blinked several times to make sure I was reading correctly. There was no orange juice here—the liquid was sherry wine! [4]

Knowing full-well neither my mother nor grandmother would have ever used an alcoholic beverage in cooking, it got me to thinking. Because I have researched my maternal family history, I was aware of a couple of relevant stories that provide an interesting backdrop to this recipe.

Worthy family lore says the family recipe originated with my great-grandmother (Granny Mann) born in 1857 in Vicksburg. Emma Worthy Mann was by all accounts a strong-willed and good-hearted woman focused on taking care of her family, no matter what. She petitioned for a divorce in 1896 because her husband was "incapable and unable to care for and maintain their children."[5] And the divorce was granted. It's been verified by several family members that my great-grandfather Worthy spent too much of his income on alcoholic drink. With such family turmoil caused by alcoholic consumption, if that had been part of the traditional recipe for Ambrosia, I can certainly imagine that Emma would have changed her household recipe! And so her version of Ambrosia used orange juice, not sherry wine.

In later years I have found other Ambrosia recipes that also did not have orange juice drizzled over the fruit layers, but a more spirited liquid. One suggested either sherry or "good Madeira wine"[6]; another suggested mixing the coconut milk and juice from the fruit with a glass of Jamaican rum. The one that I like best is "1–2 tablespoons of orange-flavored liqueur."[7] At least it maintains the fruitiness of the dish, and actually sounds good to me. To be fair, at least one of these recipes which included an alcoholic beverage also stated that it was optional.

I must include this anecdote regarding the aforementioned special family ambrosia bowl. In the *Florida Cookbook: From Gulf Coast Gumbo to Key Lime Pie*, it recounts: "Ambrosia is so important to the Christmas tradition in many Southern homes that the bowl it is served in becomes a family treasure. A Floridian whose mother died with few worldly goods to bequeath, once confided to his wife, 'Mama could have left me the ambrosia bowl!'"[8] (Sounds to me like a sad complaint.)

After my Grandma Worthy died in 1991, as long as she was able to, my Mama prepared the traditional recipe of Ambrosia served in that beautiful glass Ambrosia bowl and brought it to the annual Worthy Christmas party. Here is the Ambrosia recipe my mother passed along to me with her approximate measurements.

AMBROSIA

3 oranges
2 bananas

1 package of shredded coconut

Approx. ¼ cup sugar

Approx. ⅓ cup orange juice

Peel oranges and bananas. Separate orange sections, removing the seeds and slice bananas. In glass bowl, place a layer of oranges and coconut; sprinkle a little sugar over the layer; then place a layer of sliced bananas and a little more coconut. Repeat layers until bowl is nearly full. Have coconut on top layer. Then dredge ¼ to ⅓ cup of orange juice over the bowl. Place in fridge for 1 to 2 hours before serving.

As mentioned earlier, the recipe for this dish has evolved throughout the southern states and over the generations of many families. Especially during the past fifty years, a variety of additions and replacements have found their way into the recipe, giving it an entirely different look and flavor. I've seen recipes that instead of either orange juice or wine to dredge over the salad, would use a cup of sweet milk. Many changes made were to appeal to the younger family members, of course, encouraging some fruit into their diets. Other changes simply made it easier for the family cook.

Change likely began with the use of packaged shredded coconut rather than that dreaded chore of cracking and then grating the coconut. And the substitute of canned pineapple for fresh (for those who wanted pineapple in the recipe) soon followed, and eventually some folks opted for canned Mandarin oranges as well. Some recipes for Ambrosia have included nuts of some sort, usually pecans, which suggests a possible Texan influence.

Then there is this recipe from the *Texas Cookbook* by Mary Faulk Koock, founder of the renowned Green Pastures Restaurant in Austin and sister of John Henry Faulk, which she got from her mother-in-law. Mary Koock says that breakfast at Memaw's was "one of the most luxurious experiences our family had" on special Sunday mornings. "Some Sundays she served Ambrosia, which was also a family favorite."[9]

AMBROSIA

6 oranges, peeled, sliced and seeded
1 whole coconut grated
1 cup fresh or canned pineapple tidbits
powdered sugar to taste

Arrange layers of oranges, coconut and pineapple in a large cut-glass bowl. Pour fresh orange juice sweetened with powdered sugar over the fruit. Chill overnight.

Modern recipes of the past twenty to thirty years, however, have truly modified Ambrosia away from a fruit salad. Again, a major reason was to appeal to the children of the family, persuading them to eat some fruit at the holiday meals, I suppose. The most common of those changes was to add marshmallows (usually mini-marshmallows) and whipped cream. I've also seen one recipe with packaged instant vanilla pudding mixed with the fruit, coconut, and marshmallows. Does that sound like a fruit salad?

The two most extreme Ambrosia dessert recipes offered two very different options: (1) vanilla wafers with coconut and orange juice blended in with vanilla ice cream, topped with whipping cream—no real fruit at all included, only fruit juice; and (2) frozen fruit sherbet covered with a mixture of fruit and coconut inside the half shell of a grapefruit or orange, possibly topped with grated nuts and mint. Fruit mix consists of either grapefruit or orange, removed from the fruit's exterior, which formed the dessert's shell, along with sliced strawberries.

Conclusion: Marshmallows and pudding mix, ice cream and cookies, sherbet and strawberries! When is Ambrosia not a salad? I believe those ingredients would end any such confusion. This Ambrosia may not be the food of gods, but of mere mortals with a *very* sweet tooth indeed! But, at least some of them are eating fruit.

BIBLIOGRAPHY FOR AMBROSIA RECIPES:

1. John Mariani. *Encyclopedia of American Food & Drink*. New York: Lebhar-Friendman Books, 1999, p.5.
2. *Harper's Bazaar*. (monthly periodical, 1867–) New York: Hearst Corporation; 13 September 1879, p. 591.
3. Damon L. Fowler, ed., Recipes by Mrs S.R. (Henrietta) Dull. *Southern Cooking*. Athens, Georgia: University of Georgia Press, 1941, 2006, p. 221.
4. Mary Leigh Furrh. *Great Desserts of the South*. Gretna, La: Pelican Pub. Co., 1988, p. 124.
5. Divorce decree, Chancery Court of Warren County, Mississippi— 10 September 1896; number 2882.
6. Editors of *Progressive Farmer Magazine*, under the direction of Lena Sturges, Food Editor. *Southern Country Cookbook*. Birmingham, Ala: Progressive Farmer Books, 1972, p. 310.
7. The Junior League of Tampa. *Gasparilla Cookbook: Favorite Florida West Coast Recipes*. Tampa, FL: Junior League of Tampa, 1961, p. 289.
8. Jeanne Voltz and Caroline Stuart. *Florida Cookbook from Gulf Coast Gumbo to Key Lime Pie*. New York : A. Knopf, 1993, p. 292.
9. Mary Faulk Koock. *The Texas Cookbook: From Barbecue to Banquet— an Informal View of Dining and Entertaining the Texas Way*. Denton, Texas: University of North Texas Press, 2001, p. 17.

Erin Russell

FROM THE FARM TO THE FRYER: FOOD OF THE STATE FAIR OF TEXAS

by Erin Marissa Russell

Guests experience the State Fair of Texas as a panorama of spinning neon lights, jangly carnival melodies, and early fall Texas sunshine. But the most memorable sensory impressions the Fair offers may be the smells and tastes. Patron and one-time Wine Garden employee Sarah Browning described the smell as "all of the dinners in the world being cooked all at once." Food is entrenched in the State Fair of Texas, whether via the fried food showdown of the Big Tex Choice Awards, the offerings from concession vendors, or the food-based Creative Arts Competitions.

The Big Tex Choice Awards have brought creative cooks together since 2005 in efforts to create fried delicacies that will win the judges' favor. This iconic competition is what gave the Texas State Fair the slogan "the Fried Food Capital of Texas." Of each year's finalists, one dish is named Most Creative and another is awarded Best Taste. Top entries have included treats such as Fried Thanksgiving Dinner (Most Creative: 2013), Fried Bacon Cinnamon Roll (Best Taste: 2012), Fried Beer (Most Creative: 2010), Deep Fried Butter (Most Creative: 2009), Fernie's Deep Fried Peaches & Cream (Best Taste: 2009), Chicken Fried Bacon (Best Taste: 2008), and Fried Coke (Most Creative: 2006). Fair attendee Morgan Griffin said, "Each year, there is a new fried food the media raves about. The Fair needs fried food and the reinvention of new junk food to stay alive. The Fair fries to thrive."

The fried food smorgasbord doesn't begin and end with the Big Tex Choice Awards, though. The midway is crammed with trailers and pop-up stands offering salty, sweet, creamy, or cheesy creations. Fairgoer James Roberts said corny dogs are without a doubt the most iconic fair food, and in Texas, that's specific to Fletcher's Corn Dogs. Other favorite fair delicacies include funnel cakes (batter drizzled through a funnel into a deep fryer, cooked to golden brown, and topped with powdered sugar) and tornado taters (potatoes spiral-cut to paper thinness and deep-fried). While the Big Tex Choice Awards are dominated by food vendors who sell their creations through the duration of the fair, participants in the food categories of the Creative Arts Competitions are more likely to be home cooks. Categories range from appetizers to Southern cuisine, cobbler, homegrown vegetables, and a pre-fair chili and BBQ cookoff. Some contests are sponsored, such as the Great American Spam Championship, Bisquick, and Central Market's "Guess What's Cooking Contest," in which competitors must whip up dishes featuring a bag of mystery ingredients. For some areas with higher participation interest than can be accommodated, a lottery drawing determines the contestants. Some categories have a small fee ($2–3) associated with entry, and for some there is no charge. Prizes range from $25 to $200 for Best in Show awards, with some contests, such as the Great American Spam Championship, escalating to a national level with higher winnings.

Competitor Monica Gerlach entered the Creative Arts cooking competitions in 2001 at a friend's suggestion and won first prize in the cookie category. Gerlach said she was shocked to hear she had won— she was in conversation with other cooks and almost missed her name being called. The judges had to wait for her to finish jumping up and down before they could present her with a ribbon. "I got a blue ribbon for cookies with Blue Bonnet Margarine, not to mention a cookie press, an apron, and a check for $500," Gerlach said. "I was hooked."

However, for many competitors, the thrill does not come from the money, Gerlach said. In fact, she did not describe the environment as competitive. Entrants cheer one another on and taste one another's dishes. "It's a fun group of outgoing people who encourage each other through their wins, illnesses, jobs, relationships, families, and whatever life throws at us next," Gerlach said. When winning recipes are released in a cookbook, she said the chefs pass the books around for autographs like high school yearbooks. The Fair competitions bring these like-minded participants together into a real community, just as they have since 1886.

Gerlach was kind enough to share her recipe for Irish Cream Cheese Braid, which won Best of Show in 2013.

IRISH CREAM CHEESE BRAID

For Braid:
1 8-oz. container of sour cream
½ cup sugar
½ cup butter or margarine, cut into pieces
1 teaspoon salt
2¼ oz. envelopes active dry yeast
½ cup warm water (105–115 degrees)
2 large eggs, beaten
4 cups all-purpose flour

Combine yeast and warm water in a large mixing bowl; let stand 5 minutes. Heat first 4 ingredients in a saucepan, stirring occasionally, until butter melts. Cool to 105-115 degrees.

Stir sour cream mixture and eggs into yeast solution. Gradually stir in flour (dough will be soft). Cover and chill at least 8 hours.

Divide dough in half. Turn out each portion onto a heavily floured surface and knead four or five times.

For Irish Cream Cheese Filling:
2 8-oz. packages cream cheese, softened
¾ cup sugar
1 large egg
¼ cup Irish cream liquor

Beat all filling ingredients with an electric mixer on medium speed until smooth.

Roll each portion of dough into an 18-×-12-inch rectangle, and spread middle of each rectangle with half of cream cheese filling. Make cuts on dough from filling to edge in 1 inch strips. Fold strips toward the middle and fold ends under to seal. Place on parchment-lined baking sheets. Cover and let rise in a warm place (85 degrees) free from drafts about 1 hour, or until doubled in size.

Bake at 375 degrees for 15–20 minutes or until browned.

For Powdered Sugar Glaze:

2½ cups sifted powdered sugar

¼ cup Irish cream liquor

Stir together powdered sugar and liquor. Drizzle warm loaves with Powdered Sugar Glaze.

Fair food. Photos by Kathy Tran.

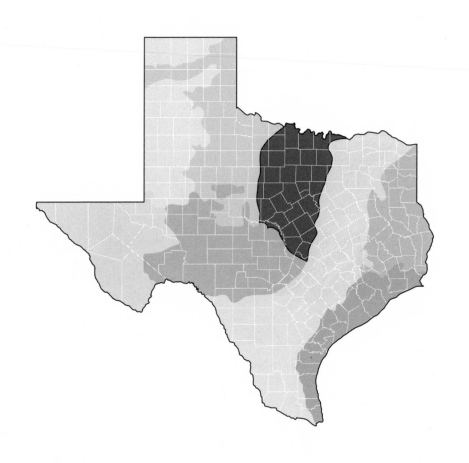

Stories and Recipes from the Cross Timbers and Prairies*

Approximately 15 million acres of alternating woodlands and prairies, often called the Western Cross Timbers, constitute this region. Sharp changes in the vegetational cover are associated with different soils and topography, but the grass composition is rather uniform.

The prairie grasses are big bluestem, little bluestem, indiangrass, switchgrass, Canada wildrye, sideoats grama, hairy grama, tall grama, tall dropseed, Texas wintergrass, blue grama, and buffalograss.

On Cross Timbers soils, the vegetation is composed of big bluestem, little bluestem, hooded windmillgrass, sand lovegrass, indiangrass, switchgrass, and many species of legumes. The woody vegetation includes shinnery, blackjack, post and live oaks.

The entire area has been invaded heavily by woody brush plants of oaks, mesquite, juniper, and other unpalatable plants that furnish little forage for livestock.

*Stephan L. Hatch, *Texas Almanac, 2014–2015*, Elizabeth Cruce Alvarez, editor (Austin: Texas State Historical Association), 115. Used with permission of Texas State Historical Association.

Jane Roberts Wood

THE PENZANCE JAM CAKE

by Jane Roberts Wood

Out beyond ideas
Of wrongdoing and right doing
There is a field.
I'll meet you there

Every family has a legendary saint. Our family's was always Mamie.
I never knew her, but I knew all her saintly qualities: I knew that
when her family left Penzance, England, she was a little girl and
told to pack her baby doll along with its clothes in a shoe box.
Mamie never married, but her acts of kindness and this recipe came
down through four generations so that we felt as if we had known
her. One of her greatest gifts was her jam cake recipe, a cake exalted
above all others because it's so delicious and so time-consuming to
make. It takes a morning to make it and an afternoon to clean up
the kitchen. Here's the recipe:

PENZANCE JAM CAKE

Heat oven to 325. You will need three greased (with butter) and floured cake pans.

Hint: A while before making, set sweet butter out
to soften.

Stir one to two teaspoons baking soda into ½ cup
buttermilk. Set aside.

Cream together 1 cup sweet butter and two cups
sugar.

Add four egg yolks, one at a time.

Measure three cups of sifted flour.

Add ¼ teaspoon salt to measured flour.

Alternating, mix buttermilk with soda and three
cups of flour.

Add ½ cup of sweet wine, homemade if possible, although good sherry is fine.

Add one teaspoon each of allspice, cinnamon, and cloves.

Add one teaspoon vanilla.

Beat four egg whites and gently fold into batter, along with one cup chopped pecans.

Divide into 3 layers and bake in greased pans at about 325 for about 30–35 minutes.

Another hint: Don't cook the cake all the way. It will cook some after you take it from the oven.

Filling and Icing:
Use one cup of blackberry jam, with seeds, for the filling. [This is sometimes difficult to find but when I couldn't find the jam with seeds, Isabel Nathaniel found two jars and sent them to me.]

Spread the blackberry jam on the second and third layers.

In a saucepan, place:
3 cups of sugar
1 cup whole milk

Cook sugar and milk until a soft ball forms in cold water. Beat with a spoon for five minutes. Warning: Do not use an automatic beater. Add one lump butter and one teaspoon of vanilla.

If icing becomes too hard, add hot water.

Cover the cake with icing. [I never have enough icing so I just put it on top and let it sort of dribble down the sides. It looks more homey that way.]

This cake will remain fresh for a very long time.

Fresh apple cake

1 cup mazola oil
2 " sugar
3 apples (cut up fine) leave peel on
3 teaspoon apples pie spice
1 cup nuts (pecans)
3 " flour
1 teaspoon B. powder
1 " soda

3 eggs
1 teaspoon vanilla
½ box golden seedless raisins

Topping

1 stick butter
⅔ cup sugar
1 cup orange or lemon juice
Come to boil & set off

Jane and Dub Wood

GOOD AND EASY COOKING

by Dub Wood

One of the most memorable dining experiences I have ever had was an eleven-course dinner served in three rooms over a four-hour period at the *Le Manor aux Quat' Saisons*. The dinner was not only a great gourmet feast, but it was accompanied by very interesting conversation and congenial company, which included my wife Jane, her twin sister Betty Dooley, and three Oxford University professors who, in the several years that we have known them, have become good friends. The *Quat' Saisons* is a wonderful restaurant and inn located in a small village not far from Oxford in England. Raymond Blanc, an ex-patriot Frenchman, who is the chef/owner, has written a "coffee table" cookbook of recipes used in the restaurant.

In his cookbook Mssr. Blanc classified each recipe as one to three *toques* (chef's hats), depending on the difficulty of preparation. I have prepared a few of his one-toque recipes and found them more difficult than a novice cook would enjoy preparing. This is the problem with many of the recipes in the almost two hundred cookbooks that I have in my kitchen. In "Good and Easy Cooking," there are no recipes that a novice cannot easily manage.

I like and enjoy cooking, but it was at my wife Jane's urging that I write these musings. I believe a truly creative mind is one that has the ability to develop new ideas and concepts, like using ingredients not usually used together. My "engineer's" mind is better at innovations and modifications. The dishes I cook are usually based on someone else's original recipe to which I have made simplification adaptations and perhaps ingredient substitutions to use more readily available ingredients.

It is interesting to me how my use of cookbooks has evolved over time. When I first developed an interest in cooking and started acquiring cookbooks I would droolingly read them and select recipes to try, diligently obtaining and accurately measuring the ingredients and following the directions carefully. As I gained more confidence, I would use the books to find recipes that had all or some of the ingredients that were currently available in my larder. Surprisingly, with a little looking, I could usually find a recipe to use what was on hand. For instance, if you are making a *bouillabaisse*, or fish stew as I usually call it, and you cannot find a specific kind of fish called for in a recipe, just substitute another kind of fish; and it makes little difference if you omit something such as live mussels that you do not have and perhaps do not like anyway.

For seasoning, I like "well-seasoned" dishes as compared to "bland" or "highly seasoned." Most recipes in mass market American cookbooks usually call for seasoning toward the bland side, and the dish will be better, in my opinion, if the seasoning is increased. One "seasoning" that I use is sherry. In most recipes calling for wine, I use sherry instead, and I have found that a dash of sherry improves many dishes that do not call for wine. I always have "jugs" of sherry for seasoning. Sherries labeled as "sherry" or "golden sherry," even the inexpensive ones, are good in all cases, and "cream sherry" is good if you want a slightly sweet taste. For instance, cream sherry is good for needed liquid when baking pork chops with fruit and onions. I do not use "dry sherry" or "extra dry sherry" because it does not add as much flavor as richer sherry. I also like to use ready mixed herbs and seasonings such as "Herbes de Provence," "Montreal Steak Seasoning," "Italian," and other mixes for seafood and chicken.

Some of my adaptations are of usually more complex recipes. Others are modified by changing ingredients, e.g. the substitution of mushrooms for lamb converts the dish to vegetarian, which was necessary for one dinner party because some of our guests were Indian and thereby vegetarians for religious reasons. Most adaptations are to simplify preparation. Although I have a food processor, blender, mixer and other appliances, I rarely use them. By the time you get them out and clean them up after use, it is usually less work to chop and mix by hand. What difference does it make in the taste of the dish if all pieces of an ingredient are not precisely the same shape and size or are finely chopped instead of pureed?

BISCUITS

I always use a prepared biscuit mix as a starter, and the baking temperature and time. Follow the package directions as far as liquid-to-dry ingredients ratio, for example, if the directions call for a cup of water or milk to a cup of dry ingredients, I use a cup of alternate liquids such as buttermilk, cream, or sour cream. An addition I make is to add about two tablespoons of corn oil per cup of dry mixture. It is not necessary to roll out and cut the raw biscuit dough. Just spoon the dough onto a baking sheet or into greased muffin pans for baking.

Possible liquid substitutions for all or part of the water for richer biscuits: buttermilk, half and half, sour cream or yogurt. If you substitute sour cream, or yogurt for part of the liquid, you need to add enough additional liquid so that the dough is still moist.

Other possible additions for variation: any kind of cheese cut into about ¼-inch cubes, picante sauce or salsa, chopped fresh or dried dill, or herbes de provence. For mock scones, add raisins and a little sugar. For multiple flavored biscuits, you can separate the dough into portions before different additions are added.

I usually make more biscuits than needed to have leftovers for later use. Guests will eat a lot of good, rich biscuits, so make plenty. Leftovers will keep for a long time if stored in a plastic bag in the refrigerator or freezer.

SCRAMBLED EGGS

I like scrambled eggs as well as omelets, and they are much easier and faster to prepare, especially when you want to serve all of your guests at the same time. By adding other things before cooking you can have all of the ingredient combinations that you can have with an omelet. For something simple, just add cream or sour cream or yogurt, and season with herbes de provence, pepper, and salt before cooking. Other single ingredients which are good in scrambled eggs are cubed brie cheese, sharp cheddar cheese, and smoked salmon, all seasoned with salt and pepper and, perhaps, capers. About a tablespoon per two eggs of picante sauce or salsa is also good in or on scrambled eggs.

GRITS

My father's family moved from Birmingham, Alabama, to Texas about the time he graduated from high school. In the Southern tradition, grits were a dietary staple in his family, and I grew up eating grits. My mother usually fixed them plain, to which we added a lot of butter at the table. This is a good way to fix and serve grits, but I now prefer to add cheese, of any kind, when I cook grits, which is more or less the way that my friend Johnny Moore served grits at brunches at his house. I cook grits according to package directions except that I use chicken or beef broth instead of water. Canned broth or bouillon cubes added to water are okay. If you use bouillon cubes do not add salt. In addition to cheese, I like to add chopped garlic or garlic powder and picante sauce as seasoning. Sun-dried tomatoes may be substituted for the picante sauce.

There are some Southerners who insist that the only good grits have to be prepared in special ways and stone ground, but as far as I am concerned both "instant" grits and the kind that need longer cooking that you get in the grocery story are good—that is, if you like grits.

RICE CASSEROLES AND SALADS

When I cook rice, I always cook enough to have some left over to use later for fixing hot rice casseroles or cold salads.

To make a casserole, mix in a microwavable dish the rice with one or more other things you have in the refrigerator, such as diced sandwich meat or smoked sausage, olives, cream cheese (including any kind of cream cheese spread or dip), picante sauce, or cubed or shredded cheese. The ingredient proportions are not all that important. Heat in the microwave oven until steaming hot and any cheese is melted. The casserole could also be heated in the oven.

More or less the same mixture as for a hot casserole can be served cold as a rice salad. Cold rice salad is good for a picnic lunch if you keep it cold in an ice chest until serving.

Brandied Fruit

Put pint of starter in a crock
+ add 1 can of drained
fruit + 1 cup sugar each
week as follows:

① 1 large bottle Maraschino (drained)
       cherries
       1 cup sugar
② drained peaches
       1 cup sugar
③ drained apricots
       1 cup sugar
④ drained pineapple chunks

Do not cover tightly —
Keep off ice —

Joyce Roach

FROM *EATS: A FOLK HISTORY* *OF TEXAS FOODS*

by Ernestine Sewell Linck and Joyce Gibson Roach*

Pioneers brought with them knowledge of edible plants, fruits, and nuts already learned from Indians back on the Upper South. Lamb's-quarters, wild lettuce, curly dock, nettle leaves, dandelion greens, sorrel, and poke were picked when the leaves were young and tender and then boiled with salt pork. Even the early spring shoots of tumbleweed and thistles could be boiled until they were edible.

A vendor at the Weatherford Trade Day one spring in the 1960s was overheard to say as he sold his last mess of poke that when word got around he had some, he sold out in thirty minutes so eager were folk for it. It was hard to find, he went on; in fact, he had to put on his waders to go into the swamps to get it. He warned his customers that it had to be "parebiled"—that is, boiled and drained and boiled again—or "it's sure pizen. The Safeway stores," he added, "didn't know it was pizen. They had so many calls for poke that they got some and canned it. Those people who bought it all got sick, and Safeway is still in court trying to settle all the cases brought against them just because they didn't know enough to parebile their poke."

Jim Byrd of Commerce says, "Folks just don't know about poke. Some think it grows around outhouses and 'hawgpens,' but it will grow anywhere the soil is rich—along roadsides, even—and it is not hard to find." He says the poison stories are exaggerated. The Cherokees advise that the leaves be picked when they are no more than three or four inches long and, when they are prepared properly, they are sweet and delicious—no poison. Besides, they are

*Ernestine Sewell Linck and Joyce Gibson Roach. *Eats: A Folk History of Texas Foods* (Fort Worth: Texas Christian University Press, 1989), 20–23. Used with permission of Texas Christian University Press.

a good tonic and restore youthful vigor. They make you feel "frisky as a snake that had shed its skin," one informant told him.

Poke is most often spoken of as "sallet." The settlers no doubt poured hot bacon grease over greens and called the dish sallet—not to be spelled s-a-l-a-d. Byrd says folk speech in Tennessee and East Texas uses sallet to refer to almost any kind of greens.

Mrs. J. B. Yates, of Wolfe City, gave him the recipe which follows:

POKE FOR THE MOST DISCRIMINATING TASTE

Simply pick the tops of tender buds. Wash them. "Pare-boil" them about half an hour and drain. The boiling and draining will get rid of a strong taste as well as a supposed poison. Put in half a cup of bacon drippings. Cook until all water has been evaporated. For every two cups of cooked poke, stir in five beaten eggs and scramble. Add salt and pepper. Serve with corn bread.

Wild fruits were abundant: mustang grapes, wild plums, blackberries, muscadines, mulberries, may apples, may pops, and mayhaws. When flour and leavening were available, persimmon pulp was used for cookies and cakes.

Among the Cherokees mustang grapes were used for a dumpling dish that became traditional for weddings. (The groom's family had to provide venison.) The recipe assumes the cook knows proportions:

CHEROKEE MUSTANG GRAPE DUMPLINGS

Bring mustang grapes to a boil and add sugar to sweeten to taste. Make dumplings of flour, lard, a little sugar, and some leavening. Dampen the flour mixture with a little grape juice. Drop the dumplings by spoonfuls into the boiling juice and cook covered for 10 or 15 minutes.

In Elithe Hamilton Kirkland's *Love Is a Wild Assault*, the historical Harriet Page, abandoned in the Brazos swamps, keeps her children alive by feeding them haws. Marcia Thomas of Jefferson has written a one-woman play about the indomitable Harriet and her tumultuous romance with the deceptive Robert Potter of Texas Republic fame. Marcia concludes her performances with a tasting party of mayhaw jelly, which she has served to such noteworthies as James Michener, Suzanne Morris, Elithe Kirkland, Mary Costa, and Ladybird Johnson. Mrs. Johnson knows about the haws and what good jelly they make, as her childhood home was a plantation alongside Caddo Lake near Jefferson. All speak of the jelly in eloquent terms and associate it with old-fashioned homemade biscuits, fresh-churned butter, and the reputation that old Red River port had for fine food.

This is what Marcia writes about the haws:

> Since I grew up here in Jefferson, I was always aware of mayhaws, and earliest recollections being memories of blacks coming along the highways to the back door to sell them by the gallon. They had always been in abundance until recent years, though they were always a bit hard to get to since they grew in swampy areas of our bottomlands. Today it is very difficult to find them—I believe the ecology is changing—and even more difficult to find someone to harvest them. Fortunately, there have always been some folks around who can get enough for jelly-making, and I have been able to keep an adequate supply for the last several years.

When Marcia began dramatizing Harriet's story, her interest in mayhaws became more than casual. . . .

> My grandmother used to make the jelly yearly and, while I was too young to be involved I do remember it was an all-day affair which put her in a somewhat grouchy mood the whole day. Now I know why. The following is a recipe from Cissie McCampbell and "Sister" Wagner. Cissie was the long-time

manager/chef of the Excelsior Hotel until her death a few years ago. "Sister" is still living and makes the jelly every few years. First, a large container is required to "juice-out" the berries, preferably porcelain or granite. It is prudent to start with only a couple of gallons so as not to overwhelm your ambitions. Rinse berries thoroughly, discarding all debris and bad fruit, but do not remove green berries as they contain the pectin that makes the jelly "roll." You can, of course, use "sto-baught" pectin if you want. Cover the berries with just enough water to cover completely and bring to a boil. Cool until the juice turns bright pink (about 15 minutes). Pour juice and berries into a cheesecloth bag or old flour sack, hang it on a nail or other holder and place a large container underneath to catch the liquid that drips through. After first skimming off the foam (be sure to squeeze the bag thoroughly to get every bit of juice), boil the juice again to a high rolling boil (about 220 degrees), add two cups sugar to every three cups juice, and boil for exactly one more minute. Take from heat and pour quickly into sterilized containers. When cool, seal with paraffin or if you want, you can store the juice for an indefinite period in the freezer—though I have noted that the juice tends to fade in color over the months and color is part of the beauty of the product.

The haw deserves its place in the history of our state for it is obvious that humans and animals alike survived on the little marble-sized fruit during hard times in those early days. Like Texas' pioneers, it was born a fighter, struggling for available space with a fierce determination to survive the elements.

The Gibson Girls of TFS: Joyce, taster; Ann, master chef; Delight, apprentice and heir apparent.

James Ward Lee

HIS RECIPES*

by James Ward Lee

Here is a word of warning. If you cook by the local church cookbook—and I hope you don't—you might as well stop now. You won't find "a can of mushroom soup" or "a ten-ounce package of frozen broccoli" mentioned here. As a matter of fact, you may have to kill a hog. But that is fine with me; as Mr. Bob Dole used to say, "Whatever."

So you've been warned.

Okay here are three of the best recipes in the world.

NECKBONES AND LIVER

Kill a hog and take the liver on in the house. Let somebody else worry about butchering and rendering lard and making cracklin's and cleaning out the chitlin's. You have better things to do. Killing a hog may not be necessary if you live where the grocery store sells pork liver. I used to, but then they took to selling tofu and radiche and foreign stuff, so pork liver disappeared from the meat case. They still have plenty of calf's liver—probably old cow's liver—but it is not at all like pork liver. I mean a cow's liver works the same way in the cow that a hog liver works in a hog, but forget that.

Now throw a pound or two of liver in a great big stewer full of water and commence to boil it. This is going to take you about two hours and you are going to have to keep skimming the foam off the top of the water. Don't ask me what the foam is! I know, but I am not going into that.

After two hours of steady boiling add an onion or two, a teaspoon or two of salt, some pepper, and a pound or two of neckbones. I am lying about the neckbones. You hardly ever see neckbones in

*Deborah Douglas, editor, *Stirring Prose: Cooking with Texas Authors* (College Station: Texas A&M University Press, 1998), 144–147. Used with permission of Texas A&M University Press.

the butcher case, but since you are killing a hog anyway. . . . The thing is, neckbones are not nearly as good as what the butchers call "country backbone." But if you are too poor to buy backbone, neckbones will do. That's how this dish got started. Among poor people. Now you have one hour more to cook this most wonderful of country dishes. Pour some of the juice over cornbread—if you don't already know how to make cornbread, go back to your Junior League cookbook and leave me alone. Now take the liver and mash it up with the juicy cornbread. The liver is now almost exactly the same consistency as the cornbread. Now don't be comparing this liver to calf liver; they are nothing alike.

A Note: When I say some salt and pepper, that's as far as I am going. If you can't cook and taste as you go along, you are not going to be able to fix any of these dishes anyway. Get you a Martha Stewart Cookbook and turn fancy.

> 1 lb. pork liver
> 1 lb. neckbones
> 1 large onion
> some salt
> some pepper

FRIED CORN

Now fried corn may look a little like that dreadful creamed corn you see in cans in the store or in the cafeteria line, but don't be misled. Creamed corn is not fit to eat, but fried corn is the best summer dish in the world. Take five or six ears of fresh corn—preferably sweet corn—but any kind will work as you will see if you keep on reading. We used to call these young fresh ears of corn "roast nears," which I think was a fast way of saying "roasting ears," though no country people I ever knew roasted one.

Anyway, back to business: take five or six—or eight—ears of corn, shuck them, hold them under running water while you take a brush and get every last bit of corn silk out of the rows of corn. About this time, fry four or five rashers of bacon (that is "strips" to city folks) in an iron skillet and set the bacon aside while you cut the corn off the ears. Wait! Not so fast here. Don't just cut the kernels off the cob. First, take a sharp knife and cut a line (longways) down each row of kernels. Now, rotate the corn while you shave—I said shave—the corn off the cob—again from top to bottom—into a big bowl. If you do this right, it will take you seven or eight turns of the corn cob to get the corn sliced off right. Okay now, take your knife and holding it perpendicular to the cob, scrape the last of the milk from the cob. Do this to all six or eight ears of corn or until you are worn to a nub—like the corncobs now are. Nubs, I mean.

Now rest a few minutes. Put all the corn in the bacon grease and turn up the fire. Cut up an onion—I mean cut it fine—and throw it in with the corn and grease. Crumble the bacon into the corn and cook away. You are going to need a little salt, a little pepper, a little water or milk (or both) and some sugar if the corn is not naturally sweet. (See I told you it didn't have to be sweet; you can fix that.) Now stir and cook, stir and cook, stir and cook, adding whatever is necessary to keep it from drying out. I never said this dish was easy. If you fix this dish and fix it right, you are going to agree with everybody else that old James Ward is the finest country cook in Texas—maybe in the whole South.

> 8 ears of fresh unshucked corn
> 5 strips of bacon
> 1 small onion
> some water
> some milk
> some salt
> some pepper
> some sugar (maybe)

COLLARDS AND RAPE

First, go to the seed store and buy some rape seeds and plant them. You are never going to find rape in the store. (Rape is a kind of greens; they grow it all over Europe to get rape seed oil. I don't know—and don't care—what rape seed oil is for. I am a cook, not a botanist.) Okay, time passes, the rape will get grown about the same time the collards do. (Did I forget to mention that you need to plant some collards, too?) Well, if you do this—and I know you are not going to—you are ready to make the world's best greens. Okay. You don't want to fool with planting rape? Here is what you do. Buy two bunches of collards at the store and one bunch of mustard greens. Wash these greens eternally—or until you get all the grit out. Then get the big veins out of the collards and cut—or tear—the collards and rape (mustard greens) up. (Here is some news. You have always heard that collards are bitter until after the first frost, right? Well, my Aunt Rene got around that: she put the torn up collards in the freezer just long enough to "frost" them good, and "voila!" as we used to say back in Alabama, all the bitterness was gone.)

All right. Throw the collards and the rape (or mustard greens) into a pot and put a cup or two of water in the pot. Fire it up and then throw a piece of fat meat (hog jowl, fatback, sow belly, salt pork, or whatever you call it) into the pot. You'll need a piece about as big as a package of Pall Malls. Now some salt and pepper and—do I need to say that?—some sugar. Cook away. You'll know when it is done. Just keep tasting it. You might even put a spoon or two of vinegar into the pot. To quote Mr. Dole again, "Whatever."

> 2 bunches of collards
> 1 bunch of mustard greens (rape if you can
>   get it)
> 1 chunk of fat meat
> some water
> some pepper
> some salt
> some vinegar (if you want to)
> some sugar (if you have to)

Now, put all three of these dishes on the table with a wheel of cornbread—even Martha Stewart probably knows how to cook cornbread—and some iced tea. The only other things you may need are pepper sauce and a few slices of sweet onion (hot onions can be sweetened by soaking them in iced water for a long time. See, I know everything!)

If you are on a diet, forget this. My local grocery store still sells tofu and kumquats and stuff, and yours probably does, too.

Norse kitchen

FROM *NORSE KITCHENS,*
OUR SAVIOR'S LUTHERAN CHURCH,
CLIFTON, TEXAS,
HOME OF THE NORSE SMØRGASBORD*

The smørgasbord is as old as the Viking Saga. It was the custom of the ruthless, conquering Vikings, their kings and leaders to hold these feasts in elaborately decorated halls. The Scandinavians say *"skål,"* which literally means skull. It is said that the Vikings drank out of the skulls of their foes. But today *"skål"* means best wishes for your health and every good thing in life. The tradition has come down from Sweden and the other Scandinavian countries. It took 500 years to create this gastronomical triumph—an artistic achievement and a gourmet's ritual. In the land of the midnight sun, towering mountains, fjords, lakes and forests, the smørgasbord became a form of traditional celebration at christenings, weddings and at many other events.

The first Norse Smørgasbord was held at Our Savior's Lutheran Church in November 1949. Since this community is predominantly Norwegian they chose the gayest of Norwegian peasant costumes— the Hardanger—for the workers to wear at the feast. Some of the foods at the smørgasbord are prepared by recipes brought by the early pioneers who came to Bosque County. The food is prepared by recipes passed down from generation to generation, and each new generation learns the details.

FLAT *BRØD* (BREAD) NO. 1

Flat *brød* has been a staple diet for the Scandinavians for centuries. As it does not contain a leavening agent—or little or no shortening—it will keep indefinitely. In the old countries, that *brød* was made on a *takke*—a thin, round iron about 24 inches in diameter, over wood coals. The immigrants brought *takkes* with them and used them during the pioneer period. Later the *brød* was made on the top of a wood

*From *Norse Kitchens.* Our Savior's Lutheran Church, Women of Our Savior's Lutheran Church, Clifton, Texas. Used with permission.

burning stove. This method is still used here. A grooved rolling pin was also used and is a prized possession today.

Flat *brød* and cheese of any variety make delightful companions. Flat *brød* can also be broken into milk like crackers.

> 6 cups flour (3 sifters)
> 2 cups whole wheat
> 2 cups corn meal
> 5 cups water or thereabouts
> 2 teaspoon salt
>
> Sift ingredients together and add water until the mixture forms a hard dough. Pinch off a piece about the size of an egg. Roll it on a well-floured cloth or board until it is paper thin. Using a long, smooth, thin spatula-like wooden stick, roll the dough on it, then unroll it on heavy foil and bake in oven about 350 degrees or until it is a light golden brown. When cool it will be very crisp and nutty in flavor. Keep in a dry place. If it becomes tough, reheat just before eating.
>
> —Mrs. Milton Solberg

LUTEFISK (FISH)

Lute fish is another highly prized Norwegian food eaten during the winter season. It is astonishing what a dried lute fish (belongs to Cod family) becomes after days of preparation. It looks like a stick when purchased. The average lute fish is about 2 feet long and 4–6 inches in width at the head and is as hard as a dried stick—weighing about 1 pound. With a hacksaw it is cut into pieces about 4" long. Then it is skinned by just pulling the skin off.

There are a number of recipes, but this one is probably the oldest and most authentic method of preparation.

> Place pieces of fish in a 2 gallon crockery jar as the fish will swell more than twice its size. Cover with cold water and change water 2 or 3 times a day for 3 days. On the 3rd day put on lye water. This is made from wood ashes, preferably live oak.

While the fish is soaking, make the lye by pouring boiling water over 4–5 gallons of ashes in an earthen or granite container. Use enough water to make enough lye to cover fish. Stir ashes a time or two. Let it stand overnight, then strain lye water through a cheese cloth. Drain fish; pour on lye water until fish is covered. Let stand from 12–15 hours. Then wash thoroughly. It has increased in weight 5–6 times. If left in lye water too long, it will become soft. All waters must be cold. Ice may be added. Remove fish and wash thoroughly. It is now ready to prepare for the big meal.

Since the fish is very delicate, it is well to place as much as your family will eat in a cheese cloth bag. Drop into a large kettle (granite or steel) of heavily salted water. When the water comes back to the boiling point, leave the fish in for about one minute (if cooked too long, it will become soft and unpalatable). Lift bag out and drain. Place on warm platter. Serve immediately with either a generous amount of drawn butter or a rich, thin white sauce from separate containers. Steaming boiled potatoes are a required accompaniment (not mashed). A meal fit for a king! If you like *lutefisk*. The fish that is not used can be placed in an airtight container in refrigerator. Uncooked fish can be frozen.

—Mrs. Ole J. Hoel

White Gravy for Lutefisk

2 tablespoons butter
2 tablespoons flour
1/8 teaspoons pepper
1 cup milk
½ cup light cream
¼ teaspoon salt

Melt butter and blend in flour until smooth. Add milk gradually. Stir in seasonings and blend. Place over hot water to keep hot and cover tightly to prevent film from forming. These proportions make only a small amount. Double or triple if desired.

Barbara Pybas

THE FRIED CHICKEN SAGA

by Barbara Pybas

During the depression years of the 1930s there was very little spending money, but our family was quite resourceful and we had plenty of food. During the spring and summer, we had fried chicken every Sunday.

There was a running joke about the preacher coming to our house for Sunday dinner. A strutting rooster flapped his wings and flew up to a fence post, and crowed loudly. He was visible from the dining room window and the preacher exclaimed, "I believe old Red Rooster is very proud of himself!" And the response by the mother of the family was, "He ought to be proud, he has a lot of sons in the ministry!"

However, great thought, planning, and work was needed to succeed with the end result—the best fried chicken in the world. Mother directed the steps to final completion. We raised our own chickens. There were many assigned chores for every kid, large or small.

I lived on a wheat farm in southwest Oklahoma. Cooperton Valley was wonderful blackland, farm land surrounded by an outcropping of small extensions from the Wichita Mountains. A country girl, I was blessed with a truly loving nuclear family, my grandparents, uncles and aunts and cousins living on nearby farms. Many times we shared Sunday dinner together, the women putting the food together, the men talking farming on the porch, and the kids playing outside until Uncle Beryl whistled for us to come in.

We were served by a rural mail route. Every March, Mother ordered baby chicks from a produce sale catalog. The mail carrier brought them out on the route. What fun to see the peeping, fuzzy chicks crowded together in the cardboard carton as we lifted the box top.

It took a lot of work to get the brooder house ready in the spring. First, there was an oil lamp under a tin dome only a foot or so from the floor. After 1940, when the REA built the lines, we used an electric light to provide the heat. The fluffy chicks would huddle together for warmth. The trick was to keep them warm but not too hot, and never wet or cold. They would surely die after that. The shallow water trays with small openings on the cover had to be cleaned and filled each day. The chick feed was also put in long holders. Sometimes, in the springtime, Mother would have me cut the tops of wild onions that came out early along the fence rows. Finally, the chicks would begin to feather out. Soon they would be big enough to put in a pen and a new batch ordered to put in the brooder.

Mother always tried to have fried chicken for Mother's Day, the second Sunday in May. At about six weeks we might find some large enough. But from then on, all summer we had fresh dressed chicken, beautifully fried chicken, that we never tired of.

As the oldest kid, the job of killing and scalding the chickens for dressing fell to me. Mother liked to have them prepared on Saturday, so they were nicely chilled in the icebox and ready to cook for Sunday dinner. I would take the chicken catcher, a long wire with a hook to snare a chicken leg, and pull one flapping and squawking out of the flock. It depended on how many Mother needed; "The preacher's coming tomorrow, better dress three."

First, I put on a big teakettle of water to heat for scalding. Then I caught the chickens and tied the feet together so they couldn't move. Next, I carried them way down past the lot fence. The most difficult step was to kill them. There are many ways persons choose for this procedure: wringing the neck until the head comes off, using an axe on a log of wood and chopping the head off, slitting the throat, and skinning the whole chicken. One method was hanging them on a fence and cutting the head off to let the blood drain out. But my most satisfactory method was one Mother showed me. I used a hoe handle. I placed the chicken's neck under the handle, and placed my feet firmly on the handle, on each side of the chicken. I got a good grip on the feet, then I shut my eyes and pulled with all my might— pulled, pulled until I felt the body loosen and the head come off. Still holding onto the feet with both hands, I pitched the carcass forward as hard as I could so that it laid twitching and bleeding on the grass. It was necessary to let it bleed before scalding.

By that time the water would be boiling back at the house. I poured it into a three-gallon bucket. Also, I added some cold water. Mother said if you got the water too hot, it would break the skin and melt the fat. If you could dip your fingers into water three times without burning, it was just right. It would only loosen the feathers. I scalded the chickens, dipping them completely three times, saturating all the feathers. That was a stinky job, the smell of the blood and wet feathers. I put the feathers in a burn barrel and placed the picked chickens in a dishpan to take to the kitchen for Mother to dress them.

She was very meticulous with the cleaning, washing thoroughly and removing any pin feathers that had not developed to full feather. She had a certain way she liked to cut up a fryer. First, the wings and legs and connecting thighs were removed. Both these were cut in two, making eight pieces. Next, she removed the pulley bone (breast plate) from the breast. (You won't find any pulley bone in modern market, refrigerated aisle chickens). Next, the breast was removed and divided in two parts. The carcass was then broken in two, for the pieces of back, which no one liked, but I did. There was always a fight about who got the pulley bone but frankly, I didn't care that much.

Mother sometimes prepared the fried chicken before church if we were to have guests. But most times it was after we returned. She liked the cast iron skillet but had to be careful about the temperature, as we used a gasoline stove. It was actually one with a tank and a pressure generator, which had to be lit and warmed before the burners would ignite, a truly dangerous invention if one was not careful to operate it properly.

This is the way I remember Mother's recipe:

Pan Fried Chicken

2 small fryers cut in serving pieces
¾ cup flour
1 ½ teaspoon salt
½ cup milk
shortening or oil

Dip the chicken pieces in milk.

Place flour in a flat pan and mix with salt.

Roll the pieces of chicken in flour until all are well coated, and set aside.

In a heavy skillet melt shortening to ½ inch depth.

Carefully place chicken pieces in hot fat (Remember that the fat will splatter when you put the chicken in the hot grease.)

When the first side is browned nicely, turn with a fork and brown the other side.

Turn the heat down and cook a few more minutes until nice and crispy.

Remove from the skillet and place on a platter.

After church, I read the cartoons to the little kids from the Sunday paper delivered while we were gone. Lying on the floor on our stomachs with the funny papers spread before us, I could hear the sizzling and smell the mouth-watering aroma of fried chicken.

Even with my unpleasant Saturday task, the Sunday-dinner platters of golden fried chicken were wonderful. Mother truly was the best ever at that.

Cookbooks from the Texas Woman's University Collection

Menus from Texas Woman's University Collection

FOLKLORE AND FOODLORE TREASURY: THE CULINARY COLLECTION OF TEXAS WOMAN'S UNIVERSITY

by Phyllis Bridges

—◆—

"Then I commended mirth for a person has no better thing under the sun than to eat, to drink, and to
be merry."

Ecclesiastes 8:15

Essential to life is food. Central to folklore are the acquisition, preparation, and rituals of food. Culinary history tells the lore of the
people and the community. Folklorists recognize the importance of
geography, economy, weather, sociology, psychology, religion, and
other folk elements in food availability and choices. Taboos regarding food are also central to understanding a folk group. Associa-
tions with food give a history of a people and often illuminate the
legends of a community.

The ancient Greeks, for example, believed that the strength of
Achilles came from his diet of intestines of lions. Peruvians feast
on guinea pigs, a dish not found on menus of other cultures. The
Peruvians consume approximately 60 million guinea pigs per year.
Asian cultures, particularly the Chinese, prefer dog and cat meat,
and run mills to supply their tables. When Lewis and Clark reached
the Pacific in their explorations, they traded their dogs to the Indians for salmon. The explorers would not eat dog and the Indians
were tired of salmon, so the deal worked out. The Irish during
the late 1700s had little for sustenance besides potatoes, so they
ate about ten pounds of potatoes per person per day. Adolph Hitler was a vegetarian, and he had planned ultimately to require his
Aryan society to comply. His sure defeat at hand, Hitler took his
own life and never managed to drive the Reich into vegetarianism.
His vegetarian cook, Fraulein Manzialy, disappeared the same day
Hitler died.

Rituals regarding food are keys to folk culture. In the early Christian church, for example, diners cut their repasts in four pieces—one for each member of the Trinity plus one for the Virgin Mary. They drank their wine in five swallows to represent the five wounds of Christ. Later, when tableware came along, many placed their knife and fork in the shape of a cross on the table as reverence. The people of the Muslim and Jewish faiths often do not get along well, but they are united in their prohibition of pork. The Seventh Day Adventists also refuse pork as part of their faith practices.

Catholics, Episcopalians, and Lutherans include sacramental wine with communion while their Protestant brethren substitute grape juice. The change from wine to grape juice required some linguistics gymnastics for the Baptists, Methodists, Presbyterians, and other groups who were vehement against alcohol. Since the first miracle of the Lord was the changing of water into wine at the wedding feast and one of His last acts on earth was the blessing of wine at the Last Supper, it was difficult to argue that wine was not scriptural. The ones who wanted to go with grape juice asked translators to come up with a new interpretation. They got what they wanted when the linguists decided that the translation could be "fruit of the vine" instead of wine. During Prohibition in the United States, wineries and breweries were forced out of business. An exception in the Volstead Act permitted sacramental wine in those churches which had historically used it. The Act also permitted licensed physicians to prescribe liquor to patients. Wineries that catered to the wine-imbibing churches flourished. New "churches" which would have been mere covers for the distribution of alcohol were not permitted.

Feasting and fasting, two rituals of many religions, are keys to the folk practices of a group. Lent for the Catholics, Ramadan for the Muslims, and Yom Kippur for Judaism are examples of the impact of food rituals on a religious group. Feasting days to commemorate holy days with special symbolic foods are observed within a folk group. Other folk dietary laws govern the preparation of food throughout the year. In the Jewish tradition, kosher governs. Among the Muslims, the rule is halal.

The intersection of folklore and food is a compelling area of study. There is a major depository of research available in Texas for those who wish to pursue scholarship in the area. The Cookbook Collection at the Texas Woman's University in Denton is one of the largest in the world. Housed in Special Collections in the library, the collection includes over 31,000 cookbooks, approximately 10,000 pamphlets and leaflets, and about 2,500 menus from all over the world. Near-complete runs of such magazines as *Good Housekeeping, Ladies Home Journal, Southern Living, Better Homes and Gardens,* and other periodicals which feature culinary sections are available. The information included in this essay is derived from the resources of TWU.

The TWU Collection was begun in 1960, with a major donation from Mrs. Marion Summerville Church of her personal collection, followed by the donation of Julie Bennell, food editor of the *Dallas Morning News* for many years, of her library of cookbooks. Other major donations include those from Katherine A. Francillon, Barbara Land, Nell Morris, Mrs. Thomas Scruggs and her daughter Margaret Cook, and Anne Simmons. Thousands of other cookbooks, menus, and vendors' pamphlets have been added since the founding in 1960. Almost daily new donations come in. The library rarely purchases cookbooks, except for bibliographies, and relies upon gifts to build the collection.

The Collection offers tremendous variety and scope. One cookbook called *The Playboy Gourmet* has chapters such as Happy as a Clam, Fair Game, Currying Favor, and All Shook Up (recipes for smoothies in a blender). The risqué playfulness of *The Playboy Gourmet* shares shelf space with *The Bible Cookbook, Modern Recipes Related to Biblical Persons or Places,* a tome which promises "food for the body; food for the soul." There is one whole section on how to say grace.

One of the most charming of the cookbooks in the collection is a very small one called *Eskimo Cook Book.* The small paperbound book was compiled by elementary school students for the benefit of the Alaska Crippled Children's Association in 1952. Twenty-one members of the Student Council directed the project. The recipes center on dishes of Alaska available in the 1950s. Elementary school student Bert Tocktoo gave this recipe for Loon: "Take off the feathers and clean the loon. Wash and put into cooking pot with plenty of water. Add salt to taste. Do not make the loon soup."

A rare and unusual book in the collection, published in Oklahoma, contains recipes from American Indians. The front and back covers are made of wood and die cut in the shape of an Indian man's head. From that book is the recipe for roasted wild duck: "First: to dress a duck—pick them dry, as clean as possible. Then run a little powdered alum on and rub real hard with a dry cloth, singe and wash. Baking: to each large duck put 1 large apple in center of duck. Sprinkle with flour, salt and pepper, celery salt and onion cut fine, to suit taste. Add a little sage if liked. Cover half over with water and large pieces of butter. Bake 2 to 3 hours, depending on size of duck."

Recent additions to the collections respond to the rush of modern life with little time for the careful and patient preparations of the past. The Bun and Run society can still find good recipes that take into account the pressure of time with such titles as *Great Meals in Minutes, Quick Fixes with Mixes, No Time to Cook,* and *The Instant Epicure.* Fine dining is not forgotten, however. Top French chefs and iconic Texas celebrity cook Helen Corbett of Zodiac Room fame at Neiman Marcus are favorites of visitors to the collection, their recipes sought enthusiastically. Highly specialized cookbooks have a place in the collection, as well. Whole books are devoted to the tomato or to pasta dishes only. Ethnic cookbooks are included. The collection has scores of Tex-Mex cookbooks. In addition, a patron could peruse *Polish Cooking, The Art of German Cooking,* or *Recipes from the Russians of San Francisco.*

Food fashions and trends can be traced through a study of cookbooks from various eras. Lard was common in kitchens in earlier times in America. Gluten-free diets were not mentioned in early cookbooks. The close tie of health and nutrition has brought a new awareness to food consumption, but even the ancients had made a link. Hippocrates said, "Let your food be your medicine, and let your medicine be your food." Michael T. Murray in his *The Healing Power of Foods*, published in 1993, included a comparison of food consumption in the early 1900s with recent patterns. For example, annually Americans on average consumed eighteen pounds of poultry per capita in the early 1900s to seventy pounds per capita now. Butter went from eighteen pounds per capita earlier to only five pounds per capita per year in the 1990s. White potatoes, once consumed at 182 pounds per year per capita, were down to fifty-five pounds. Refined sugar shot up from fourteen pounds per capita in the early 1900s to ninety pounds in recent times. Health issues associated with consumption draw the attention of clinical dieticians and nutritionists as well as health food stores. The nutrition labs of TWU have brought new food stuffs from cotton seed to market and to cookbooks. Evolving dietary studies will bring new learning and new recipes.

The oldest cookbook in the collection at TWU was published in London in 1661. It is titled *The Queen's Closet Opened: Incomparable Secrets in Physick, Chyrugery, Preserving and Candying*. It is a leather-bound volume measuring 3½ inches by 6 inches. Like most cookbooks of its time, the *Queen's Closet Opened* contains advice on health, etiquette, and miscellaneous subjects. One section is on Doctor Butler's Preservative Against the Plague, an important topic in disease-ravaged Europe when one-fifth of the population died of the plague. There is an *Approved Medicine for the Spleen*: "Drink for three mornings together pure whey as it comes naturally from the Curd: the first morning two pints, the second morning three pints, the third morning four pints. The best exercise after it is gentle riding."

The book contains a recipe for the making of Queen Elizabeth's Perfume: "Take eight spoonfulls of Compound water, the weight of two pence in fine powder of sugar, and boil it on hot Embers and Coals softly, and half an ounce of sweet majoram dried in the sun, the weight of two pence of the powder of Benjamin. This perfume is very sweet, and good for a time." There are guides for cooking in the book as well. Here is how to make a chicken pye in 1661:

CHICKEN PYE

Take four or five chickens, cut them in pieces, take two or three sweet breads parboyl'd and cut the pieces as big as walnuts; take the udder of veal cut in thin slices, or little slices of Bacon, the bottom of Hartichoaks boiled, then make your coffin proportional to your meat. Season your meat with Nutmeg, Mace, and Salt, then some butter on top of the Pye, put a little water into it as you put it in the oven, and let it bake an hour, then put a leer of butter, gravy of mutton, eight lemons slice, so serve it.

The earliest cookbooks published in Texas in the collection are indexes of food preferences before the turn of the twentieth century. Dishes that were staples of the time are carefully recorded. From *The Texas Cookbook: A Thorough Treatise on the Art of Cookery*, edited by the Ladies Association of the First Presbyterian Church of Houston, Texas, in 1883, is a recipe for the standard relish of the day: Chow Chow:

CHOW CHOW

One head cabbage, chopped fine, six cucumbers, six onions, one pint green tomatoes, one pint snap beans, chopped fine, two tablespoons salt and pepper (black and red) to suit taste. Cover with vinegar, let it boil down to about half. When taken off fire, add teaspoon sweet oil.

—Mrs. J. R. Hutchinson

The *Household Manual and Practical Cookbook Embracing Many Hundreds of Valuable Recipes, Contributed and Endorsed by the Best Housekeepers of Texas and Other States with Numerous Miscellaneous Suggestions Invaluable to Housekeepers* was gathered and published by the Ladies of St. Paul's Guild, Waco, Texas, in 1888.

Frog legs were a popular dish of the day, and the recipe for turkey dressing was typical of the time.

FRIED FROGS

The hind legs only are used. Put them in salted boiling water, with a little lemon juice, and boil them three minutes; dry and dip them in cracker dust, then in eggs; pepper and salt them, then in the crumbs again. When they are breaded clean off the bone at the end; put them in a wire basket and dip in boiling lard to fry. Place them on a hot platter and serve while hot and crisp.

—Maria Parole

DRESSING FOR TURKEY

Take stale bread crumbs, with water in which the turkey is boiled, sufficient to soften; put in butter the size of a hen's egg, a spoonful of pulverized sage, a spoonful of black pepper (ground) and add a teaspoon of salt. Mix thoroughly and stuff turkey.

—Aunt Harriet

In addition to the recipes, the cookbook included a poem of Thanksgiving in tribute to pumpkin pie, and then provided a recipe for the holiday dessert:

POETRY OF PUMPKIN PIE, by JOHN G. WHITTIER

Ah, on Thanksgiving Day, when from east and from west,
From north and from south come the pilgrim guest,
When the grey-haired New Englander sees 'round his board
The old broken links of affection restored;
When the care-wearied man seeks his mother once more,
And the worn matron smiles where the girl smiled before;
What moistens the lip and what brightens the eye,
What calls back the past like the rich Pumpkin Pie?

Pumpkin Pie

Stew and mash a quarter of a small pumpkin;
add

2 tablespoons butter

1 cup cream, or milk

4 eggs, yolks, well beaten

Spice with nutmeg, and sweeten to taste

½ cup good brandy

Mix and add whites of the eggs, frothed, and the pie is equal to a New England make. [*sic*]

—Mrs. Congressman Bayne of Pittsburg

Another early cookbook, published in Austin in 1899, by the Ladies of the Albert Sidney Johnston Chapter of the Daughters of the Confederacy provided guidance on *olla podrida* (Spanish stew):

Olla Podrida

Fry one small onion, cut fine, in 1 tablespoon of butter, until it is light brown; add one pint each of green corn, okra, butter beans and tomatoes, and enough water to cook tender. Add gravy if preferred. Season highly with red and black pepper and salt, if desired. Add finely chopped chicken or beef.

—Mrs. Charles D. Walsh

Our Home Cookbook from Austin, printed in 1891, offered recipes for the Dixie Biscuit and Vinegar Pie, favorites of the time:

Dixie Biscuit

Three pints of flour, two eggs, two tablespoons of lard, one cup of yeast, one cup of milk. Mix at eleven o'clock, roll out at four o'clock, cut with two sizes of cutters, putting the smaller one on top; let rise until supper, bake twenty minutes.

—Mrs. Paul Thornton

VINEGAR PIE

One cup sugar, one cup molasses, two eggs, one half-cup water, one half cup of vinegar, two teaspoons of flour.

—Miss Mollie Flaniken

The Robert E. Lee Chapter of the United Daughters of the Confederacy No. 278, headquartered in Los Angeles, California, like other UDC chapters in other states, turned to the publication of cookbooks as a fundraiser to assist those Southerners with afflictions suffered in the Civil War. The Robert E. Lee Chapter cookbook came out in 1905. It was called *Echoes from Southern Kitchens.* The cover has the image of a black cook with a bandana on her head. The recipe for croquettes in the book would have been attractive to cooks all over the South:

CROQUETTES

One cup of cold minced chicken, one cup of cold minced veal, one cup of boiled brains, one cup of sweet milk, one heaping tablespoon of butter, rubbed into two of flour. Add butter and flour to milk and cook until thick. Season with white pepper and salt and one half-teaspoon of mustard. Place in flat dish on ice and let stand until firm enough to roll into shapes. Roll in egg and roll in bread crumbs and fry in smoking hot lard.

In addition to a variety of recipes for food, the book contains an appendix of helpful hints for household chores. For examples, here are good tips:

An excellent furniture polish: One part of raw linseed oil mixed with two of turpentine.

Disinfectant for a sick room: Put ground coffee in a saucer with a piece of camphor in the center, to which set fire. Very healthful and refreshing.

Soot on carpets falling from an open chimney may be swept up with the slightest trouble by sprinkling lavishly with salt at first, and then sweeping.

With the abolition of slavery, cooking chores were no longer assigned to those held in bondage. However, the landowners and their families still valued the dishes that had come to their tables from slave hands. The white women of the houses were not skilled in the culinary arts in most cases. From that set of circumstances arose a new industry—prepared mixes for pancakes shipped in a box. The Aunt Jemima line of food came from this moment in history. Sharp-eyed entrepreneurs took the initiative to develop a mix that required only the addition of water to make pancakes. The name of Aunt Jemima came from an old song sung in minstrel shows called "Jemima." The company hired persons to appear as Aunt Jemima at fairs and shows to pitch the product. The image of Aunt Jemima on the boxes and ads—a heavy black woman in a bandana—changed over time to the point that the model Jemima morphed into a new image to reflect a movement away from stereotypes. The whole Aunt Jemima story is told in a book called *Slave in a Box* in the TWU collection.

The TWU cookbook collection has recipes from all over the world over five centuries. Any Texas folklorist can easily mine the collection for special recipes associated with the Lone Star state from the 1880s to 2014. Texas food is world-famous. The many landscapes of Texas and the various ethnic cuisines provide a diversity that no other state can claim. There are standards of Texas cooking from the jerky of the cowboys to the barbecues of the pits to the chicken fried steak of small cafes or home kitchens to chili to pecan pie.

Jalapeno-Cheese Cornbread

If Texas had a state bread, it might well be cornbread. With the blended cultures of Texas, jalapeno cornbread is a natural. The following recipe was shared by Governor Ann Richards.

1½ cups cornbread mix
¾ cup milk
1 egg
½ green onion, chopped
½ cup creamed corn
¼ cup chopped jalapeno pepper
¾ cup grated cheese (combination of cheddar
   and Monterey Jack)
1 tablespoon sugar
2 tablespoons oil
chopped bacon
chopped pimento

Combine all ingredients and mix well. Pour into buttered baking dish and bake at 425 degrees for about 25 minutes. Can double recipe for a 9 × 13 pan and it still cooks in 25 minutes.

Beans, According to J. Frank Dobie, the Lion of the Texas Folklore Society

In *A Taste of Texas*, J. Frank Dobie is quoted as observing, "On the oldtime ranches of the border country where I grew up, frijoles were about as regular as bread, and in some households they still are." Dobie "always insisted that beans should be cooked plain and appreciated without a lot of extras. At his most extravagant, he would mash a couple of wild chile pequins on his plate, mix the beans with the chiles, and top them with a little chopped onion." (*The Tex-Mex Cookbook* by Robb Walsh, 2004)

MA FERGUSON'S PECAN CREAM PIE

The first woman governor of Texas was Miriam Ferguson, often called Ma. Maisie Paulissen, a member of the Texas Folklore Society and an expert on Ferguson, shared the recipe for Ma's famous pie. The pecan is the state nut of Texas.

1 cup sugar
½ cup chopped pecans
2 tablespoons all-purpose flour
2 eggs, separated
1 cup milk
2 tablespoons butter or margarine
2 teaspoons vanilla extract
1 pastry shell
¼ cup sugar
¼ teaspoon vanilla extract
2 tablespoons finely chopped pecans

Combine 1 cup sugar, ½ cup pecans, and flour in a heavy saucepan; stir well.

Combine egg yolks and milk in a mixing bowl; mix well.

Gradually add milk mixture to pecan mixture, stirring until well blended. Cook over medium heat, stirring constantly until the mixture thickens and comes to a boil. Cook one minute, stirring constantly. Remove from heat; add butter and 2 teaspoons of vanilla, stirring until butter melts. Pour into a pastry shell.

Beat egg whites (at room temperature) until foamy. Add ¼ cup sugar, 1 tablespoon at a time, beating until stiff peaks form. Beat in ¼ teaspoon vanilla. Spread meringue over filling; seal to the edge of the pastry. Sprinkle with pecans. Bake at 400 for 10 minutes or until golden brown.

RECIPE FOR JERKY

From *Cowboy Chow*, published by Judy Barbour of Bay City, Texas, in 1988.

Cut deer, elk, or beef meat into ¼ inch-thick strips. Put in 2-quart glass dish. Put meat strips in layers and on each layer sprinkle the following in order:
Liquid smoke, granulated sugar, seasoned salt, coarse pepper, onion and garlic powder.

Cover and let set in the refrigerator overnight. Put meat in strips on foil-covered cookie sheets. Place in a 200-degree oven. Cook 4 hours, turn over and cook 4 more hours.
Store in sealed containers.

These classics of Texas cooking are just a few samples of the many thousands that are available in the Cookbook Collection of Texas Woman's University, a site which is open to all visitors. Researchers from across the world are in residence, constantly exploring this rich resource. Those interested in exploring the collection are welcome to schedule a tour. Those who would like to contribute a recipe or cookbook to the collection are invited to do so.

ACKNOWLEDGMENTS

Kimberly Johnson, Coordinator of Special Collections, TWU Library; Bethany Ross, TWU Librarian; Erica Block, TWU Librarian; and, Ann Barton, TWU archival staff (retired).

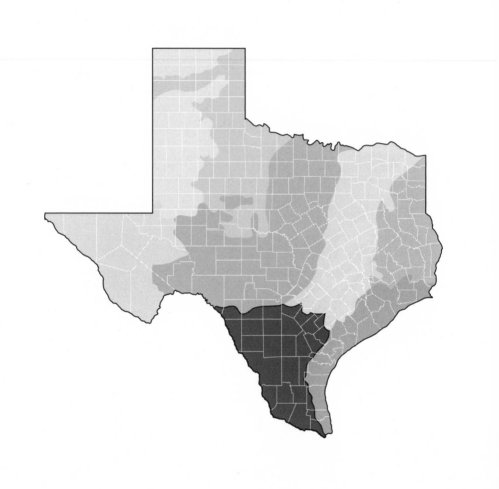

Stories and Recipes from the South Texas Plains*

South of San Antonio, between the coast and the Rio Grande, are some 21 million acres of subtropical dryland vegetation, consisting of small trees, shrubs, cactus, weeds, and grasses. The area is noteworthy for extensive brushlands and is known as the Brush Country, or the Spanish equivalents of chaparral or monte. Principal plants are mesquite, small live oak, post oak, prickly pear (Opuntia) cactus, catclaw, blackbrush, whitebrush, guajillo, huisache, cenizo, and others that often grow very densely.

The original vegetation was mainly perennial warm-season bunchgrasses in savannahs of post oak, live oak, and mesquite. Other brush species form dense thickets on the ridges and along streams. Long-continued grazing has contributed to the dense cover of brush. Most of the desirable grasses have only persisted under the protection of brush and cacti.

There are distinct differences in the original plant communities on various soils. Dominant grasses on the sandy loam soils are seacoast bluestem, bristlegrass, paspalum, windmillgrass, silver

*Stephan L. Hatch, *Texas Almanac, 2014–2015*, Elizabeth Cruce Alvarez, editor (Austin: Texas State Historical Association), 115. Used with permission of Texas State Historical Association.

bluestem, big sandbur, and tanglehead. Dominant grasses on the clay and clay loams are silver bluestem, Arizona cottontop, buffalograss, common curlymesquite, bristlegrass, pappusgrass, gramas, plains lovegrass, Texas cupgrass, vinemesquite, other panicums, and Texas wintergrass.

Low saline areas are characterized by gulf cordgrass, saltgrass, alkali sacaton and switchgrass. In the post oak and live oak savannahs the grasses are mainly seacoast bluestem, indiangrass, switchgrass, crinkleawn, paspalums, and panicums. Today much of the area has been reseeded to buffelgrass.

2 cups Sugar
1/2 cup water
boil untill it strings
add 1 pint berries
boil 10 min
add 1 pt + 1 cup Sugar
10 more Minutes
Shake + skim let cool & put in jar.

Berries recipe

Mary Binz Froh and Riley Froh. Bill Binz was almost 60 when his only child, Mary, was born

Bill Binz, government packer

GOVERNMENT PACKER GRUB

by Riley Froh

My father-in-law, William Valentine Binz, was over fifty when his only child Mary Pearl Binz was born on October 29, 1939, so I had an interesting link with the past when Mary and I married in the early 1960s and I gradually got to know Bill Binz. He was seventy-one when I met him in October of 1960, and, although he was not a talker, I am, and over an extended period I was finally able to extract a good deal of his story.

Once, I was driving him north on Broadway out of downtown San Antonio and right before we hit Alamo Heights he pointed to a lovely grove of oaks still a part of the landscape today. "I used to herd cattle along here when I was a boy," he stated simply. It was the opening I needed to ask questions. "I only went through the second grade," he told me. "There was only one school in all of San Antonio back then," he continued in a rare show of verbosity. "Look at all the schools we have today. You know, as kids, we used to play in the ruins of the Alamo back before they fixed it up," he concluded, lapsing back into his usual silence. But I did find out enough about him to learn that one reason he was so good with horses and mules was that he had grown up on horseback. Binz-Engleman Road, a San Antonio landmark thoroughfare, leads to the location of the old Binz ranch, now covered by houses, Fort Sam Houston, and assorted other neighborhood structures.

I came to believe that he made too much of his limited formal education, for he spoke German, Spanish, and English fluently. He could read and make sense of complicated insurance forms that mystify some college graduates. He read out loud, slowly and deliberately, but he remembered the printed words verbatim. He was studying *Compton's Picture Encyclopedia* (a gift to Mary when she entered junior high school) from A to Z when I met him. And he was well informed about current events since he read the daily San Antonio newspapers front to back.

Actually, I discovered more about his limited, one-dish culinary delight before I got into his biography. About once a month he would ease into the kitchen in that quiet way he had and create an iron skillet brimming with his German Hash, a plain but hearty stew which he had eaten on the trail between San Antonio and Laredo in his government packer days. He put it together roughly in the following manner, and he had a secret ingredient.

German Hash

1 pound of meat (hamburger or left-over roast
    in town; rabbit, venison, javelina, quail, or
    dove on the trail)
1 baked potato thinly sliced
1 onion
salt and pepper to taste
1 carrot (if available)

Secret ingredients handed down in old German families
    in Texas:
1 tablespoon vinegar
⅓ cup water
1 tablespoon sugar (or, to taste)

Pour over and let simmer in covered iron skillet until the potatoes are well cooked. The starch from the potatoes thickens the hash.

He needed plenty of quickly cooked and plain but simple food for his round trip between San Antonio and Laredo, so he carried dozens of corn fritters made his way:

Corn Fritters

1 cup corn meal
1 teaspoon baking powder
pinch of salt

Pour boiling water to form a thick consistency and fry by spoonfuls in hot oil or bacon grease.

When I knew Bill Binz, he would prepare his real delicacy about once every three months: boiled and pickled cow's tongue, in this simple manner:

BOILED AND PICKLED COW'S TONGUE

Boil a tongue and remove skin.
Slice tongue and pour ⅓ cup vinegar and 2 teaspoons
  sugar over tongue.
Soak and refrigerate for several days.

These three dishes, plus the large pot of coffee he made every morning, made up the sum total of his enterprises in the kitchen. He saucered and blew his first cup of scalding hot Java. The rest he drank cold all day long just as though he were back on the pack trail.

It took Bill the better part of a week to lead his pack mules along the old trail to Laredo that ran more along old cattle paths than the modern highway route today out of San Antonio; and it is difficult to imagine that so much of South Texas was open, unfenced country in 1909, but it was exactly that, not much different from when God first made it.

He met few residents and encountered even fewer travelers as he rode south and back, camping out along the way at whatever place his mules thought best. This life of solitude, I believe, had a lot to do with his lack of verbal communication in later life. By habit he just didn't converse. This rectitude is typical of cowboys, ranchers, and government packers who had no one to talk to other than the animals for days on end.

On that lonely trek of W. V. Binz, one would think that highwaymen would abound in the early part of last century, yet Bill was never held up or robbed during his half-decade of service in the capacity of government packer. As far as I know, he didn't even carry a firearm other than the ever-present carbine most solitary horsemen seemed to rely on back then.

Unfortunately, one cannot boast about a lack of crime on a journey to Laredo today. Drug trafficking has made the hundred-mile radius around the city one of the most dangerous areas in Texas. Actually, proximity to Mexico is unhealthy from Brownsville to El Paso, and when driving south from central Texas, the closer one gets to a border city, the less one's chances of survival becomes. Gringos nowadays tend to shy away from venturing down Mexico way. For example, the very popular Dale Goss Rodeo of Del Rio, right up the river from Laredo, was cancelled permanently last year because of lack of attendance. Nuevo Laredo still carries bravely on with its George Washington Day Celebration and Festivities, but fewer and fewer Texans show up from north of town. It just ain't safe on the border, and one's heart doesn't lie south anymore unless it's dead and buried in the hundreds of unmarked graves in the barren soil around Nuevo Laredo.

Not that there weren't border disturbances back in Bill Binz's government packing days. He told me that the Mexican army was once quelling an outbreak of some sort in Nuevo Laredo while he was in town resting up for the return trip to San Antonio. A friend climbed up a telephone pole for a better look across the river. Either a stray shot or a pot shot tumbled him down in a crumpled heap right at Bill's feet. Characteristically, Bill was doing the smart thing and lying low. Telling me the story brought a short laugh from him, especially when he got to the part about his friend's foolish invitation to catch a bullet.

Bullets started flying worldwide in 1914, and America's eventual entrance into World War I ended Bill's government packing days. By 1918, he was a soldier employing his skill with animals for the U.S. Cavalry. He used to show me the spot on the railroad where he took charge of a trainload of horses bound for New York City to be transported by freighter to Europe. Originally, he was to accompany these steeds "over there," but a top officer watched him unloading and working the stock and changed the orders. He put Bill Binz in charge of all remounts for the European war effort.

There in the Big Apple, Bill would decide which of the horses that came in would be shipped overseas. It was a huge job of incredible responsibility, but he warmed to the task, for he was in his element, working night and day with horses and mules.

At the end of the war he was offered an opportunity to become an officer, but he felt his second-grade education would stand in his way, and he mustered out of the cavalry. He left with three letters of recommendation. Once, during a very rare display of revealing something of himself, he showed me these collector's items, written on beautiful stationery provided the officer corps of the old mounted service. (Whatever happened to these priceless documents we will never know, for I could not find them after his death in 1966.) In summation, the testimonials all went something like this: "William Valentine Binz is the best man with horses and mules that I have seen during twenty-five years in the United States Cavalry."

While in New York, Bill courted and married an older woman with a grown daughter, but he always planned to return to Texas. Back in San Antonio with his wife and step-daughter, he sought further employment with the government. He went to work as a Civil Service employee, mainly supervising construction and upkeep at Fort Sam Houston. During World War II, he came in very handy; because of his fluency in German, he took charge of all POWs working on the Fort Sam Houston premises. He said they were good workers and they got along well. Most of them begged him to use his influence to allow them to stay in Texas after the war. Hitler's Germany held bad memories for them.

Although he stayed in some sort of government service, he did get away from his first marriage. Of course, he never spoke of this experience, just like he never spoke much about any of his background, but his nephew told me it was a mismatch from the start and neither could adjust to the other.

He also left the Catholic Church, or rather, the Church left him. When he could no longer receive the benefits of the Church because of his divorce, he severed all connections to organized religion. Characteristically, he revealed little about the breakup, nor did he ever criticize the Catholic Church or any other religious group. Like so many other topics in Bill Binz's life, we will never know his thoughts on the matter. But the fact that he never again darkened the door of any church house spoke volumes about his attitude.

Bill later married into a tribe as silent as the Binz clan. Lona Gunn could go days without speaking a word. That's why their daughter Mary and our son Noble King Froh don't have a whole lot to say. It runs in the family—or in the families, to be more precise. They also have a strange power over animals. Dogs, horses, and mules seek them out and want to get close. Mary did not use this native ability much, but Noble breaks and trains roping horses. He reminds me of his grandfather, whom he never saw, in many ways, particularly with his non-verbal communication, his natural inclination to work with animals, and his ability to hide his thoughts. His favorite cousin, Marci Froh, declares, "Noble is not a man of few words. He is a man of no words." I don't know what Noble says to horses, but he and his animals definitely communicate in some strange language beyond me.

Noble's grandfather spoke out during our times together about one other notable event: the televised funeral of John Kennedy. Long before the sanctimonious announcers and commentators began to intone about the horse being led in the procession, Bill said, "See those boots stuck in the stirrups backward? That was done for a cavalry officer's funeral." But he was disturbed that the spirited, difficult to control horse chosen for the occasion was not historically accurate. "They would lead the officer's favorite mount or one like it," he pointed out. According to Bill, the well-trained cavalry horses of the past would march proudly and solemnly, fitting into the somber nature of the ceremony and quite aware they were doing so. Many of these favorite mounts sickened and died soon after their master's funeral—or so legend would have it.

Bill was only a couple of years away from his own funeral as we watched television that day. The countless Prince Albert cigarettes he rolled and smoked ("So roll your own with good P.A., and take a puff or two; you'll get that added smoking joy, Prince Albert brings to you.") over seven decades finally gave him the lung cancer that ended the career of the old cowboy, government packer, and cavalryman in March of 1966. He lies alongside Lona in Sunset Memorial Park, a distinguished spot of real estate in Old San Antonio. R.I.P.

Robert Flynn

LION STEW
(FOR THE LION-HEARTED)*

by Robert Flynn

The way to Ewaso Ngiro was so rough I bounced off the seat and bumped my head on the roof of the vehicle. It was so rough my wife said the thing she most regretted not bringing to Africa was a jogging bra. Led by our Kikuyu guide, we were driving into Masai territory, into an area few non-Masai ever saw.

This is not a Kenya game reserve. This was the Ewaso Ngiro Plain unmarked by roads. Masai herdsmen watched us pass, as did herds of zebra, impala and wildebeest. We drove across the plain until we reached a riverine acacia forest on the edge of the Loita Hills. The Bantu drivers guided the truck and two vans around acacia, thornbush, and deep holes left by anteaters, and stopped in a thicket.

Two vultures watched our arrival with veiled interest. Sunlight filtered dimly through the trees. The earth was invisible beneath high grass and low bushes. I looked out the window in disbelief. This couldn't be our campsite; this was a jungle.

As a native Texan I had an in-bred suspicion of brush and high grass that could harbor centipedes, scorpions, spiders and snakes. Most snakes, I knew, were non-poisonous in Texas. In Kenya, the only non-poisonous snake was the python.

When John Ochieng, our guide, told us to get out, I, like the others, left my belongings inside the vehicle. I wasn't convinced this was going to be our camp until the drivers dumped the tents on the ground and the cooks, armed with machetes, chopped a "kitchen" out of the undergrowth beneath a tree.

*Deborah Douglas, editor, *Stirring Prose: Cooking with Texas Authors* (College Station: Texas A&M University Press, 1998), 86–91. Used with permission of Texas A&M University Press.

Ochieng, who spoke fluent English, Swahili and several tribal dialects, led us around the campground to put us at ease. He was a teacher, naturalist and survival instructor, and he gave us English and Swahili names for the birds, trees, and bushes and laughed at our concern for snakes in the high grass. "Go slow and single file," he advised us. "They'll get out of your way. If you crowd up and trap them between you they'll coil and strike."

I joined the end of the single file as Ochieng led us on a hike to a spring and along the river. Weaver nests hung from the trees. A yellow-billed stork waded in the shallow water. It was a peaceful scene and when we returned, camp didn't seem so hostile. Ochieng pointed out the toilets—men to the left of the tents, women to the right, no one toward the spring, and all tissue paper was to be brought back to camp and burned. Ochieng was also an ecologist.

Under his direction, we set up our tents in a close semi-circle and rolled out our sleeping bags. The tent was of the utilitarian variety. It was high enough that I could crawl in, long enough that I could stretch out my full six feet, and wide enough for two intimate friends and one duffel bag. It contained the essentials—a fly for deflecting rain, netting for keeping out flies and mosquitoes, a floor to provide separation, if not total protection from water, scorpions, ants and snakes, and canvas sides that were impervious to lions. That was what Ochieng assured us. And he was an experienced guide and survival instructor.

Ochieng suffered a recurrence of malaria and after inspecting the location of the tents he went to sleep, telling us we could explore the area as long as we did not go alone, told the others where we were going, and kept in the clearings and away from the bush. My wife and I walked out of the forest to explore the plains. Masai cattle kept the grass short, and we avoided the occasional thickets. We saw ring-necked doves, rabbits, and dik-dik. We picked up two skulls and three jawbones and tried to identify the animals they had belonged to. Two Masai wearing red togas and beaded necklaces, and carrying clubs and short stabbing spears, began following us. They shouted, waved, and made gestures which we interpreted as warning us away from something, perhaps their herds. We returned to camp.

Two other Masai, who looked like teenage boys, came to the camp to stare curiously at our pale faces. The Masai, who have little body hair, felt the hair on my forearm. A young woman with shoulder-length brunette hair drew their attention. They touched her hair and examined it with their fingers. One of the young men had two wives, five children, and 150 cattle, and was interested in the brunette for a third wife.

The brunette, who was going to be a Teaching Assistant at Ohio State University in the fall, believed her father would be flattered at the offer of 150 cattle until one of the drivers explained that the Masai had not offered all his cattle. Negotiation with her father was still to take place. The brunette abandoned the courtship and withdrew to her tent.

After the Masai left, I walked a short distance behind the tents, and watched the sun set through the flat-topped thorn trees. The sky went blue, to pink to orange to crimson, and the insects and long-tailed hoepoes went quiet.

Before the sky turned to black I joined the others at the folding tables the cooks had set up in a clearing they had hacked out between our tents and the cook area. John Mbogo, chief cook, brought lentil soup, which was salty but delicious. The soup was always salty but delicious. I had almost finished mine when a lion roared just beyond the cook area. The cooks and drivers reassembled at our table, grabbing our lanterns and pointing flashlights at the bushes on three sides of the kitchen. Mbogo saw a lion beside the truck that carried the food and tents.

It wasn't the presence of the lions that was frightening, it was the fact that the cooks and drivers were scared. They started two roaring bonfires, one near our table and the other near the kitchen. Mbogo had two flashlights in one hand and appropriated mine because it was more powerful.

"We know the lions in the game reserves, " he explained. "We know what they'll do. These lions aren't used to people. We don't know what they'll do." He played the flashlight beams on the darkness beyond the dim light of the lantern.

A lion was in heavy brush and all we could see was the glitter of his eye, first one eye and then the other as the head moved through the brush. The lion was walking toward us. While Mbogo and I watched the glittering eye, a big lioness walked through the beam of the flashlight. The lioness was twenty yards away and as soon as it disappeared into the darkness, Mbobo and I backed up to the fire.

We turned for advice to Ochieng, who was drowsing at the table. He assured us that the lions would not come into the camp with all of us yelling and running around, and that lions would not come into the tents. We searched the darkness with our flashlights for several minutes and then gathered around the fire. It took longer for the cooks to return to the cook fire because the kitchen had brush on three sides. While Mbogo finished dinner, Elijah watched.

Mbogo and Elijah brought fresh salad, sweet and sour pork, and fresh corn and peas to the table, but we were slow to settle down enough to eat. We all wanted to tell what we had seen or heard. Only a few of us had seen the lions but everyone had heard them. No one was certain how many lions there had been but Mbogo thought there were two lionesses and some younger lions.

I had scarcely tasted my dessert of fresh fruit cocktail when a lion roared from the bush outside the kitchen. We deserted the table again to look for the lions. I'm not sure why we were looking for the lions but the cooks and drivers ran from one side of the camp area to the other flashing their lights in the darkness, so we joined them. I think no one wanted to see the lions but everyone wanted to know where they were.

A lion roared on the other side of the camp. They had circled and were now behind our tents. The cooks and drivers threw wood on both fires and we returned to the table, fetched our chairs, and dragged them to the blaze. We finished dessert and took our coffee or hot chocolate and huddled around the fire. The evening was cool but we huddled more for spiritual than physical comfort.

We sat by the fire, watching our backs and trying to scare each other. Ochieng slept in his chair. He roused from time to time to assure us that lions would not come into tents, and in an act of mercy we insisted that he go to bed, as he had a high fever.

We lingered by the fire drinking coffee and hot chocolate, listening to the lions that had stilled the other sounds of the night. No one really wanted to go to bed. We enjoyed our coffee, one another's company, and the roaring of the lions. No one wanted to walk to his or her tent alone.

After a time the women organized a trip to the powder room and trooped off together. I watched them leave with some disappointment. My wife was among them, which meant I would walk to the tent alone. After a few jokes about women traveling in herds, we men said goodnight, and manfully walked alone. I talked the whole way to the other men, who were also talking. I wanted everyone to know where I was, and my mouth prepared to scream.

I zipped up the mosquito netting but let the outside covering open so that I could see. I couldn't see the lions, but they got so close Mbogo drove a vehicle behind the tents to drive them away.

I went to sleep and was awakened by the roar of a lion that sounded like it was between our tent and the kitchen. My wife and I got out of our bags to look through the mosquito netting but could see nothing. We could, however, hear it padding behind the tent. Then we heard one of the vehicles start, and drive behind the tents. After that, we heard the lions but never again so close.

As early as two o'clock I regretted the two cups of coffee mocha I had enjoyed in the camaraderie of the campfire. By three o'clock I was in heavy internal debate as to the prudence of leaving the tent. By three-thirty I was envisioning the headlines I would make after being dragged away by a lion while attending nature's call. Was that the way I wanted my life to end, victim of healthy kidneys? By four o'clock the debate was over, but I didn't go far and with one hand I kept the flashlight beam making a constant, if not steady, 360-degree sweep.

I was up early the next morning, eager to recount the sounds of the night over a cup of coffee. As recompense for waking my wife during the night to ask her to listen for any strangled screams or sounds of a heavy body being dragged through the brush, I promised to bring her a cup of coffee in bed. However, I was the first one up. The cooks and drivers had abandoned their tents and were asleep in the vehicles. Only we tourists had known the security of the canvas tents.

I sat in one of the camp chairs and relished the tranquility of the morning. I revived the fire, and thought over the excitement of the night and the adventure of the day to come. And the lions that would return at nightfall. I decided I liked it. I decided I would be disappointed if the lions didn't return. I decided to limit all liquids after four o'clock in the afternoon, and no coffee after dinner.

Ingredients:
two pounds of diced lion or other hearty meat
(fat trimmed)
two cans of non-fat chicken broth
two large cubed potatoes
two large sliced carrots
one large sliced onion
two cans of Rotel diced tomatoes with jalapeño peppers
one can of whole kernel corn
one can of beans
one tablespoon Worcestershire sauce
pepper and Mrs. Dash (extra spicy) to taste

Boil water in a dutch oven. Lots of water. Length of boiling time is determined by the cleanliness of the dutch oven. If you are cooking at home and your hands and your pans are clean you may dispense with this step.

Dispatch a lion. Note: venison, elk, buffalo, or beef may be substituted. If beef is substituted, dispatch your own cow or obtain meat from a licensed butcher.

Cube two pounds of lion meat, preferably backstrap or hindquarter. Let meat drain thoroughly.

Put meat in the dutch oven. Add two cans of chicken broth and simmer until the meat is tender.

Add two cans of Rotel diced tomatoes with jalapeno peppers and liquid from a can of green beans and a can of whole kernel corn.

Add cut onion, potatoes and carrots and simmer until the vegetables are tender.

Add remaining green beans and whole kernel corn, a tablespoon of Worcestershire sauce, black pepper and Mrs. Dash (extra spicy) to taste.

Simmer, stirring frequently to prevent sticking, until the stew has reached desired thickness.

Refrigerate for two days; heat and serve.

Served with hot cornbread, this recipe will serve six. It can be frozen.

Jean and Robert Flynn

ROADKILL DINNERS*

by Jean Flynn

Wild game is a specialty around our house because after hunting season we can't afford anything else. But cooking the game is a natural for me. Dad was a sharecropper in Northwest Texas, which means he owned nothing put a passel of kids—six of his own and two orphaned nephews. When he could, he brought home rabbit, squirrel, frogs or fish. He had an aversion to opossum and armadillo.

My parents never turned anyone away at mealtimes. Mama could stretch a meal farther than anyone I have ever known simply by adding more milk or water to the gravy and making the biscuits a little smaller. Or I've seen her add more dumplings to the pot where a squirrel or rabbit had cooked off the bones.

But, becoming a big city person, I have tried to sophisticate my cooking as well as myself. One of the things I have not changed and recommend to anyone who is cooking wild game is to let the meat drain thoroughly before doing anything with it. If meat has been frozen, I let it thaw in a colander (with a pan under it, of course) in the refrigerator. Now the meat will smell, so wrap the whole thing in a tightly closed plastic bag to keep from getting nauseated when you open the refrigerator door. Once you discard the juices from the meat, it will smell just like it was store-bought. One of my sophisticated recipes follows.

Burgundy Venison

2 pounds venison, round (cut into one-inch cubes)
1 garlic clove (minced)
3 medium onions (diced)

*Deborah Douglas, editor, *Stirring Prose: Cooking with Texas Authors* (College Station: Texas A&M University Press, 1998), 80–81. Used with permission of Texas A&M University Press.

4 tablespoons butter or margarine (I use canola oil)
salt, pepper, flour
¼ teaspoon marjoram
¼ teaspoon oregano
½ cup burgundy wine (I use chilled so I can
   sip as I cook)
1 cup sour cream (I use nonfat)
4 oz. can mushrooms (drained unless you need
to thin gravy)

Tenderize cubed venison and set aside. Sauté garlic, onions in butter (or oil) until soft and brown. Remove onions and garlic from pan. Brown venison slowly in drippings. Return onions and garlic to pan. Add flour and water to thicken gravy (and to make as much as you want). Add salt and pepper to taste. Simmer 1–1½ hours (covered, but stir occasionally). Add mushrooms, herbs and wine. Simmer 15 minutes. Add sour cream and serve over wild rice (or plain white rice). Serves six.

When I was growing up, we ate what was on the table and then asked, "What was it?" But in the sophisticated world we now live in some people who have been invited to a Roadkill Dinner at our house ask, "What is it?" before they take a bite. Or the really sophisticated ask, "What are you going to serve?" before they will accept an invitation to dinner.

We occasionally have buffet dinners for as many as sixty guests. I always prepare one store-bought meat for those who get sick at the thought of eating wild game. One guest was so suspicious at a Christmas party that the only thing he would eat was turkey. It was the only wild thing on the table. That has been several years ago and if he were told today that he ate wild game, he would throw up just to prove his point.

Our wild game dishes range from a rattlesnake appetizer (depending on the last time Bob stepped on one) to sweet-and-sour venison meatballs (depending on Bob's luck the last time he went hunting) to barbecued pork (depending on the last time Bob ran over a wild hog) with a host of others in between. All wild game should be served with squash or eggplant casserole, twice-baked potatoes, corn pie, pinto beans, and jalapeño cornbread topped by some kind of Texas pecan dessert.

And to show how sophisticated I have become, we eat by bamboo torch light under the trees by the patio. That way guests can't see what they are eating and have to wait to ask, "What was it?"

Even in a sophisticated world everything in life goes full circle.

MULTI-SHOT, INC.
DIRECTIONAL SURVEYING
Magnetic/Gyroscopic/Inclination/Orientation/Surface Recording Gyro

Buttermilk Pie

3 eggs slightly beaten

2 cup sugar

1/4 cup flour

3/4 cup Buttermilk

1 Stick oleo, melted

1 tsp. Vanilla

1 10" pie uncooked

Slow oven @ 325°

HOUSTON	DALLAS	LAFAYETTE
713/894-5157	214/771-2646	318/232-8596
1-800-641-7468	SALES	1-800-259-2867

PASSING ALONG FAMILY RECIPES

by Mary Margaret Dougherty Campbell

My grandmother Leona Harrod Dougherty Grimsinger, whom everyone called Nonnie, was an excellent cook. I was fortunate to spend time in her kitchen from my earliest years until her death just after my 40th birthday, which was a few months shy of her 93rd birthday, first observing, then helping—but always learning.

At the age of twenty-one, Nonnie married F. X. Dougherty and moved to the Dougherty Ranch in southern Live Oak County. At the ranch, she prepared meals for her family, the cowboys who came to work cattle, and a host of others. My grandparents loved entertaining and seemed to always have guests of one type or another in their home: friends who came out to the ranch to hunt deer or turkey, family and friends from nearby ranches and communities or from greater distances who came to visit, ladies from the study club or church in nearby Orange Grove who came to discuss the topic of the day, etc. My grandfather loved to play poker, so weekend poker games around the dining room table were not uncommon. All of my grandparents' various guests knew they would enjoy plenty of food at the Dougherty Ranch and that the food would be delicious.

After my grandfather died and Nonnie remarried and moved to Karnes City, she continued entertaining with her husband A. F. Grimsinger, whom the grandkids called Grimmie. They had lively New Year's Eve parties, birthday parties for friends in the neighborhood, and other get-togethers. In town, Nonnie's guests came to include more of the ladies groups because living in town, Nonnie being involved in church, civic, and social clubs was more convenient.

I say all of this to point out why Nonnie's repertoire of dishes and meals was as diverse as it was. She could cook a hearty lunch of chicken fried steak, mashed potatoes, gravy, green beans, homemade rolls, and a choice of pie for eight to ten cowboys one day and the next a delicate meal of chicken salad, congealed salad, and assorted cookies for the ladies in her bridge club. And she was always looking for and trying new recipes.

At any given time, Nonnie had some sort of sweet on her buffet. It might be a cake or a pie or a batch of cookies—none of which came from a store or bakery. On holidays, she made at least two pies. Chocolate pie was the favorite among my brothers and boy cousins; my dad's pie of choice was mincemeat, a pie I just could not make myself sample. My favorite was coconut. Every year from a time I cannot even remember, Nonnie made a coconut pie for my birthday and somehow seemed to get it to me, no matter where I was. The last coconut pie she made was for my birthday just three weeks before she passed away. Boy, do I miss those pies; I have not found any other that tastes quite the same.

But it's not about the chocolate or the mincemeat or the coconut that I write. As an adult, I discovered Nonnie's buttermilk pie. Apparently, I had spent so much time scoffing at the mincemeat and savoring the coconut that I had overlooked her buttermilk pie. Immediately upon finishing the last bite of that first slice, I asked for the recipe. She dictated a list of ingredients and said to cook the pie in "a slow oven," a term she defined upon my asking: approximately 325 degrees. No instructions, just a list of ingredients, typical of Nonnie's cut-to-the-chase manner. My husband Jody took the dictation; he had loved the taste of the pie as much as I had.

Because the pie was already made that day, I did not have the luxury of watching her make it. After numerous attempts of trial and error—and phone calls to Nonnie, asking this question or that—I finally made a buttermilk pie that looked and tasted like hers. However, I have never had the courage to make a pie crust from scratch. I have watched it made many times by accomplished cooks, but the cautions about tough crusts just scared me away. Thankfully, the grocery store refrigerated and frozen sections have ready-made crusts that I can simply fill with the buttermilk deliciousness.

Over the years, Nonnie's buttermilk pie has become my specialty pie, which I make for holidays and as birthday gifts. After I "got it down," I made the pie for Jody's birthday and his father's birthday, a tradition that continues to this day even though Jody and I have been divorced since 1996. When Jody married Karin and she got a taste of his birthday pie, an addition to the tradition began: Karin gets a buttermilk pie for her birthday, as well. Yes, I know it is out of the ordinary, but there's little about our family's relationships that is ordinary, anyway.

Some of my nieces and "adopted" nieces, who call me MeMock, have come to me for Nonnie's buttermilk pie recipe, which I eagerly share. The tradition of passing along family recipes should continue, recipes from grandmothers, mothers, aunts, and other relatives (including males!). Recipes like Nonnie's buttermilk pie and the stories behind them are part of who we are as a family and as a culture. Stories regarding the acquisition of the recipes can be as important as the recipes, themselves—especially if the recipes are in the giver's own handwriting—as well as photos from the occasion or of the giver. When we pass down recipes, we pass on culinary traditions and customs as well as genealogy and a bit of ourselves.

NONNIE'S BUTTERMILK PIE

3 eggs, slightly beaten
2 cups sugar
¼ cup flour
¾ cup buttermilk
2 sticks oleo, melted
1 teaspoon vanilla
1 10" pie crust, uncooked

Stir all ingredients together in a mixing bowl. Pour into the pie crust. Bake in a "slow oven" at 325 degrees until golden brown on top (about an hour).

MeMock's Tips:
Be sure to add the melted butter SLOWLY into the other ingredients so the two temperatures have a chance to meld well.

I pour the vanilla into the measuring spoon over the mixing bowl and let the vanilla overflow the spoon.

To test doneness of the pie: If the pie jiggles, the filling is not completely cooked.

If you use a frozen pie crust from the grocery store: The 9" crust is too small; you'll have filling left over. The deep dish takes forever to cook (I prefer NOT to use these). They have started making a "large" crust—that's the one I try to find; it's closest to the 10" pie plate. Of course, the best crust is the crust from scratch.

Tetrazzini
(from Grandmother Nonnie)

8 oz. spaghetti
14 oz. can mushrooms
4 tablespoons butter
3 cups chopped onion
½ teaspoon celery salad
¼ cup marjoram
1 can cream of chicken soup
1 tall can milk
2 tablespoon chopped pimento
2 cups chopped turkey or chicken

Vermicelli Salad
(from Mom over the phone)

My mother, Anne Pickle Dougherty Mangham, has shared many family recipes with me over the years.

Cook 2 boxes vermicelli; drain into colander.

In a bowl:
4 tablespoons salad oil over vermicelli
3 tablespoons lemon juice
1 tablespoon accent
1 tablespoon Lawrey salt

Stir well.

Add:
1 chopped onion
chopped celery
chopped bell pepper
med. jar chopped pimentos
small can chopped ripe olives
real mayonnaise—small jar

Stir.

Add pepper.

Chill.

Roast a la Baboo
(from KK)

This handwritten recipe from my Aunt Kay Kay (Donna Kay Powell) was on a 4 × 6 notecard. "Baboo" was her mother, my maternal grandmother—Margaret Morrison Pickle.

Momma always said a Sirloin Tip roast was the best cut. However, a good substitute is a rump roast.

Salt and pepper all sides. Place in a roaster with enough grease—bacon grease if possible—to brown the meat on all sides.

After browned, add water, at least 1 cup, more if needed.

At this point, Momma put a peeled clove of garlic in.

Cook at 350 degrees for 30 min. per pound. Or less, if you want it rare.

Mrs. Bob Pickle, known to her friends as Margaret, enjoys cooking many taste-tempting dishes for friends or for family, which also includes two daughters, a son, and five small grandchildren. A noted good cook, Mrs. Pickle likes to share her recipes as well as attain new ones.

For her husband, Bob, who is co-owner of a lease company, she sometimes prepares his favorite recipe, that being Osgood Pie. The recipe has been in her family for five generations, having come from her great-grandmother, and today she reveals the secret of a great dish, which originated in England.

OSGOOD PIE

3 egg yolks
1 cup sugar
1 cup sweet milk
1½ cups raisins
¾ teaspoon cinnamon
½ teaspoon cloves
¾ teaspoon nutmeg
1 cup pecans

Beat egg yolks; add milk and pour over sugar, cinnamon, cloves and nutmeg, which have been thoroughly mixed. Add the raisins and cook until thickened. Then add a teaspoon of vanilla. Put into a cooked pie shell and cover with meringue made from the three egg whites. Remember: Use no flour in the filling.

JULIA'S BEANS

This recipe is from my step-mother, Sherry Holland Dougherty Appell. Julia Gonzalez worked in the kitchen/helped/learned from my grandmother Nonnie at the Lagarto Ranch and later worked occasionally for my step-mother Sherry.

4 cups pinto beans
4 tablespoons chili powder
4 cloves garlic—crushed
1 onion—sliced
1–2 Serrano Peppers—whole
Water

Cook 2½–3 hours (simmer w/lid partially covering).

Grandchildren Ashleigh, Nathan, Seth, with Sam. Courtney at the stove in back

Sam Cavazos

FOLLOWING THE CROPS

by Sam Cavazos

How did this Mexican man and this strawberry blonde, blue-eyed Irish girl get together? My parents, Rafael Silva Cavazos and Lenora Josephine Walter—my mom's mother's maiden name was O'Toole—met this way, according to my sister. My father was working in a restaurant in the St. Louis area. There was a dance hall he liked to go to where they played Mexican music, and my dad loved to dance. My mom had an Hispanic girlfriend and since my mom liked the music as well, and she loved to dance, she would go to the same dance hall. The night she saw my dad on the dance floor for the first time, she leaned over to her friend and said that that was the man she was going to marry.

So, they started seeing each other and since my dad spoke very little English and my mom very little Spanish, the way he would let her know what they were doing on any given night was with gum. Juicy Fruit meant they were going to the park. Spearmint meant they were going to the dance, and Doublemint meant they were going to the movies. Dad sent her to Mexico for six months to live with his mom, and she had to learn the language and how to cook the food on the fly. She did not have an interpreter, so she just learned it.

My brother Raphael was born in St. Louis in 1949. They started following the crops, having children along the way. My brother Francisco was born in San Jose, California, in 1950; I was born in Oroville, California, in 1960; my younger brother Mario was born in 1964 in Portland, Oregon. We moved back to the Rio Grande Valley for good in 1964 because one of my dad's sisters called him and said that their mother was on her death bed and they needed to get back right away. Fortunately, that was not the case and all was fine, but we ended up staying in the Valley. According to my sister, we would never have left Oregon otherwise.

After that non-crisis we continued to follow the crops from the Valley. When we left to go work the crops, there were nine of us— Mom and Dad, Rafael Joseph (Ralph), Francisco Miguel (Frank), Cristela Ann (Crissy), Cesario Antonio (Tony), Daniel Walter (Dan), Samuel James (me), and Steven Mario (Mario), in order of age. We traveled in a pickup with a camper. There were usually three in the cab, and the rest of us would be in the back. When Dad got tired, he would find a safe place to park, climb in back, and get the rest he needed. There were also a couple of migrant camps, which had bathrooms, showers, and basic sleeping accommodations that we stopped at a couple of times. As soon as the school year was over we would head out, and we would always spend about two to three weeks in school while we were up north, before we came home.

In my earliest memory of being up north, we were in The Dalles, Oregon, living in a cherry orchard in the back of a pickup with a camper. There were a bunch of cherry bins lined around a perimeter, as kind of an outside room, and Mom was cooking on a Coleman stove. That's the year I got chicken pox.

Everybody went to the field to work unless we were under-age, then we would handle the household duties. Of course, lots of times we would just go out and play all day, which the older siblings hated. Mom went out in the fields as well. That is what is so amazing to me about her. She would get up, cook breakfast for the entire family, and also pack a lunch; most fields were not in close proximity to where we were living, so we mostly ate lunch in the fields or orchards. Then she would come in after a full day of picking and cook dinner for everybody.

We always started out the year in Powell, Wyoming, working for Mr. Johnson in the sugar beets. My younger brother Mario and my other brother Dan and I could not work because we had to be at least sixteen years old to work farm labor in that state. So we took care of all the housework, and watched over any cooking Mom may have had on the stove. (Boy! Don't burn the beans. That will get you something you do not want. Been there, done that!). The thing I loved about working for Mr. Johnson is that he had a cabin just outside Yellowstone National Park, and he would always take us for a weekend while we were there. One year he even took us out on his boat and we got to fish Yellowstone Lake, as well.

Once that season was done, we would head to Ohio to pick tomatoes. I never saw such long fields of "maters." It seemed like they were never-ending. Besides picking them, the three older brothers—Rafael, Frank and Tony—would load the bushels we filled that day on a flatbed truck and take them to the processing plant. Ohio was also the first place we had ever seen a shopping mall. Mom always bought our school clothes up there. She could get things you couldn't get back home because we were so behind-the-times for shopping when we got back to the Valley.

After Ohio was Michigan, where we picked cucumbers, cherries, and apples. I always loved Michigan because no matter where we were, there was always a very cool lake to go swimming in. We also had some interesting experiences there. Dan and I were going to school at the time and there was a big tree right next to where we would wait for the bus. The tree had a really long vine attached to it, and after we worked on it for a few days we finally were able to cut through it. What a time we had swinging on that vine—that is, until the bees attacked. Apparently, there was a hive up in the tree that we did not see. It was cold that morning and we had coats on, but by the time we got back to the house, the bees were inside our coats, inside the clothes under that, in our hair, everywhere. Needless to say, we did not make it to school that day.

One day the owner of the apple farm where we were working came to my dad and expressed to him what great workers we were and that he did not mind if we ate all the apples we wanted. He just asked that first the apples be picked off the trees from which we ate them. It seems my oldest brother Rafael chose one tree in the orchard that he ate his apples off of, but he did not pick them. So here is this tree with the lower half pretty much covered in eaten apples, which unfortunately is not good because of the rot and pests it attracted, and it also made the tree look pretty weird.

The last year we did farm labor, which was the year I was entering the sixth grade, we ended up going to New York to work in the lettuce fields. We picked apples, pears, and even cherries. At some point my dad was not happy with this place and was going to leave, but the owner was so desperate to keep us that he built a shell of a house for us to live in. It actually had a shower and an inside bathroom, which was unheard of in our line of work. It was like staying at a luxury hotel for us, even though it had concrete floors and bare walls, but we had an "INSIDE BATHROOM!"

After that, we ended the season by going to Alabama to pick pecans. I had never seen pecan trees so big. For the life of me I could not figure out how we were expected to pick them, until the tractor showed up, wrapped its arms around the tree, and shook vigorously. It was unbelievable how much that thing could shake the ground around you while it shook the pecans out of the trees.

One thing I always appreciated about my mom was that when the school year started, no matter where we were, she would enroll us in school. So, I have been to school in Wyoming, Michigan, New York, and Alabama. That way I didn't have to go into the Migrant Worker Classes when we got home, which were longer days, and ended past the regular school year. I also think it helped in making us more well rounded, as opposed to friends that I knew from the Valley who hardly ever left the area. To me, it was a great experience.

Sam's Salsa—The Best!

I use Roma tomatoes, which I boil in water until the peel starts splitting. Then you can just peel it off once it cools a little. In a sauce pan, I put about a tablespoon of Extra Virgin Olive Oil (or however much you need) to cook down your onions, garlic to taste and cilantro (just a few leaves. I add the rest when I throw in the "maters.")

Once you have the onions cooked the way you want, start adding the tomatoes. I just usually crush them as best I can with my hands, but you can chop them or even put them in a food processor—your call.

Once I get all the ingredients in, I add one cube of Caldo De Tomate for the extra "mater" flavor. Or you can use a Caldo de Res for the beef flavor, which everybody likes, too. And remember, it will thicken after you finish cooking, so depending on what consistency you like, you may have to add a little water.

I do not like it too spicy any more, but for both of these recipes, if you like it spicy add as many jalapeños, serranos, or whatever your chile of choice is.

SAM'S PICO

Chop: Roma tomatoes, green onions, cilantro
Add: salt, pepper, garlic powder to taste

As far as measurements, it just depends on what size of a batch you're making, and I always make to taste.

LENORA'S MEXICAN RICE

(from Karen Cavazos, learned from Lenora,
    with the addition of onions. Rafael would
    not allow Lenora to use onions.)

1 onion, chopped
2 cups Mahatma long grain rice
2–3 tablespoons oil
3 cubes Caldo de Tomate

Put oil in a large skillet. Add chopped onion and saute 2 to 3 minutes. Add uncooked rice. Saute in oil/onion until rice is golden brown. This can take about 15 minutes. Add 4 cups of water and the Caldo de Tomate. Make sure the cubes are dissolved and mixed well with the rice.

Once you see "boil" bubbles in the water, reduce heat to the lowest setting, cover the skillet, and set the timer for 45 minutes. DO NOT CHECK THE RICE UNTIL THE TIMER GOES OFF. (This is the secret.)

Petra Vela

FROM *PETRA'S LEGACY: THE SOUTH TEXAS RANCHING EMPIRE OF PETRA VELA AND MIFFLIN KENEDY**

Jane Clements Monday, Frances Brannen Vick

In Brownsville, Petra Vela de Vidal Kenedy planned her family's meals and she or her servant shopped each day, which was required due to the lack of refrigeration. Early in the morning the market-place was filled with the aromas of ground coffee beans, fresh vegetables, baked breads, and herbs. Shoppers bargained for prices and filled their baskets. The market offered meats and fowls for roasting, and fish. Fresh vegetables, goat cheeses and fruits filled the stalls with splashes of color and fragrances. Bakeries provided fresh breads and homemade tortillas. Fine European wines and Cuban cigars were brought in for the gentlemen. The women shoppers exchanged the latest news of the day as they made their way up and down the aisles. Typically the men would have a roll and coffee about nine in the morning at the Market, and they too exchanged the latest news. At noon the market bell sounded, signaling lunchtime. The town's shops closed and some people went home for lunch. The poor ate a small meal of rolled tortillas with a filling of beans or perhaps meat, then rested on a small mat for their siesta. Frijoles (beans) and tortillas were the sustenance of life to the Mexicans, and were served for breakfast, dinner and supper. These two foods identified the Tejano way of life.

The wealthy merchants went home for a formal dinner, starting with soup followed by a plate of seasoned rice or garbanzo beans; roasted cabrito (goat), beef roast, beef steak, or fish; and vegetables such as peas or green beans. Fruit was often on the table and flans or

*Jane Clements Monday, Frances Brannen Vick, *Petra's Legacy: The South Texas Ranching Empire of Petra Vela and Mifflin Kenedy* (College Station: Texas A&M University Press, 2007), 52–53. Used with permission of Texas A&M University Press.

custards were served for dessert. The women drank orangeade or lemonade, many times from fresh fruits off the trees in their yards. The men drank wine or had a cordial. A siesta followed during the heat of the day and activity would resume about three in the afternoon. Supper in the evening was light, consisting of a cold plate and a dessert of custard or flan. Carriers provided household water on a regular basis, or families drew from their cisterns, except during drought when they used street vendors. These street vendors attached a rope to a rolling water barrel and delivered the water throughout town.

Descendants of Petra's daughter, Luisa Vidal Dalzell—Susan Seeds and Janis Hefley—contributed the following recipe for Mexican Rice that has been handed down through Petra's family.

MEXICAN RICE

Oil to coat a medium saucepan.
1 cup rice
1 chopped onion
1 can whole tomatoes, including juice
    (adapted to contemporary times)
1 cup water

Saute the onion and rice in oil until light brown. Add tomatoes, smashing in your hands. Add 1 cup water. Simmer on low about 20 minutes.

Mary Josephine Dalzell Hefley was Luisa's daughter. The family called her Mayme. This recipe was in Mayme's handwriting. Janis Hefley and Susan Seeds are sisters and descendants of Mayme and Petra.

MAYME DALZELL HEFLEY'S CHARLOTTE RUSSE RECIPE

1 pint heavy cream (for filling)
1 pint heavy cream (for top)
1 cup sugar

1 tablespoon gelatin
1 tablespoon vanilla
1 cup milk
3 eggs (separated)
1 pkg. Lady Fingers

Whip cream until stiff—Cream sugar and egg yolks—Dissolve gelatin in milk to simmering, not boiling—Stir dissolved gelatin with yolks and sugar—Stir this into whipped cream—Add vanilla—Last, add beaten egg whites—Pour into mold lined with Lady Fingers—Top with whipped cream and sprinkle with glacé cherries.

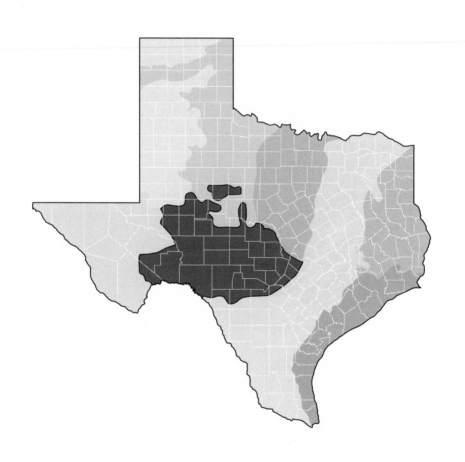

Stories and Recipes from the Edwards Plateau*

These 25 million acres are rolling to mountainous, with woodlands in the eastern part and grassy prairies in the west. There is a good deal of brushy growth in the central and eastern areas. The combination of grasses, weeds and small trees is ideal for cattle, sheep, goats, deer, and wild turkey.

The limestone-based area is characterized by the large number of springfed, perennially flowing streams that originate in its interior and flow across the Balcones Escarpment, which bounds it on the south and east. The soils are shallow, ranging from sandy to clays, and are calcareous in reaction. This area is predominantly rangeland with cultivation confined to the deeper soils.

In the east-central portion is the well-marked Central or Llano Basin, centering in Mason, Llano, and Burnet counties, with a mixture of granitic and sandy soils. The western portion of the area comprises the semi-arid Stockton Plateau. Noteworthy is the growth of cypress along the perennially flowing streams. . . . These

*Stephan L. Hatch, *Texas Almanac, 2014–2015*, Elizabeth Cruce Alvarez, editor (Austin: Texas State Historical Association), 116. Used with permission of Texas State Historical Association.

trees, which grow to stately proportions, were commercialized in the past.

The principal grasses of the clay soils are cane bluestem, silver bluestem, little bluestem, sideoats, grama, hairy grama, indiangrass, curly-mesquite, buffalograss, fall witchgrass, plains lovegrass, wildryes, and Texas wintergrass. The rocky areas support tall or mid-grasses with an overstory of live oak, shinnery oak, juniper, and mesquite. The heavy clay soils have a mixture of tobosagrass, buffalograss, sideoats grama, and mesquite. Throughout the Edwards Plateau, live oak, shinnery oak, mesquite, and juniper dominate the woody vegetation.

Texas Pecan Cake

3 C. sugar   5 C. flour
1 lb. oleo   1 2-oz. lemon ext.
7 eggs beaten separately   { 1 tsp. soda dissolved in
                                       { 4 tsp. warm wine

1 qt. chopped pecans
1 lb. candied pineapple cut fine
1/2 lb.   "   red cherries

   Cream oleo & sugar well, add well
well-beaten egg yolks. Add a little flour,
then wine, soda, lemon ext. & half
of the flour. Add fruits & nuts which
have been dredged in balance of flour.
Then fold in beaten egg whites stiff.
Bake in tube pan or loaf pan which
has been lined with wax paper. Use foil
under & over pan while baking. Bake 3½
hrs. at 250° Makes a big cake, but
can be kept ages.

Jean Andrews

THE PEPPER TRAIL AND PEPPER COOKBOOK

by Jean Andrews

Jean Andrews writes a cultural history of a food—peppers, a food she fell in love with years ago. She traveled the pepper trail from Bolivia to the Far East, Tibet to Timbuktu and back, tracking the pungent pod. She tells how and why the American capsicums moved from their prehistoric Bolivian place of origin and traveled around the world affecting the foodways of both hemispheres, and also, how to hone Capsicum cooking skills. She writes:

> This is a cultural history of a food with recipes—put together by an inquisitive scholar, gardener, cook, traveler, and artist who fell in love with peppers more than twenty years ago. During that time I attempted to learn what they are, where they came from, where they moved, and how they affected the cooking in the places they went. . . . As I delved deeper into the directions taken by the Capsicum peppers after Christopher Columbus discovered them, it appeared that as peppers followed the ancient trade routes they had a great effect on the cuisines of the lands along the way. Once capsicums reached the Old World they fell into the hands of spice merchants. I began to wonder why the spice trade went one way and not another five hundred years ago? How it went and what it went in? Who carried it? Why some people responded to the introduction of peppers and others didn't? Why cuisines have certain characteristics and not others? and on and on. These questions took me not only to libraries but also to many countries along the pepper trail including much of Africa, the Middle East, Central Asia, and Monsoon Asia—India, Nepal, Bhutan,

Tibet, Sri Lanka, Thailand, Indonesia—plus Xinjiang, Sichuan and Hunan in China as well as Latin America. . . . The manner in which food is selected, prepared and served is always the result of the culture in which it occurs, as indeed are the accessories and rituals that accompany the rudimentary activity of eating.*

The Pepper Lady's Chile Con Queso**

This is about as Tex-Mex as it comes, but an informal gathering in these parts of Texas wouldn't be the same without it.

Makes 8 to 12 Servings (more as a dip).

1 2-pound package Velveeta® cheese, cut into
    1-inch cubes
1 pound sharp cheddar cheese, shredded, light
    if available
1 10-ounce can Rotel® diced tomatoes and
    green chiles
2 fresh poblanos peppers or long green/red
    chiles, roasted, skinned, deveined, and cut
    into fine, 2-inch strips
Salt and freshly ground black pepper to taste.
Ground cayenne or Aleppo pepper to taste.
canned, evaporated milk for thinning

Melt Velveeta® cheese in a microwave or in a large double boiler, or crock pot, being careful not to scorch. Add

---

* Jean Andrews, *The Pepper Trail: History and Recipes from Around the World* (Denton: University of North Texas Press, 1999, ix–x. Used with permission of University of North Texas Press.
** Jean Andrews, *The Peppers Cookbook* (Denton: University of North Texas Press, 2005). Used with permission of University of North Texas Press.

cheddar cheese gradually; stir until melted and completely mixed with Velveeta® cheese. Add the can of tomatoes to melted cheeses; mix well. Add chopped fresh poblano or long green/red chile. Stir until well mixed. Add seasonings to taste. Thin to desired consistency with canned evaporated milk; stir well. Serve immediately with freshly made corn tortillas or tostados.

In the Southwest, chile con queso is served warm from a chafing dish or fondue pot as a dip with toasted tortilla chips.

EASY JALAPEÑO CORNBREAD

This should never be a sweet cornbread. It is great topped with stewed tomatoes and lots of butter—real country style. Another country favorite is cold left-over cornbread crumbled into a glass of sweet milk and eaten with a spoon—called "crumble-in" or "crumblin."

Makes 4 to 8 servings.

3 canned or pickled jalapeños, drained and chopped

1½ cups yellow stone-ground cornmeal

½ cup all-purpose flour

1 teaspoon granulated sugar, or up to 1 tablespoon depending on taste

½ teaspoon baking soda

1 teaspoon salt

2 teaspoons baking powder

2 large eggs, at room temperature

1 cup buttermilk

1 tablespoon vegetable oil, plus enough to grease pan

Preheat oven to 400°F. In a mixing bowl, combine cornmeal, baking soda, sugar, flour, salt, and baking power;

set aside. In a separate bowl, mix eggs, buttermilk, and oil; stir until smooth and creamy. Add jalapeños; mix. Stir liquid into cornmeal-flour mixture. Blend with a spoon to form a smooth batter; do not overstir. Grease a 9-inch pan (preferably cast iron) with oil and preheat in oven. Remove; pour batter into the hot pan. Return to oven; bake for 20 to 30 minutes, or until a toothpick inserted in the bread comes out clean. Cut and serve immediately.

OLD TIME TEXAS FAVORITES

FRITO PIE

The incomparable, favorite chip, Frito, was originated about 1932 by Elmer Doolin in San Antonio, Texas, in a little old house on South Flores Street. His wife, Daisy, made the first Frito pie when she dumped her bowl of chili directly into a bag of Fritos. Her handy innovation caught on with kids of all ages and is still going strong—but has graduated to a bowl. You can use chili made from a recipe or just open and heat a can of Wolf Brand® Chili without beans. Wolf Brand Chili is also a native of Texas but now owned by ConAgra.

Makes—depends on the amount of chili on hand.

Fritos
chili con carne
onions chopped
longhorn cheddar cheese, shredded
salsa picante

In each individual bowl spread about ¾ cup Fritos and sprinkle onion equally on top. Put equal amounts of hot chili on top of the Fritos and top with cheese. Pass the salsa at the table.

Originally, a small individual bag of Fritos was split down one side and spread open to allow entry of chili. The other side was flattened so the package of Frito pie would sit on a table.

PEDERNALES RIVER CHILI (PRONOUNCED: "PURR-DIN-ALICE")

The late Frank Tolbert reported in his *A Bowl of Red*, that President Lyndon B. Johnson said: "One of the first things I do when I get home to Texas is to have a bowl of red. There is simply nothing better." This recipe got its inspiration from the chili made at the LBJ Ranch, which is located on the Pedernales River near Johnson City in Blanco County, Texas. In the late 1950s, Frank and I were Dallas neighbors. Our pre-teen sons played together for years.

A word about chili con carne. Most evidence points to its beginnings in Texas, probably in San Antonio, in the early nineteenth century and becoming known in the 1880s when chili queens sold cooked chili con carne from caldrons at dusk in downtown plazas. This practice continued until about 1943. O. Henry was the first to write about the chili queens.

Makes—a lot!

4 pounds of chili meat, coarsely cut beef, or
   venison (deer)
4 tablespoons vegetable oil
1 large onion, chopped
4 garlic cloves, peeled and minced
1 teaspoon oregano
1 teaspoon cumin seeds, ground
7 teaspoons chili powder, more if desired
   (Gebhardt's® preferred)
2 16-ounce cans of tomatoes, diced
2 cups of boiling water
cayenne pepper, to taste
salt and freshly ground black pepper, to taste

In a large skillet or Dutch oven heat oil. Add ground meat, onion, garlic; sear until a grayish color. Add the rest of the ingredients; bring to a boil and lower heat. Simmer for an hour, covered. Skim off grease. Cooked pinto beans or black beans may be added, but never kidney beans!

CHILI PEPPER JELLY

Tasty, savory, tangy, piquant, appetizing—this jelly is all these things. Once you have introduced it to your repertoire of delectable treats you'll find you must have it to serve with chicken and meats, as well as on hot breads, waffles, and pancakes.

Makes 7 cups.

¼ cup fresh chili peppers, chiltepines, jalapeños, or habaneros, seeded and chopped
¾ cup bell peppers; use same color as the chili
   peppers
6½ cups sugar
1½ cups white vinegar
6 ounce pouch liquid pectin (Certo®)
Food coloring, same color as peppers (optional)
Paraffin

Peppers can be chopped in a food processor if care is taken to not get them too fine. Mix peppers, sugar and vinegar together in a 6 to 7-quart non-reactive pan; boil for 2 minutes. Let cool 5 minutes. Add pectin; 1 or 2 drops of food coloring, then bring to a rolling boil and boil for 1 minute (do not exceed recommended time).

Pour into hot, sterilized jelly jars to ½ inch from the rim. Wipe rims with a clean damp cloth; seal immediately with melted paraffin. Place scalded lids on the jars and tighten. Place on a rack to cool. Store in refrigerator once opened. If jelly turns to sugar, melt it and use it to baste fowl or as a sauce or glaze for meats or in salad dressing.

The flecks of pepper are attractive but for a clear jelly, strain mixture after it has boiled for 2 minutes; return to pan, bring to boil; continue as directed.

Any chili pepper—jalapeños, habanero, datil, serrano, chiltepines—can be used but don't mix them if you want a distinct flavor typical of that variety.

Alternative: Try a chili pepper jelly that is not from scratch.

2 habanero or scotch bonnet chili peppers, or
    4 jalapeños, 4 serranos, or 8 chiltepines (or
    to taste); stemmed, seeded, and chopped
1 cup white vinegar
1 cup sugar
4 10-ounce jars apple or current jelly

Mix chili peppers, vinegar, and sugar in a 4 to 5-quart non-reactive sauce pan. Bring to a boil over high heat and boil; stir until mixture is reduced to about ⅓ cup, about 7 minutes. Remove jelly from jars with a sterile spoon; stir it into the pepper mixture. Boil, stirring until jelly melts. Ladle hot jelly back into unwashed apple jelly jars to within ¼ inch of the rims. Wipe rims clean with damp paper towel; tighten lids onto jar. If there is any jelly left over, put it into a covered dish for immediate use. After 1–2 hours agitate jars to redistribute pepper pieces. When jelly is cool, store it in the refrigerator up to 4 months.

Margaret Anna Cox

FUDGE RECEIPT

by Margaret Anna Cox

On a bright day in May, 1918, Evelyn Murray was born in Eden, Texas. Her parents, Zack and Annie Murray, barely moved into town from the ranch before their daughter's arrival. They rented the Fred Ede house briefly before buying their own home on the Old Paint Rock Road. Evelyn was always proud to tell everyone that she had been born in the first home of the founder of Eden, Frederick Ede. The English cattleman had deeded forty acres for a town site in 1882, and the town was called Eden in his honor.

After the Murrays settled on their place on the Old Paint Rock Road, two little brothers later joined Evelyn in sharing an active life in a home that was only a mile or two from downtown Eden. In rural Concho County most families kept chickens, hogs, cows, sheep, turkeys and other livestock, and Evelyn and her brothers were always in the middle of the action—especially when their mama called for them to "Go run down a chicken!" They knew that meant the Baptist preacher was probably coming after church, and they would have fried chicken for Sunday dinner. (That meant noon, as supper was always the evening meal.)

The act of catching the bird was a major enterprise. And after the children cornered and handed it to Mama, she very adeptly wrung off its head and popped it, headless, into a pot of boiling water to soften the feathers for plucking. In spite of all that effort, and having to watch the poor bird die, the fried chicken always tasted delicious, and everyone felt the frenzy was worth it. What a far cry from modern folks who can purchase their chicken from the supermarket already dead, sorted, and wrapped in plastic. It seems that only the fun of the chase is missing.

Chicken wasn't always the featured meal. Evelyn, my mother, told me of a supper of butterbeans, ably prepared by a good cook, Annie. They had as a guest, an old uncle who suffered from a case of palsy. His hands were very shaky, and the three children watched in wide-eyed wonder as he attempted to eat butterbeans off his knife or fork. He would get the bean nearly to his mouth, then it would drop back into his plate. Their giggles prompted their father to send them away from the table. This allowed the old uncle to eat his butterbeans in peace.

Milk often was the source of comfort food. I'm not sure who in the family was the designated cow milker. I suppose each family member played a part. First, the cream had to be churned for butter after it sat a while in the crock and rose to the top of the milk. Buttermilk, fresh with tiny flecks of butter, was delicious to drink. Clabber, which was the result of letting the milk sour and become solid like yogurt, was an extra-special treat for my father, and later for me. I haven't tasted good clabber in years. Cold sweetmilk poured into a glass of warm cornbread makes a delightfully comforting and tasty mush, and is a good meal for someone recovering from a bout of the measles or mumps. My mother prepared milk-toast for all her children. She poured hot milk over a simple slice of buttered toast, and that brought the ailing child back to good health quickly.

And, don't get me started on the vegetable garden, or the corn patch. My grandmother was great with plants, as was my mother, and they raised a bountiful amount of fodder and foliage for the family. Once, my grandmother became so agitated with a group of hens scratching in her flowerbed that she grabbed one and actually spanked its little tail feathers. The garden provided a surprising source of income during the Great Depression for my mother's youngest brother. One day he loaded as many vegetables as his little red wagon could hold and pulled it the two miles to town. He didn't tell his mama he was going to do this, and she became frantic when he turned up missing for several hours. Later in the day, the little cotton-headed boy was seen coming in the front gate, pulling an empty wagon and yelling: "Sold out! Sold out!" I don't think my grandmother had the heart to discipline him after that valiant effort.

Growing up during the Great Depression gave my mother ample opportunities to witness the evolving rural life around her. As a creative cook she personally experienced many challenges in her attempts to stir up something delicious with meager resources.

She had to rely often on a traveling peddler of Raleigh or Watkins home products to complete her recipes. The peddlers sold things like vanilla and various patent medicines. When she didn't have cash, she traded chickens or other produce to the Raleigh man.

Many years later she composed a Fudge Receipt (circa 1931), as a micro-view of the era in which she grew up and flourished. She called it "receipt" not "recipe," because that's how many old-time cooks referred to it. She wanted to shed some light-heartedness on the tough times that faced many rural cooks.

Fudge Receipt: Circa 1931

First gather a bucket of hard-shelled pecans the size of English Pea or a bucket of Black Walnuts. Crack with a hammer. Pick out ⅕ cup nuts.

Go to woodpile. Bring in wood and chips. Build fire. Or, if you live in town and use oil stove, take gallon can, walk to town and get gallon coal oil. Bring home with potato on spout. Fill oil stove.

Use gray granite pot.

Mix together:
2 cups sugar
2 tablespoons cocoa
½ cup water (because cows had either gone dry, or mint weed or gourd vine had spoiled the milk)
1 tablespoon hog lard

Bring to boil. And boil and boil and boil. Add ⅕ cup nuts. Grease platter with hog lard and pour quickly before it hardens. Let cool, cut in squares (if knife is sharp).

Eat if possible.

Note: If the Raleigh man (Old Man Wilks) has been around, and you had chickens to trade for vanilla, add ½ teaspoon to boiling fudge.

Laura and Gary Lavergne. Photo courtesy of Walt Maciborski

"BECAUSE IT WAS GOOD!!"

by Gary and Laura Lavergne

One of the funniest stories we have ever heard about Cajuns and eating was told to us by an aunt of ours from St. Landry Parish. It seems she knew of a man who had to be rushed to Opelousas General Hospital for immediate medical attention, not because of an accident or disease, but for the self-inflicted trauma of having eaten four pounds of boudin in one sitting.

"Why on Earth did you eat so darn much boudin?" the incredulous doctor asked.

"Because it was good," his patient replied.

We think that was a GREAT answer!

That brings us to Cajun Cooking Rule #1: If you can't take salt, pepper, sugar, cream, and fat, then just enjoy being a trendy American and leave us Cajuns alone. As authentic Cajuns, we can't imagine pralines made of nutra-sweet, or meat, fish, or even vegetables without seasoning of some sort. No other group cooks like Cajuns. Think about it: Roux is skillfully-burned flour. Without seasoning, it looks like milk chocolate and tastes like discarded cigarette butts. But eventually, with love and seasoning and more skill, it will become a gumbo, and that is much different. So, we Cajuns just relax and remind others that, one day, no matter how long you deprive yourself of the delight of eating something that actually tastes good, and even after decades of carrot sticks and dry lettuce, sooner or later we will all end up in the same place.

We admit to adapting Cajun Cooking Rule #2 from a Rita Rudner joke: Cajun men, especially, enjoy cooking as long as danger is involved. Around Thanksgiving time insurance companies feel compelled to remind us of the dangers of deep frying whole turkeys: "It will . . . burn your house to the ground." Cajun bar-b-ques and an authentic Cochon de Lait don't seem authentic unless there is a huge pit of glowing, fiery hardwood—enough heat to smelt iron. There is little comfort in knowing that the whole event is often loosely monitored by intoxicated adults and children at play. For Cajun cooks, indoors provide no safety; in Cajun homes, who hasn't seen the perilous movement of a cauldron of gumbo that's too hot to touch and too heavy to lift? Who hasn't seen a Cajun dip a tablespoon into hard-boiling gumbo, only to grimace and reply, "Oh, that's hot!" Why on Earth do we do such things? Well, because it's good! So, in order to protect our American citizenship, and with a concern for the safety of our American readers, we submit a meal that, literally, could be made with anything you have left over: a Jambalaya. We'll use chicken and sausage.

CHICKEN AND SAUSAGE JAMBALAYA

1 large sweet onion, diced

1 cup each celery and/or bell pepper (unless your sons won't eat the green stuff)

2–3 pounds of deboned chicken thighs, diced into bite-sized chunks (breasts are okay, but much drier)

2–3 pounds of pork sausage (if you are close to a Cajun meat market get the "Hot Pure Pork")

a couple of teaspoons of olive oil (or bacon drippings, if you're Gary)

2–3 cups of cooked long-grain rice

Cajun seasoning, like Tony Chachere's, or your own concoction of salt, cayenne, black pepper, and paprika

a bit of teriyaki sauce

1 can of some kind of cream soup (golden mushroom is good)

In a large pot, brown the chicken and sausage. If you like, glaze it with a little sugar cane or maple syrup. Throw in the diced veggies. Cook until the veggies are of the consistency you like. Add the rice, the teriyaki sauce, and the soup. Stir. Eat it while it's hot because it's good.

J. Frank Dobie

DOBIE, WEBB, AND BEDICHEK DINNERS, FROM *THE TEXAS COOKBOOK*

by Mary Faulk Koock*

‸‸

Mr. J. Frank Dobie, late famous writer and folklorist; Dr. Walter Prescott Webb, noted historian; Dr. Roy Bedichek, writer and naturalist; and Dr. Mody Boatright, professor of English at the University of Texas, would often come to Green Pastures with their wives, who are very talented and distinguished in their own rights. When my brother John Henry Faulk was at home from New York he was always invited to join them for dinner. They came early and stayed late, and needless to say, never for a second did their stimulating and fascinating conversation lag. They all loved good food and good wine. We usually put their table in a small dining room where in the winter we keep a good fire cracklin' in the fireplace. One night they particularly enjoyed:

Cup of Beef Bouillon

Fresh Fruit Salad

Breast of White Guinea Hen, with Artichoke Sauce

Baked Rice

Baked Tomatoes filled with Spinach Vera Cruz

Hot Crescent Rolls

Sherry Almond Pudding

Before Green Pastures was taken into the city we used to raise chickens, turkey and guineas—guineas with black-and-white speckled feathers. They were fairly wild and when Mama wanted to cook guinea for Sunday dinner, I remember my brothers, Johnny or Hamilton, would shoot them as they flew up from the ground over the oak trees. Those guineas were all dark meat, and had to cook

* Mary Faulk Koock, *The Texas Cookbook* (Denton: University of North Texas Press, 2001), 23–28. Used with permission of University of North Texas Press.

slowly for a long time. Not too many years ago, our friends Mr. and Mrs. Parks Johnson started raising white guineas—the first I ever heard of in Texas. Parks will be remembered for his popular nation-wide radio show *Vox Pox*, before television days. When he retired from show business, he and Louise moved to their ranch near Wimberley and thought these birds had great merit. The white guineas have all white feathers and all white meat, rather like a Cornish game hen, only larger. Now that Parks has turned to other projects, we get our supply from Bill Modene and serve only the breast for dinner; the rest goes to make delicious chicken salad.

BREAST OF WHITE GUINEA HEN

(may also be prepared with breast of chicken)
For 6 breasts: (approx. ¾ lb. each)
3 tablespoons butter
salt to taste
1 teaspoon white pepper
2 tablespoons flour
½ teaspoons Beau Monde seasoned salt
1 garlic clove, mashed
1 tablespoon parsley, chopped very fine
1 tablespoon green onion (white and green
    part, chopped very fine)
3 cups rich chicken stock (all fat removed)
1 tablespoon imported parmesan
1 teaspoon Maggi Seasoning
2 tablespoons dry sherry
¾ cup sliced sautéed mushrooms
Baked Rice [see below]
hearts of artichoke
butter

Remove skin. Rub breasts with melted butter, salt and pepper, brown lightly in heavy iron skillet and then place in roaster, meaty side down.

Make sauce by melting butter and flour and simmering 10 minutes browning only very slightly. Add Beau Monde, garlic, pepper and salt to taste, parsley, onion and chicken stock. Then add parmesan, Maggi and sherry and whip till smooth. This should be rather a thin sauce, so a little more chicken stock may be added if necessary. Pour over guinea breasts; cover and cook in 275° oven for 2 hours. Remove breasts; strain sauce and add sautéed mushrooms. Place breasts in center of Baked Rice; place hearts of artichoke on each side of guinea and glaze with sauce. Pass remaining sauce. Serves 6.

BAKED RICE

2 tablespoons oil
1 cup rice
¼ cup chopped onion
1 ½ cups hot chicken stock (with fat removed)
¾ cup sautéed sliced mushrooms (optional)
1 cup cooked wild rice

In a heavy skillet heat oil till hot and add rice and onion. Stir till they are very light brown. Add chicken stock and mushrooms and place in 350° oven uncovered for approximately 30 minutes. Stir during cooking time and add more liquid if necessary. (Never let any rice overcook; grains should be tender and stand apart.) Add 1 cup of cooked wild rice; stir and season to taste.

I really think that this and the guineas are my original recipes!

TOMATOES FILLED WITH SPINACH VERA CRUZ

1 small packet frozen chopped spinach
6 medium-sized firm tomatoes
salt
3 strips bacon
¼ cup chopped onion

1 cup sour cream
dash of Tabasco
freshly ground black pepper
5 slices mozzarella cheese

Thaw spinach and blanch in hot water, let drain in colander. Cut out centers of tomatoes, leaving firm outside wall. Sprinkle with salt and turn open side down to drain. Chop the part of the tomato removed from center and let it drain also in a strainer.

Fry bacon until crisp, remove from pan and drain on paper. Pour off excess bacon fat, retaining 2 tablespoons. Sauté onions in bacon drippings over low fire; add spinach which has been squeezed dry. Add the chopped well-drained tomatoes, add sour cream. Season with salt, a dash of Tabasco and freshly ground pepper. Stir well and add 2 slices of the cheese, cut fine, and stir in the bacon, which has been crumbled. When heated through, fill cavity of tomatoes. Place in slightly buttered baking pan. Top each tomato with triangle of cheese. Just before time to serve run in oven long enough to heat through (15 minutes).

This is very pretty, and I think terrifically good; it is important not to let the tomatoes get soft by cooking too long.

HOT CRESCENT ROLLS (POPULAR AT GREEN PASTURES)

½ cup sugar
½ cup soft butter
1 teaspoon salt
2 eggs
¾ cup scalded milk (scalded and then cooled
    to lukewarm)

2 cakes of yeast

4 cups sifted all-purpose flour

Mix sugar, butter, salt and eggs together. Beat with rotary egg beater. Stir in milk. Crumble yeast into the mixture; stir until dissolved. Beat in the flour with a spoon. Scrape dough from sides of bowl. Cover with damp cloth and let rise until double. Roll dough on floured board to ½ inch. Make pie wedges. Brush with melted butter. Roll in circles. Cut in triangular pieces. Roll and twist into crescent shapes. Let stand till double in bulk. Bake for 15 minutes in 425° oven. Makes 4 dozen rolls.

SHERRY ALMOND PUDDING

2 tablespoons unflavored gelatin

½ cup cold water

1 cup hot water

⅓ cup sherry

½ teaspoon almond extract

¼ teaspoon salt

6 egg whites

1 ½ cups sugar

1 cup heavy cream, whipped

Sherry Sauce [see below]

¼ toasted shredded coconut

¼ cup toasted almonds

Soak gelatin in cold water. Dissolve in hot water. Cool 15 to 20 minutes. Add wine, almond extract and salt. When mixture begins to thicken beat until frothy. Beat egg whites until foamy. Gradually add sugar and beat till stiff. Fold egg whites and whipped cream into gelatin mixture. Pour into individual molds and chill till firm. Turn out, cover with sauce and sprinkle top with 1 tablespoon each toasted coconut and almonds.

Sherry Sauce

6 egg yolks
¼ cup sugar
1 tablespoon flour
2 cups milk (scalded)
¼ cup sherry
1 cup heavy cream

Beat egg yolks thoroughly. Mix in sugar and flour. Gradually stir in milk. Cook over low heat until thickened, stirring constantly. Cool 15–20 minutes. Add sherry. Chill. When ready to serve, whip cream and fold into custard.

After everyone had polished the bones of the guinea hens, Frank Dobie said, "Seeing these clean bones around the table reminds me of the time when I was a boy and living on our ranch in South Texas, and there was a lot of quail around. We never shot the quail, but would catch lots of them in a homemade trap. One day, my mother made a great big Quail Pie for our dinner. Shortly before the time to serve, our neighbor Andrew Jackson Wright and his brother, from a nearby ranch, stopped in, and as was customary, they were asked to stay for dinner. This meant that we children had to wait for the 'second table.' As we patiently waited we peeped through the door; the guest already had a big pile of bones by his plate and was lifting another of the succulent birds from the pie. Mama was getting uneasy—and so were we! Finally he pulled the napkin from his collar, wiped his mouth and hands, and said: 'Mrs. Dobie, that was a mighty fine quail pie, but I think it would have been better if you'd fried the quail first.'"

Quail Pie

Split 12 quail down the back and rub with salt pork, salt and pepper. Roll in flour and brown on both sides in a little hot Crisco in a heavy iron skillet. Pour 1 quart chicken stock over and cover. Let simmer slowly about 30 minutes, then remove to a casserole which has a sliced onion medium-sized. Lay the birds close together and pour the hot gravy over them. Add about 1 tablespoon flour mixed smooth with a little water, ½ cup wine and a cup of small canned green peas. Cover with rich pastry dough and bake in 350° oven till crust is brown. Allow 3 quail per person—unless you have a greedy guest for dinner.

Mr. Dobie called me one morning and asked if I had a good recipe for beef hash. He said his mother used to make it on cold mornings and served it with hot biscuits and he knew of nothing he liked better. He had recently been a guest at the White House, and former President Harry Truman was also visiting there at the same time. President Johnson had very graciously asked Mr. Truman and Mr. Dobie to sit in on some of the conferences. It was about two o'clock when the three of them went up to the family dining room on the third floor of the White House for lunch. Mr. Dobie said they had a lovely lunch, but he couldn't remember anything in particular except the hash. He said it was the best he'd ever eaten; it tasted like it had a little jalapeno pepper. I wrote Zephyr Wright at the White House, who was probably the one who made it and asked how she made that hash.

White House Hash

Zephyr said there wasn't a definite recipe, but that it was very necessary to use only the best meat available, and make lots of gravy. She adds a few potatoes and onions, and—Mr. Dobie was right—a few jalapeno peppers. The President and his visitors from Texas always like this little hot accent!

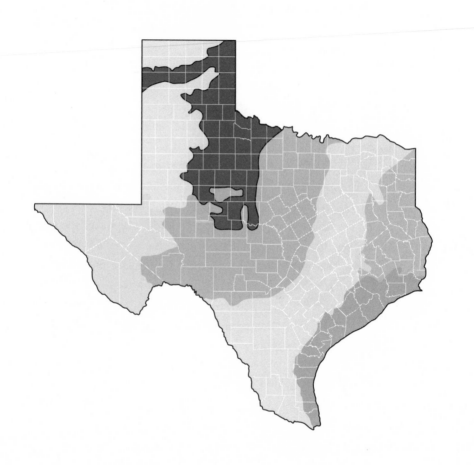

Stories and Recipes from the Rolling Plains*

This is a region of approximately 24 million acres of alternating woodlands and prairies. The area is half mesquite woodland and half prairie. Mesquite trees have steadily invaded and increased in the grasslands for many years, despite constant control efforts.

Soils range from coarse sands along out-wash terraces adjacent to streams to tight or compact clays on redbed clays and shales. Rough broken lands on steep slopes are found in the western portion. About two-thirds of the area is rangeland, but cultivation is important in certain localities.

The original vegetation includes big, little, sand and silver blue-stems, Texas wintergrass, indiangrass, switchgrass, sideoats and blue gramas, wild-ryes, tobosagrass, and buffalograss on the clay soils. The sandy soils support tall bunchgrasses, mainly sand bluestem. Sand shinnery oak, sand sagebrush, and mesquite are the dominant woody plants. Continued heavy grazing contributes to the increase in woody plants, low-value grasses, such as red grama, red lovegrass, tumblegrass, gummy lovegrass, Texas grama, sand dropseed, and sandbur with western ragweed, croton, and many other weedy forbs. Yucca is a problem plant on certain rangelands.

*Stephan L. Hatch, *Texas Almanac, 2014–2015*, Elizabeth Cruce Alvarez, editor (Austin: Texas State Historical Association), 117. Used with permission of Texas State Historical Association.

George Owens

FROM THE JOURNAL
OF ROBERT WILSON BOOTH

by George Owens

—◆◆—

I spent the winter and spring of 1878 working in a saloon at Rath City, recovering from injuries and privation suffered in an ill-advised attempt to hunt for buffalo hides on the staked plains. The "restaurant," as it was styled by its owner, I. F. Hackney, served to slake the hunters' thirst for ardent spirits and female company. It was built picket style of cottonwood logs and local stone with a wagon sheet roof. There were two Mexican women in the place, Hackney's wife Agustina and her cousin Lucie, both of whom were employed in the old profession. I was brought to these people in very poor condition, unable to speak or do much else than eat, and that sparingly. Allowed to remain at first as a sort of curiosity, with time I was put to work at menial tasks. Although I was regarded by most as a half-wit the women were kind to me, and as I recovered my ability to speak they taught me the rudiments of the border regions' peculiar Spanish dialect. Lucie was not much of a talker, but Agustina enjoyed conversation so much that Hackney eventually told me if I continued to monopolize her time I would have to pay the going rate.

I was able to help with the cooking, done at a mud hearth filling one end of the building's single low room. The food we supplied was of necessity simple, beans and tortillas supplemented with meat from various sources, flavored with a condiment I have since regarded as a staple, a rough sauce of tomatoes, onions, fresh peppers, garlic and spices. The "salsa picante" was kept in snuff-bottles stacked in the root cellar. Not long before leaving Rath City I helped the women put up a batch of the stuff and committed the method of its preparation to memory.

Fresh ingredients were grown in the back yard of the store. Coriander leaves came from a plant that filled half an old whiskey barrel near the rear door. Cumin seed and tiny limes, hard as a green peach, were acquired from a trader who came up from the south in late spring, following an old Comanchero trail.

Tomatoes were blanched, peeled and cored, then sliced into small cubes about a quarter-inch on a side. Onions and green peppers were likewise cut up with garlic and a handful or two of the leaves of the coriander plant. Quartered limes were placed in a square of cheesecloth folded over to form a bag, which was beaten lightly with a bottle to help release the juice. The loose ends of the cloth were wrapped around a stick and twisted above the pot, straining the lime juice into the mixture as it cooked over a medium fire. The pot was allowed to come to a boil for two or three minutes, then a handful of salt and a small amount of cumin seed, roasted and finely ground, was stirred in and the pot covered. After a brief rest the steaming mixture was ladled into snuff bottles and sealed with melted tallow. Agustina told me that if the bottles were kept out of the sun the salsa would retain its color and flavor for as long as six months.

Around the first of July I had regained the ability to shift for myself, so I went to Mr. Hackney to ask if I owed him anything. He said I had earned my keep. With account squared I hired on with a freight-hauler pulling for the Pease River country. I was without money or possessions and my hunting companions all dead. I was friendless in Texas, or so I thought. As the wagon crested the rise that would put the camp out of sight I turned, and in my last view of Rath City saw Lucie standing alone in the dust of the road, one hand raised in silent farewell.

I chanced to return to that area some years later, by which time the buffalo business had devoured itself, and found the building very nearly gone, its fallen walls overgrown with brush. The story I heard was that when the hunting was over, the Moaar brothers packed what they could on freight wagons and moved all to Camp Supply in the Indian Territory. Sure enough, the little temporary town was gone; my only company that day was the wind rushing by on its way down the Double Mountain Fork's broad, ancient valley.

DOUBLE MOUNTAIN SALSA

(With contemporary ingredients substituted.)

6 fresh jalapeno peppers, cored and chopped
3 habanero peppers, cored and finely chopped
1 medium green bell pepper, cored and diced
2 yellow onions, finely chopped
4 cloves garlic, finely chopped or pressed
1 tablespoon chopped fresh cilantro
juice of 2 limes
12 Roma tomatoes, peeled, cored and chopped
10 ounces spicy hot V-8 juice
2 medium (14.5 ounce) cans petite diced
    tomatoes
season salt

In a large saucepan, combine the canned tomatoes and
V-8 juice and bring to a boil. Add the chopped peppers,
onions and garlic and cook, stirring, until the mixture
returns to a boil. Add the fresh tomatoes, cilantro, lime
juice and a healthy dash of season salt and stir well. Cover
and turn off heat. Allow to sit for five minutes, then ladle
into clean mason jars. Refrigerate when jars are cool
enough to handle. Makes 5 pints.

Bumgardner Recipes

"GRANDMA IN ABILENE"—ANTICIPATING GOOD EATS

by Scott Hill Bumgardner

I must say that as a kid I was preoccupied, hyperactive, and a little dumb. I'm not sure I really even knew my "Grandma in Abilene" had a name. My Houston citified grandmother had a name; well, it was hand-picked, "Bamie." Bamie was picked because of the "Bambi" deer drawings she and I would work on together. But, my countrified "Grandma in Abilene" was just Grandma. Oh, how she could cook! Each summer I would spend a week or two with her in Abilene. The trip from Houston to Abilene was mighty long, about seven hours. But that was seven hours of anticipation for grandma's chicken and dumplings and chocolate pecan pie.

Those trips were great. For a number of years I was placed on a Greyhound bus where I traveled alone. Times were really different; these days you can't even imagine having an eight-year-old boy travel alone on a bus. One year for some reason I had to transfer from one bus to another in Austin. These long, lonely, nerve-racking trips helped to build my confidence, making me self-sufficient. Upon arrival my reward was waiting. The reward was a loving grandmother with some dang good food.

Heck, I might have been a teenager by the time I learned Grandma's name. Her name even got confusing, because she had worked her way through a variety of men. She was born in Comanche, Texas, in 1897, with the name of Mayme Jobe. As a young mother when the Depression caused unemployment of her first husband, "Cash" Bumgardner, she became a struggling single mother. Cash dropped Dad and Grandma off at her mother's home in Abilene. He left them to find work and became a virtual stranger. Through the years she bore other men's names: Sipe, Brown and Lowrance. I mostly remember her with a good old man named Walter Brown.

Much of this family's survival was based on Grandma's cooking skills. She had also worked some non-cooking jobs to feed the family. Around 1938, Mayme spent a time at Abilene's Banner Ice-cream factory, where she was paid one dollar per day to wrap ice cream sandwiches. But most of her life was spent in diners. My dad spent much of his youth sleeping in the back storeroom of her cafes. Grandma had started several cafes or diners in Abilene and other West Texas towns. She was becoming moderately successful with Mayme's Cafe on Abilene's Butternut Street, until she lost the lease. Another effort made down the street just never took off. Mayme, with her husband Ruel Sipe, opened Sipe's Cafe on East 2nd in Odessa in the later 1940s and made a reported whopping loss of $684.03 on their 1949 income tax report. Lack of success led them back to Abilene by 1951. Another effort was made with the City Cafe at 933 North 3rd about the time Ruel died.

I remember Grandma as a senior citizen waitress at the Dixie Pig cafe on the corner of Butternut and S. 14th. Her home was on S. 15th just a couple of blocks from the Dixie Pig. The backyard was a regular little farm. She had a mess of hens, berry vines, fruit trees, and three pecan trees. Her pecan trees were named after my family: Scott, JC, and Betty. Every morning of my visits we would have fresh eggs. The hens occasionally made it into the pot for her special time-honored chicken and dumplings. One dim memory I have is of one of her beheaded hens charging around the yard. I must say that bird became a delicacy.

Man oh man, each floury dumpling was rolled out with love while her fat hen would be boiling away, filling the house with savory aromas. Over the years she never would share the recipe, possibly believing that if you could not figure it out then your attempt would not be good anyway. My dad and I could eat a ton of them. No wonder I am what we might call "stout." We ate till we were miserable. But I have never been too miserable to turn down Grandma's chocolate pecan pies.

Our meals used all fresh ingredients; vegetables were grown at another urban garden. She had a lot by a couple of her rent houses that was chock-full of well tended vegetables. We would tend the gardens together, weeding and such, then pick what was needed for the next meal or two. One of the sweetest, yet most painful jobs was picking dew berries from those thorny vines—ouch. Gathered at the kitchen table, Grandma and I would make the preparations for our meals. I helped cut the veggies, snapped the peas, and we endlessly shelled her home grown pecans.

Mayme's chocolate pecan pie was, as we say down South, sinful. She would have a couple of them waiting for my arrival each year. They were truly unique, and each pie was solid and never runny. The pies were sweet, rich—but not overpowering. As if a pie or two during my visit was not enough, she would whip two or three more together to send off with my parents and me as we headed back to Houston.

Most Texans might think that a pie is best served up with ice cream, but in this rare case I must disagree. Her pie was perfect without any additions. But, we did have our share of ice cream. Even going back to the age of four or so, I can remember working hard for my share of Grandma's hand-churned homemade peach ice cream. She never did get an electric ice cream maker; we had to crank the handle. I recall sitting on the maker and struggling to turn the handle with both hands as the bucket seemed to want to walk out from under me. The mixtures of cream, vanilla, and sugar were added to the inner metal container along with plenty of fresh, hand-picked sliced peaches. Once the container was sealed and placed in the wooden bucket, it was surrounded by ice with plenty of rock salt thrown in and then the crank mechanism was attached. Now it all came down to one human power to turn the crank for thirty minutes or so. The final product was a cold fantastic summertime treat that was even better because you had to work for it.

Grandma was pure country with little real sophistication, but a loving heart. When she passed in 1986, my parents and I cleaned out her home and discovered a few of her recipes in one of Dad's old elementary school notebooks. Included in this notebook were even a couple of the home remedies that she had always sworn by. Generally, they involved fat and vinegar. Mayme was a big proponent of the power of vinegar; she even swallowed a spoonful daily. We discovered that she was still making her own lye soap. (No wonder I never could seem to get lathered up.)

It has been many years since I was a youngster hanging out with Grandma. I still think back fondly on those long-ago days when the greatest showing of love was the love poured into the preparation and sharing of meals. When I drive out across Texas, I am often transported back to the days when I was filled with anticipation of arriving in Abilene for Grandma's great cooking.

CHOCOLATE PECAN PIE

(This was in Mayme's notebook, as a magazine-
supplied recipe.)

2 squares unsweetened chocolate
3 tablespoons butter
1 cup light corn syrup
¾ cup sugar
3 eggs, slightly beaten
1 teaspoon vanilla
1 cup coarsely chopped pecans
1 unbaked 9 inch pie shell

Melt chocolate and butter over boiling water. Boil syrup and sugar together 2 minutes. Add chocolate mixture. Pour slowly over eggs, stirring constantly. Add vanilla and nuts. Turn into shell, and bake at 375° for 45 to 50 minutes.

PECAN PIE

(Handwritten and marked "2 delicious.")

¼ cup of butter
1 teaspoon vanilla
½ cup karo syrup

1 cup sugar
¼ teaspoon salt
pecans
3 eggs well beaten

Well, that was it; use some trial and error.

Date Loaf

(Written on a Dixie Pig receipt, as a "Bessie recipe.")

1 cup chopped dates
1 cup chopped nuts
1 teaspoon vanilla
2 cups sugar
¾ cup milk
2 tablespoons butter

Boil milk and sugar to a soft ball, add vanilla and stir until it boils slowly and dates are well mixed. Add nuts and heat until you can pour and roll in a damp cloth. Then place in cool place to harden.

Elmer Kelton

LINZERTORTE*

by Elmer Kelton

First of all, let me say that I am not a cook. I proved that more than fifty years ago during a couple of summers when I was in high school. My father had a ranch leased west of Crane, Texas, and after school was out he sent me there to watch over it while the regular caretaker took the summer off. My three younger brothers would come to help me, one at a time. It was strictly a batching outfit, and I did the cooking.

My brothers could only stay about a week at a time before they starved out. They rotated, under protest, one week with me and two weeks at home to recuperate on Mother's cooking.

The years have not improved my performance in the kitchen. When I boil water, it smells scorched. But my Austrian-born wife Ann is a good cook. The most popular recipe she has is for a type of Austrian cake known as the Linzertorte, named for its city of origin, Linz, where I was stationed a few months in 1946 as a go-fer, a lowly Pfc. She has made a few minor modifications from the original, for instance using pecans rather than almonds or walnuts, because pecans are much more readily available in Texas. We grow our own.

The torte is a little tricky to make, and some people have trouble getting the proper consistency in the dough the first time they try. It must be kneaded, preferably by hand, until it is soft and sticks together well. People are sometimes tempted to add extra flour. That makes the dough too dry. It crumbles and will not stick together.

The cakes keep well if wrapped in airtight foil or plastic, and they also freeze well. Ann usually makes up a large number before

*Deborah Douglas, editor, *Stirring Prose: Cooking with Texas Authors* (College Station: Texas A&M University Press, 1998), 134–135. Used with permission of Texas A&M University Press.

Christmas. Any leftover tortes are put in the freezer, and we have thawed them as late as the following summer with good results.

A word of caution: don't make the slices too large. This is definitely not a low-cal dessert.

LINZERTORTE

2 cups (very fine) ground pecans (or almonds or walnuts)
2 sticks butter
2⅔ cups flour
1⅓ cups sugar
1 whole egg and 2 yolks
1 teaspoon cloves
1 teaspoon cinnamon
2 teaspoons ground lemon peel
1 cup plum jam

Mix in a large bowl.

Cut butter into the flour as for a pie crust, then mix sugar, pecans, spices and lemon peel in with the flour. Make a well in the center, then, add the eggs. Mix thoroughly until it sticks together, then place on a dough board and keep working it until smooth. (The dough will be sticky, but don't add flour.)

Press ⅔ dough into a 9-inch spring-form cake pan (don't grease the pan). Spread 1 cup jam evenly over the top, ½ inch from side of pan.

Roll remaining dough pencil-thick and arrange it around the side of the pan and criss-cross over top of the jam.

For a cake, bake one hour at 350 degrees.

For cookies, press dough into small balls and press center with ⅛ teaspoon to make indentation, put jam inside indentation; bake 15 minutes at 350 degrees.

Wax's Pecan Cake

6 egg whites   1½ t. baking powder
1 box brown sugar   ¼ t. salt
3 c. pecans   1¾ c. flour

Mix sugar & egg white. Add
sifted flour, baking powder, salt.
Add pecans. Bake 1 hr. 275°-
300° in 9×13 pan.

oh yea Darlyn
had a real good Vinegar
Cobbler when I was eating
I was thinking of her, and
I am sending the way I make
them. no 1 — 1½ cups Sugar → Hot
  3 — " " water
  ½ " vinegar
real short pie crust —
mix sugar well in Hot water
then add vinegar, cook in 4 or
over 35 m
well I made a mess but
you can make it out.
you know I love all very
much, will say good night

Love ya

Evelyn —

Handwritten recipe for Vinegar Cobbler

VINEGAR COBBLER

by Darlyn Neubauer

Maggie Free was my grandmother, a descendant of a Cherokee mother and an Irish father. I didn't get to know her, but the family stories tell me she was a very strong-spirited and independent lady. My mother was born on September 13, 1913, and Maggie became a single parent on October 13, 1913, with the death of my grandfather, J. W. (Bill) Lee. Maggie, being in ill health, had been told she needed to go West to a drier climate. A controlling family member wanted her to put the children in a children's home to be better able to take care of herself. She knew she was not going to lose her children, and began to formulate a plan.

With the assistance of one of her brothers, she obtained a covered wagon, a team of horses, and a cow. In or about 1920, she set her sights West with her wagon and team of horses, her children, one pet chicken, and the cow. The children ranged in age from six to fourteen years of age, with my mother being the six-year-old. She often stated that her strongest memory of the trip was of walking barefoot in the wagon tracks all the way to Texas. The next to oldest girl "owned" the pet chicken, which she had to butcher for the families' food on the trip. She could NEVER eat chicken again during her lifetime. The oldest daughter became a caregiver, the second became the protector, and the boy, at age eight, became the hunter, fisherman, and food provider.

Those children grew up telling us these stories. They settled at the edge of Mertzon, Texas, on Spring Creek, where the rails were being laid. Grandmother Maggie pitched a tent for the family, enrolled the children in Mertzon public schools, and earned her income by cooking and feeding the railroad workers during the day, storing water, tea, and lemonade in the shady creek that ran nearby.

My Grandmother Maggie passed away in San Angelo, Texas, in 1928. Even though I didn't know her, the children she raised and the stories I've heard tell me she inherited her spirit and strength from her parents, and she worked herself to death to keep her family together. She was able to save enough money to buy a frame home on the west side of San Angelo, where she "lived until she died."

At the time of her death, the children ranged in age from fourteen to nineteen, and their roles in the family remained similar to the earlier years. The oldest the caregiver and provider, becoming a beautician; the second the protector, watching over the family like a pit bull dog; the boy went to work on the BARS ranch in Barnhart, Texas at fourteen years of age; and my mother (the baby) became a "shampoo girl" to her beautician sister. They lived together, remaining extremely close their entire lives, never living over 100 miles apart in and around San Angelo. As they aged, they split up, following their children, but they always had that family "intuition" about one another. It was not uncommon in our family for the phone to ring day or night with one of the siblings or parents on the other end, having had a dream (or not being able to get us off their minds), calling to make sure everything was alright. Even today, we children rest well, knowing our parents are all together in Heaven and keeping a very watchful eye over each of us.

Following is a copy of the original vinegar cobbler recipe, given to me in a letter from my Aunt Evelyn when I married. She was oldest of Grandmother Maggie's children and passed away in 1986, still residing in the original house that Maggie bought upon her arrival in San Angelo. This recipe was a huge hit in our family, and was a wonderful sweet to many children who didn't have the money for much else. It was always said that it also served as a wonderful Depression recipe when some things were scarce. One of my greatest memories is how much my dad loved this cobbler. I think he would have eaten three of them had they been set in front of him.

She wrote, "Ah yes, Darlyn had a real good vinegar cobbler. When I was eating I was thinking of her, and I am sending the way I make them."

VINEGAR COBBLER

1½ cups sugar
3 cups water Hot
½ cup vinegar
real short pie crust*

Mix sugar well in hot water then add vinegar, cook in oven 35 ms.

"Well I made a mess but you can make it out." You know I love all very much. Will say good night.

Love ya,
Evelyn

*A short crust has a higher ratio of flour to fat than a traditional pie crust so it is lighter and more crumbly, like a shortbread cookie, rather than flaky. You can use either pie crust or puff pastry; both will be delicious, just different from the short crust. Actually, I prefer either of those to short crust, because I find the crumbly nature of it more difficult to eat!

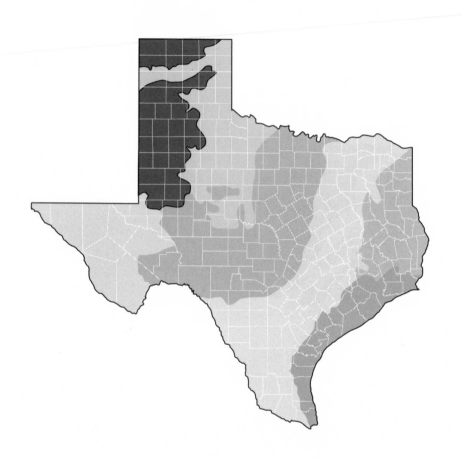

Stories and Recipes from the High Plains*

The High Plains, some 19 million treeless acres, are an extension of the Great Plains to the north. Its level nature and porous soils prevent drainage over wide areas.

The relatively light rainfall flows into the numerous shallow "playa" lakes or sinks into the ground to feed the great underground aquifer that is the source of water for the countless wells that irrigate the surface of the plains. A large part of this area is under irrigated farming, but native grassland remains in about one-half of the High Plains.

Blue grama and buffalograss comprise the principal vegetation on the clay loam "hardland" soils. Important grasses on the sandy loam "sandy land" soils are little bluestem, western wheatgrass, indiangrass, switchgrass, and sand reedygrass. Sand shinnery oak, sand sagebrush, mesquite, and yucca are conspicuous invading brushy plants.

*Stephan L. Hatch, *Texas Almanac, 2014–2015*, Elizabeth Cruce Alvarez, editor (Austin: Texas State Historical Association), 117. Used with permission of Texas State Historical Association.

Sweet Potato Pie

1 C. S. potato

3 whole eggs   1 C sugar
2 tbsp flour   ½ stick butter
dash Nutmeg - Cinnamon - Salt
1 tbsp vanilla
1½ C. scalded S. milk

Beat eggs until light yellow and
add sugar & flour gradually. Scald
milk & add to this mixture slowly,
beating as the milk is added. add
butter & stir until melted. add
spices, salt & vanilla. stir in
mashed potatoes until very smooth
Pour in unbaked pie shell & bake
at 375° for 20 min. Reduce heat to
275° Continue baking to until firm
Serve plain or with whipped cream

Sweet Potato Pie

SWEET POTATO PIE—MINNIE BELLE DAVIS'S RECIPE

by Kenneth W. Davis

❦

Here is a recipe that has been in our family since before I was born. I am eighty-three years old. It was written on tablet paper by my mother. I think it is a memorial reconstruction of my grandmother Laura Jane Perkins' recipe. If so, it came to Texas in the late 1870s or early 1880s.

My grandmother and to a lesser extent my mother were "pinch and dab" cooks who seldom relied on written recipes. I do not remember seeing my grandmother use a written recipe. She had a phenomenal memory, and was justly famed for her cooking skills. She taught my mother and my aunt the basics of good southern cooking.

I do not know when my mother wrote out the version I transcribed below. The use of "stick" with the amount of butter suggests the 1950s, perhaps. This pie was my father's favorite. My mother cooked it often when sweet potatoes were in season.

SWEET POTATO PIE—MINNIE BELLE DAVIS'S RECIPE

1 cup mashed sweet potatoes
2 whole eggs
1 cup sugar
2 tablespoons flour
1 half stick butter
dash nutmeg, cinnamon, salt
1 tablespoon vanilla
1½ cup scalded sweet milk

Beat eggs until light yellow and add sugar and flour gradually. Scald milk and add to this mixture slowly, beating as the milk is added. Add butter and stir until melted.

Add spices, salt, and vanilla. Stir in mashed potatoes until very smooth.

Pour into unbaked pie shell and bake at 375 for 20 minutes. Reduce heat to 275 and continue baking until firm.

Serve plain or with whipped cream.

I have baked this pie, and I added half a cup of finely chopped pecans. Good river bottom Central and East Texas pecans are welcome in many desserts.

"Orange Slices"

4 eggs beaten all together

2 Cups brown Sugar

1/2 teasp soda in 1 tbs water
and mix two cups flour in
the egg mixture

1 teasp Vanilla

1 Cup pecans

1 Cup diced Orange Slices (the
gum drop kind).

Bake in moderate oven
in a large bread pan (Square)
then Cool and Cut in squares
or oblong pieces and roll
in powdered Sugar.

John R. Erickson. Photo by Bill Ellzey.

FROM *THROUGH TIME AND THE VALLEY**

by John R. Erickson

In an isolated piece of the West, the Canadian River stretched before John Erickson and Bill Ellzey as they began a journey through time and what the locals call "the valley." They went on horseback, as they might have traveled it a century before. For 140 miles they followed the course of the river from the Turkey Track Ranch to the redland prairies of the Oasis Ranch, from Adobe Walls and the ghost town of Plemons to the little cowtown of Canadian. They talked, worked, and swapped stories with the people of the valley, piecing together a picture of what life has been like there for a hundred years, including tales of such real-life characters as Kit Carson, Quanah Parker, Billy Dixon, and Ishatai. John's book with Bill's photographs was a result—*Through Time and the Valley*.[1]

In the book, John cooked dinner at the first night's camp on Carson Creek, named after Kit Carson, who in 1864 led a force of soldiers down the Canadian River Valley and was surprised by one of the largest armies of Plains Indians ever assembled. John kindled a fire and put the evening meal on to cook: rice and jerked beef simmered in bouillon broth, fried bacon, raisins, and sassafras tea. "Jerked beef, once a staple in the diet of pioneers, can now be purchased in almost any quick-stop grocery store. I made our jerky from a recipe given to me by my grandmother, the late Mrs. B. B. Curry of Seminole, Texas. One summer evening, as we were sitting on her front porch, she told me about her childhood in the old Quaker community of Estacado in Crosby County, where she often saw strips of beef hanging on lines to dry in the sun."[2] All I put on my jerky was garlic salt and flies, John writes of his recipe.

*John R. Erickson, *Through Time and the Valley* (Denton: University of North Texas Press, 1995). Used with permission of University of North Texas Press.

He added that "the Panhandle climate, especially the last three years, is wonderful if you want the life and juice sucked out of something, so making jerky is easy. Sometimes our faces begin to resemble jerky, not to mention our dispositions. My grandmother not only survived under those conditions, she remained a beautiful woman into her eighties, and used a large quantity of what my mother used to call "coal cream" or "cold cream."[3]

"I encountered sassafras tea in *Tom Sawyer* in the fourth grade. Tom drank it on camping expeditions, so I had to get some. It was not easy to find, because nobody in Perryton had ever heard of it. I think I found some at a pharmaceutical company that advertised in a trapping magazine, *Fur Fish and Game*. I ordered some. It came in a bottle and resembled red sticks of wood. You boiled it in water and added sugar. It wasn't bad and had the taste of root beer. I guess that was my way of tipping my hat to Tom Sawyer, whose fingerprints are all over the Hank the Cowdog books."[4]

Endnotes

1. From the dust jacket, John Erickson, *Through Time and the Valley* (Denton: University of North Texas Press, 1995).
2. John Erickson, *Through Time and the Valley* (Denton: University of North Texas Press, 1995), 20–22.
3. Letter written to Frances B. Vick.
4. Ibid.

Ice water pickles

Six lbs med size cucumbers
each cut in 4 to 8 pieces
according to size of cucumbers
Soak in ice water 3 hrs - drain
pack into sterilized Kerr jars
add 6 pickling onions. 1 piece
Celery. 1 teaspoon mustard seed
to each jar   Solution

        3 qts white vinegar
1 cup salt. 3 cups sugar
bring to boil. pour over
cucumbers and seal jars. Makes 6

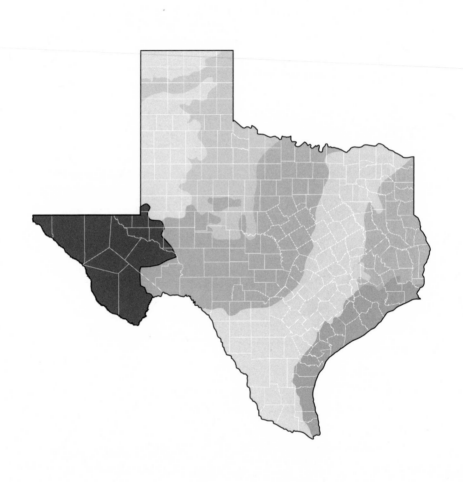

Stories and Recipes from the Trans-Pecos Mountains and Basins*

With as little as eight inches of annual rainfall, long hot summers, and usually cloudless skies to encourage evaporation, this 18-million-acre area produces only drought-resistant vegetation without irrigation. Grass is usually short and sparse.

The principal vegetation consists of lechuguilla, ocotillo, yucca, cenizo, prickly pear, and other arid land plants. In the more arid areas gyp and chino grama, and tobosagrass prevail. There is some mesquite. The vegetation includes creosote-tarbush, desert shrub, grama grassland, yucca and juniper savannahs, pine oak forest, and saline flats.

The mountains are 3,000 to 8,749 feet in elevation and support piñon pine, juniper, and some ponderosa pine and other forest vegetation on a few of the higher slopes. The grass on the higher mountain slopes includes many southwestern and Rocky Mountain

---

*Stephan L. Hatch, *Texas Almanac, 2014–2015*, Elizabeth Cruce Alvarez, editor (Austin: Texas State Historical Association), 117. Used with permission of Texas State Historical Association.

species not present elsewhere in Texas. On the desert flats, black grama, burrograss, and fluffgrass are frequent.

More productive sites have numerous species of grama, muhly, Arizona cottontop, dropseed, and perennial threeawn grasses. At the higher elevations, plains bristlegrass, little bluestem, Texas blue-stem, sideoats grama, chino grama, blue grama, piñon ricegrass, wolftail, and several species of needlegrass are frequent.

The common invaders on all depleted ranges are woody plants, burrograss, fluffgrass, hairy erioneuron, ear muhly, sand muhly, red grama, broom snakeweed, croton, cacti, and several poisonous plants.

Lucy Fischer-West

Meredith Abarca in Lucy West's kitchen with Blue, Lady &
Little Guy

HEALING BY SHARING SCALLOPED POTATOES

by Meredith E. Abarca

My brother Hugo and I are not from Texas, but Texas marked our lives. Just a narrow body of water, the Rio Bravo/Rio Grande, separated our home from Laredo, Texas. Escaping the meager conditions in which she had been raising her children, our mother arrived to Nuevo Laredo, Tamaulipas, just three months short of giving birth to her sixth child, me. In her arms she carried her two year old son, my brother Hugo, who was almost on the brink of death. It was our grandmother's labor as a housekeeper in San Antonio, Texas, that helped our mother rent a one-room apartment in Nuevo Laredo. It was our aunt's marriage to a man born in Laredo that made possible crossing the international border on a regular basis. Hugo's eventual recovery from malnourishment was in part due to our grandmother's financial support and our aunt's legal residence status in Laredo, which facilitated medical treatment for him in the United States. For my part, my aunt and uncle raised me for the first three years of my life. My brother's recovery to health and my steady healthy growth, therefore, took root in Laredo.

Texas also marked my brother's and my destiny by separating our lives forever. Places have the power to define us, and they often do so by calling us back. After twelve years of making a life between the two Laredos, my mother with her seven children immigrated to Menlo Park, California. It only took six years for Laredo, the place that brought my brother back to life, to claim him. The Davis Mountains' winds were the last ones to embrace my brother's body. His longing to return to Laredo proved fatal. Fifteen years after his motorcycle accident, Texas called me back, too. My own life's journey brought me to live in El Paso, only three hours away from the place where my brother took his last breath. Over the years, I've realized that my return to Texas has been to initiate the slow process of grieving—and eventually healing—from the profound pain of losing a loved one.

I love and care for all of my siblings. But Hugo and I had a special bond. Over the years I've wondered why this is so. Was it the proximity of our age? He was only two years older than I. Was it my subconscious way of getting closer to our mother? His critical health issues as a child caused our mother to spend all the time she had taking care of him. I, as a healthy child who actually began walking before Hugo, did not require as much of our mother's attention. Of course, it is now that I'm a woman in her mid-forties that I've come to understand a mother's need to attend a son she feared would die at a young age. Yet, as a child and teenager, all I saw was how close she was to him.

But maybe it was none of these reasons. Could it be because of my love for cooking and his appetite for eating my food—even when at the age of five all I cooked was scramble eggs with hot-dogs? Whatever the reason, the emotional and spiritual closeness to my brother Hugo was such that fifteen years after his death, I still spoke about him and the accident as if it had "just" happened. Meaning, I spoke very little about him and cooked none of the food he loved to eat—especially the dish I would prepare just for him: Scalloped Potatoes.

Less than a year after moving to El Paso, I visited the site of the accident. I went in search of letting go of the pain and in hopes of discovering ways to feel connected to his spirit. I visited the site, for I longed to learn how to share stories and memories about Hugo without shattering my heart into tiny fragments. The next day after the visit to the Davis Mountains, I played one of his favorite albums, "Purple Heart" by Prince. I then walked into the kitchen to make scalloped potatoes. I first turned on the oven at 350 degrees, took some Russet potatoes and an onion from the counter, opened a bottle of Sherry wine, and mixed some sour cream with heavy cream. I placed the black pepper grinder and sea salt next to the stove, and proceeded to take the potatoes in my hands and inhaled their earthiness. I began peeling them in such a methodical way, that now as I'm reliving the memory it feels as if I were in a deep moment of prayer.

By the time I got to peeling and dicing the onion, their sharpness was no match for the tears already cascading down my face. My senses must have taken over to continue cooking, for the tears were such that I literally couldn't see clearly. I took a pot and placed it on the stove, adding both oil and butter. Once hot, the diced onions went in to sauté until they reached a clear, translucent color. At that point, I must have added some fresh black pepper and a generous dash of Sherry wine. I have no recollection at what point I ran the potatoes through the food processor to cut them into thin slices, but I did. After the alcohol had cooked out, the potatoes went into the pot, followed by the cream mixture and salt. All was then placed in a baking dish and cooked in the oven for about an hour. Once the scalloped potatoes were cooked, I sat by myself and ate nothing but my brother's potatoes.

That day marked a new tradition in my life as I began cooking scalloped potatoes once a year to commemorate my brother's birthday. Yet, it was not until El Paso became my home that I began to share them with those who became my new family. However, it was not until October 2012 that for the first time I shared the depth of my brother's and my bond with others. It happened while I was teaching a course at the University of Texas at El Paso on "Food and Memory," in which one of the assignments was to share foods that had a significant memory and story connected to it. Since then, there have been other social occasions where I have cooked and shared my brother's favorite dish.

Each time I share this dish and stories about my brother, I always begin by explaining how scalloped potatoes came to symbolize the kind of love only siblings can feel for one another, and express with actions instead of words. I learned to make scalloped potatoes while working in a French restaurant at the age of sixteen. Since I worked Thursday, Friday and Saturday nights, it was not unusual for me to come home at one o'clock in the morning. It was equally just as common to find no one else at home awake but Hugo waiting for my safe return. Somewhere in the middle of a story I might be telling about him, I always mention that on those occasions I was upset with him and refused to cook scalloped potatoes, he often made his own out of a box mix. The story concludes with how almost twenty years after his accident, while riding on the back of a motorcycle on an open mountain road in Nepal, I reconnected with Hugo's soul. Since I was introduced to Tibetan Buddhism in Texas, and it was a spiritual pilgrimage that took me to Nepal and India, Texas, too, marks a sibling's soulful reconnection.

HUGO'S SCALLOPED POTATOES

Depending on the number of people you will be sharing this dish with, adjust the ingredients accordingly. But if the gathering is between 6–8, these ingredients might suffice.

> 6 to 8 Russet potatoes: peel and cut into thin
>   slices using a food processor
> 1 medium size white onion: peel and dice
> ¼ cup of Sherry wine (creamy)
> ½ cup of sour cream and ½ cup of heavy
>   cream: mix together
> 2 tablespoons of unsalted butter
> 1 tablespoon of olive oil
> fresh ground black pepper (to taste)
> sea salt (to taste)

> Turn oven to 350 degrees. In a heavy pot, combine butter and oil; once butter has melted, add diced onions and sauté until they are translucent. At this point add ground black pepper and Sherry wine. Once alcohol has cooked out, add potatoes and heavy cream as well as sea salt. Mix all. Transfer potato mixture into a baking dish. Bake potatoes for about an hour. Once the top is golden brown and the potatoes are cooked, remove from the oven. Let them cool a bit before serving.

Remember to always tell stories of those you love when sharing my brother's Scalloped Potatoes—they will taste better that way.

Hugo Abarca

Lentils

Lucy's Two Sisters Calabacitas

Finished zucchini dish

COMIDA RICA DE POBRES: TASTY POOR FOLK'S FOOD

by Lucy Fischer-West

My mother had a knack for making a very limited budget go far; we were as poor as the rest of our neighbors in the *barrio* where I grew up, but I was blessed with parents who loved and nurtured me in countless ways. In my early childhood, my father did construction work two or three days a week, and later had a machinist job at Falstaff Brewery, but he always found time to read to me and fill my head with dreams. My mother was very much a traditional homemaker of the era, cooking three meals a day for my father and me, having lunch on the table when I walked home from school at noontime, and feeding my father according to whatever schedule his jobs permitted. Our trips across the border to the markets in Juárez enabled her to cook delicious meals on a meager allowance.

Perhaps because of my fond recollection of all those trips coming back from Juárez loaded down with fresh produce wrapped in newspaper carried in colorful woven hemp grocery bags, there are foods that I have to stock on a regular basis. If I don't have tomatoes, onions, garlic, squash, and *cilantro,* plus corn tortillas and *azadero* cheese in the house, I feel poor, disorganized, out of sorts. Even if what I'm about to cook includes none of the above ingredients, there is something about their presence that is comforting.

Although we were not Roman Catholic, the foods my mother cooked during Lent were definitely grounded in that cultural tradition. At every Mexican market, as the season nears, there are neatly arranged displays of dried shrimp for tomato-sauced patties, *chacales* (a cracked corn which I was none too fond of), peanuts, dried coconut, brown sugar cones, and *colaciones,* (sugar sprinkles for the top of Mexican bread pudding called *capirotada*), and *lentejas*—lentils. While I developed a palate for most of the above, I have to admit that, of all the dishes I associate with Lent, the only one I crave, and cook year-round, are my mother's lentils. I realize that there are multiple varieties of them—red, brown, yellow, tiny, middle-sized, and large—but the lentils common to the markets that we frequented are flat and greenish-brown. Faithful to my mother's way of cooking, I use only that variety for the following dish:

Lentejas de Cuaresma: Mamacita's Lenten Lentils

1 lb. of plain, ordinary lentils
6–8 nice tomatoes, or however many fit into
    your blender
1 head of garlic, peeled and diced (you can use
    a mini-food processor)
a few dried bay leaves
salt and freshly ground pepper to taste
6–8 cups of water, according to how soupy
    you want them to turn out

Clean the lentils to get rid of the clumps of dirt and occasional rocks that come in the package. Wash them thoroughly—at least three times. (Somewhere, I read that there is a folk tradition that goes with this practice of three, but at the moment, the specifics escape me.) The water should be almost clear when you are done.

Drain them and put them in a stockpot with enough water to cover.

Put the tomatoes in the blender, puree them, and add them to the lentils. Sometimes, if the tomatoes are out of season, or if the lentils do not have to be strictly vegetarian, I add a couple of tablespoons of Knorr Tomato Bouillon with Chicken Flavor. That blended mixture should give you about 6 cups of water, but mind you, I long ago stopped measuring, so you'll have to eyeball it and see if the amount of liquid suits you.

Bring them to a boil, add the diced garlic and bay leaves, then turn down the flame, put a lid on the pot and simmer for 2 to 3 hours. Add salt and pepper about half way through the simmering. Taste them to make sure they are the doneness you like; I happen to like them thoroughly cooked.

Place dishes of finely diced raw onion, *cilantro*, chopped hard-boiled eggs, and lime quarters to squeeze—plus your favorite *salsa*—on the table and let people customize their soup bowls as they wish. This recipe should feed 4 people, unless they want seconds, which frequently happens at my house.

My mother used Mexican squash mostly in *Caldo de Res* and *Caldo de Pollo*, beef or chicken soup, along with cabbage, potatoes, carrots and celery to make the soup go a long way. I have to admit that I worked around the mushy slices in the soup and went for the potatoes and carrots and whatever meat was in it instead. I don't remember the taste of my mother's *calabacitas*, even though I know she cooked them. Maybe I scooted them around on the plate hoping she wouldn't notice that I wasn't eating them. It took me a long time to like Mexican squash—that pale version of Italian zucchini, but once I decided that I wouldn't be much of a Mexican if I didn't learn to cook it, over time I have developed a recipe I'm happy with. You'll need to bear with me on the measurements, because I have cooked this dish for as many as sixty people. I'd recommend starting with one medium-sized *calabacita* per person, or two if you want to have leftovers, which, by the way, reheat well in the microwave.

LUCY'S TWO SISTERS *CALABACITAS*

8 firm Mexican squash (or zucchini), sliced to a thickness of ⅜ to ½ inch and then quartered

2 big white onions, diced according to your sense of aesthetics

1 head of garlic, peeled and diced (you can use a mini-food processor)

> peanut oil or olive oil or sesame oil to sauté
>   the above
> 1–2 cans of Hunt's Petite Diced Tomatoes
> 1–2 cans of Yellow Niblet Corn
> a few dried Bay Leaves
> salt and pepper to taste
> *cilantro* if you want my Mexican version, or
>   tarragon if you want it to taste like I've
>   been making it lately
> *azadero* cheese, grated, or crumbled Feta cheese

Put a few tablespoons of your oil of choice in the bottom of a wide skillet and sauté the onions until nearly clear; when they are about done, make a space in the middle, sauté the diced garlic, and mix the two together.

The following step depends on the size of your skillet (the wider and flatter, the better): Move the onions and garlic around to the edges, add a bit of oil in the center if needed, then add as much of the sliced squash as will fit in one layer, let it cook some, then move it to the edges; keep adding until they are all coated with a little oil, start to brown, and you have mixed in the onions and garlic.

Add the cans of tomatoes, drained corn, bay leaves, chopped *cilantro* to taste (maybe one bunch)—or about a tablespoon of dried tarragon—and bring to a simmer.

Cover and cook for 10–15 minutes depending on the desired doneness.

Transfer the squash mixture to an ovenproof casserole, sprinkle it with however much of the cheese you like, and pop it into a 350 degree oven until the cheese is melted and it looks bubbly and delicious.

These are dishes that I fix on a regular basis, one by my mother's recipe, the other with my own twist on a traditional Mexican dish, using two out of the "three sisters" so named by the Iroquois who lived in New York State where I was born. My mother's recipe for beans out of the pot takes one sentence: "Clean and wash pinto beans, cook them until tender with lots of fresh garlic and salt to taste in a 45-year-old clay pot bought at the Juárez market." In my El Paso kitchen, I am constantly reminded that those "three sisters"—corn, beans, and squash—have fed us for so long, wherever in the Americas we happen to live.

Meredith E. Abarca is an Associate Professor in the Department of English at the University of Texas at El Paso. At the undergraduate level she teaches courses in Chicana/o Literature, Mexican-American Folklore, and Women in Literature. She also teaches graduate courses that examine the intersection of literature and globalism, cosmopolitanism, and food as cultural and theoretical discourses. She is the author of *Voices in the Kitchen* (Texas A&M University Press, 2006), and co-editor of *Rethinking Chicana/o Literature through Food* (Palgrave, 2013). Her work has appeared in *Food & Foodways*, *Food, Culture & Society*, and, in edited collections such as *Taking Food Public: Redefining Foodways in the Changing World* (Routledge, 2011) and *The Routledge Companion to U.S. Latino Studies* (2012). She has lectured at community and academic settings, such as the Southern Foodways Alliance Symposium in Oxford, Mississippi, and the University of Gastronomical Sciences in (Colormo) Parma, Italy.

Jean Andrews is the best-selling Texas author of books on sea shells, bluebonnets, and hot peppers. A fifth-generation Texan, Andrews was born in Kingsville in 1923, graduated from boarding school in 1940, attended Texas A&I University in her hometown, majoring in Home Economics, and later transferred to the University of Texas. She obtained her Master of Science degree in education at Texas A&I University. In 1976, she received her Ph.D. in art from the University of North Texas. She also produced the art for her books. She received the Distinguished Alumna award from both the University of Texas and the University of North Texas. Andrews began collecting sea shells in 1959, and her field guides on the shells of the Texas and Florida coasts became instant classics. Andrews taught herself botany and cultivated varieties of *chiles*. Her publications include: *Sea Shells of the Texas Coast* (1971), *Shells and Shores of Texas* (1977), *Texas Shells: A Field Guide* (1981),

Peppers: the Domesticated Capsicums (1984, revised in 1995), *The Texas Bluebonnet* (1986, revised in 1993), *An American Wildflower Florilegium* (1992), *A Field Guide to Shells of the Texas Coast* (1992), *Red Hot Peppers: A Cookbook for the Not-So-Faint of Heart* (1993), *Field Guide to the Shells of the Florida Coast* (1994), *The Pepper Lady's Pocket Pepper Primer* (1998), and *The Pepper Trail: History & Recipes From Around the World* (1999).

Phyllis Bridges is Cornaro Professor of English at Texas Woman's University. She is a past-President of the Texas Folklore Society and a former Board member of the Society. She chairs the Folklore Section of the Southwest American Culture Association. She is a native Texan and a graduate of West Texas State University and Texas Tech University. Her publications include the new publication *Marking New Trails: An Informal History of the Texas Woman's University.* Friends and former students have established a scholarship in honor of the longtime TWU educator.

Scott Hill Bumgardner is a retired Houston cop, real estate investor, rancher, grandpa, and professional storyteller. He has been spinning yarns for ages. His imagination and speaking abilities have helped him become Louisiana's Champion Liar—in 2005 and 2012. But this proclamation must be tempered, as everyone knows that Texans can really stretch the truth, and it must be admitted that politicians were not at the competitions. Scott is a three-time past-President of the Houston Storytellers Guild and currently serves as the 2014–2015 President of the Texas Folklore Society. He is an active Lifetime Committeeman serving on the Speakers and Magazine Committees of the Houston Livestock Show and Rodeo.

Mary Margaret Dougherty Campbell holds a B.A. and an M.A. in English from Texas Tech University and an M.S. in Educational Administration from Texas A&M University, Corpus Christi. She has presented several papers at annual TFS meetings and has essays in four prior TFS Publications: *The Family Saga*; *Folklore: In All of Us, In All We Do*; *Death Lore: Texas Rituals, Superstitions, and Legends of the Hereafter*; *Celebrating 100 Years of the Texas Folklore Society, 1909-2009*; and, *Hide, Horn, Fish, and Fowl: Texas Hunting and Fishing Lore*. She is a Petroleum Landman and the Executive Director of George West Storyfest. She has served TFS as Local Arrangements Chairman, Councilor, Director, Vice-President/ Program Chair, and President.

Sam Cavazos grew up in the Rio Grande Valley as a migrant worker and later moved to the Dallas area, starting work at the World Trade Center, which led to him meeting Karen, his wife. That, in turn, led to working at Ross Vick & Associates, where he became a sales rep. Karen has two daughters, Courtney and Kathy; Courtney has three children, Ashleigh and twin boys Nathan and Seth, and Kathy has two children, Emily and Chris. They all call him Grandpa, which Sam says is a great blessing. He says that he can say with all honesty that being a Grandpa is the greatest job in the world. They spend a lot of time together in the kitchen when they visit. His mom's side of the family were great cooks, and he learned to cook at a very early age. He has the Mexican influence from his dad's side, and the Midwest influence from his mom's side. Put the two together, and you get some darn good food.

Janell Croley Chesnut studied music and art education at University of North Texas. She received an award from The Texas Commission of Fine Arts in 1966–67 for distinguished service. A long-time member of the Texas Folklore Society, Janell is a native of East Texas, moving to Austin from Longview in 1991. Her family are pioneer residents of Gilmer and other East Texas towns. She has collected recipes from East Texas and around the world. When traveling, she keeps a journal of notes and sketches of places visited. She has two sons, Jim Hogg and Dr. John Hogg, and three granddaughters.

Robert Compton, better known as "Bob," grew up well-fed in Freestone County, Texas, where his great-grandfather and a brave group of Alabama families migrated in 1850, seeking their fortunes. Like Coronado, they discovered no gold, but stayed anyway and found peace and comfort in farming. Robert grew up to become a journalist, eventually at *The Dallas Morning News*, where he spent more than forty years, the last fifteen as the newspaper's fourth book editor, following such distinguished leaders as John McGinnis, Lon Tinkle, and Allen Maxwell. He retired in 1998 to cook for himself.

Margaret Anna Cox of Austin grew up in Eden, Texas, fourth generation of 1886 Concho County pioneers. She maintained close ties to Eden while working thirty-five years for the University of Texas Library. She presented papers at three TFS meetings, and has had stories in *The Family Saga* and *Death Lore* books. In addition, fourteen of her "memory" tales of growing up in the '40s and '50s were published in the weekly, *Eden Echo*. She has enjoyed assisting in the development of the Don Freeman Memorial Museum of Concho County, and the Eden Public Library. At the Library, Margaret's gift of her large Roadrunner collection is on permanent display, along with books by J. Frank Dobie and connections to Texas folklore.

Kenneth W. Davis is a past-President and a Fellow of the Texas Folklore Society. He is also Emeritus Professor of English at Texas Tech University. He is also a past-president of the American Studies Association of Texas, the Texas and Southwestern Popular Culture Association, and the West Texas Historical Association. He is an honorary member of the West Texas Historical Association and was a founding member of the National Cowboy Symposium and Celebration, an organization now in its 27th year. He co-edited *Black Cats, Hoot Owls and Water Witches* (Denton: University of North Texas Press, 1991) with Everett A. Glllis; *The Catch Pen* (National Cowboy Symposium), with Len Ainsworth; and, *Horsing Around: Contemporary Cowboy Humor* (Wayne State University, 1992) with Lawrence Clayton (republished by Texas Tech University Press, 1998, with Lawrence Clayton and Mary Evelyn Collins). He is also the author of more than one hundred essays and reviews.

Robert Gross Dean was born on September 3, 1932, in the Goodwin Community in San Augustine County, Texas. He attended public schools in San Augustine and colleges at Kilgore College, Stephen F. Austin State College (B.S. Degree), Oklahoma State University (Master of Natural Science Degree), and Texas Christian University (Ph.D. Degree in Mathematics). He taught mathematics at Texas City High School for two years, at the University of Texas at Arlington for two years, and at Stephen F. Austin State University for thirty-seven years. He has been active in numerous organizations, including the Texas Section of the Mathematical Association of America and the MAA, the East Texas Council of Teachers of Mathematics and the NCTM, the Nacogdoches Genealogical Society, the East Texas Historical Association, the Nacogdoches Photographic Association, and the Texas Folklore Society (since 1970), and he has served as a president of TSMAA, ETCTM, NGS, ETHA, and NPA. In 1980, he was a co-recipient of the Mathematical Association of America's *Polya Award for Expository Writing*; in 1995, he published *A Seventy-Five Year History of the Texas Section of the Mathematical Association of America 1920–1995*; and, in 1996, he and Ouida Dean selected the images for two pictorial history books, *Nacogdoches, Texas, A Pictorial History* and *Historic Texas, An Illustrated Chronicle of Texas' Past*. He is a member of the Missions Committee at the First United Methodist Church in Nacogdoches, and he enjoys reading, writing, helping people, and building things.

Carolyn B. Edwards has spent the last twenty-five years in the small town weekly newspaper business. She has worked in ad sales and production, and as a proofreader, photographer, columnist, staff writer, and editor. She fell in love with local history when she moved to Bandera County, the home of the Frontier Times Museum, that eclectic collection of memorabilia begun by pioneer newspaperman, book and magazine publisher, J. Marvin Hunter. Whatever her position in the newspaper office, she aimed to continue Hunter's habit of preserving history through the written word. She served a term as President of the Bandera County Historical Commission, during which time she wrote and published the commission's quarterly newsletter, "The Bandera County His-torian." Edwards grew up on a small farm in South Texas with seven brothers and sisters. The family rarely had spending money, but always ate well. She has compiled an extensive collection of family stories to pass on to her children. Edwards currently lives in Bandera with her daughter and grandson, and is planning to install a rainwater catchment system in her back yard.

John Erickson was born in Midland, Texas, to Joseph W. Erickson and Anna Beth Curry Erickson. The Curry side of the family had deep roots in Texas history. A great-great-grandmother, Martha Sherman, was murdered in 1860 by a band of Comanche Indians led by Chief Peta Nocona. To avenge the death of Mrs. Sherman, Governor Sam Houston dispatched Captain Sul Ross and his Texas Rangers to pursue the Comanches. The Rangers captured Cynthia Ann Parker, the mother of Quanah Parker. The scout for the mission was young Charles Goodnight. Another set of Erickson's great-great-grandparents were among a colony of Quakers who established the town of Estacado in 1879, the first Anglo settlement on the Staked Plains near present-day Lubbock. Anna Beth Curry's grandparents began ranching in Crosby and Lubbock Counties in the mid-1880s, and later, her father, Buck Curry, operated a ranch near Seminole in Gaines County.

Erickson finished his B.A. degree at the University of Texas in Austin and studied theology at Harvard Divinity School. At UT, he met his future wife, Kristine Dykema. After college, John worked as a ranch cowboy in Oklahoma and Texas. There, he found a balance between hard physical work and the intense, concentrated effort of writing four hours every day. In 1982, he and Kris started their own publishing company, Maverick Books, and brought out the first Hank the Cowdog book in 1983. To date, the Hank the Cowdog series has sold over 8 million copies.

Robert Flynn, born 12 April 1932 in Chillicothe, Texas, is an author and Professor Emeritus at Trinity University. Flynn's early fame came with the novel *North to Yesterday*, which was a national bestseller. His other publications include *In the House of the Lord; The Sounds of Rescue, The Signs of Hope; Wanderer Springs; The Last Klick; The Devil's Tiger* (with Dan Klepper); *Tie-Fast Country;* and, *Jade: The Outlaw.* Short Story Collections include *Living with the Hyenas; Seasonal Rain;* and, *Slouching toward Zion.* He also published *When I was Just Your Age* (oral histories edited with Susan Russell) and essays in *Growing Up a Sullen Baptist.* He is a former President of the Texas Institute of Letters, and winner of the Lon Tinkle Award for a lifetime achievement in letters.

Jean Flynn was a San Antonio teacher, school librarian and writer who began writing because she couldn't find many books that were inspirational for young people. Her books include *Jim Bowie: A Texas Legend* (1980); *Stephen F. Austin, The Father of Texas* (1981); *William Barret Travis* (1982); *Lady: The Story of Claudia Alta* (1991); *James Butler Bonham: The Rebel Hero* (1984); *Anson Jones: The Last President of the Republic of Texas* (1997); *Annie Oakley: Legendary Sharpshooter* (1998); *Texas Women Who Dared to Be First* (1999); and, *Henry B. Gonzalez: Rebel with a Cause* (2004).

Riley Froh was born in Luling, Texas, and spent his early years there enjoying the 1950s. He is descended from original settlers of the town. His great-grandfather drove cattle up the Chisholm Trail, and his great-great-grandfather was a noted Texas Ranger. He holds bachelor's and master's degrees from Southwest Texas State College (now Texas State University), and a Ph.D. in history from Texas A&M University. He is presently back in Luling after teaching Texas history, U.S. history, and British Literature for forty years at San Jacinto College. He is the author of *Wildcatter Extraordinary, Edgar B. Davis* and *Sequences in Business Capitalism,* as well as several articles on Texas history and folklore. His numerous short stories have appeared in *Louis Lamour Western Magazine,* various WWA anthologies, and other literary journals. Currently, he is writing the popular column "To and Froh" for the *Luling Newsboy.* He is married to Mary Binz of San Antonio, Texas, whose father was well known in the Alamo City as a horse trainer and trick rider.

Mary is also retired from San Jacinto College. Their son Noble King Froh continues the cowboy tradition of both families.

Nina Lou Vansickle Marshall Garrett was born in 1926 in Pushmataha County, Oklahoma. In 1944, she graduated from the Boswell High School in Choctaw County, Oklahoma, as the class Salutatorian. During 1945, she worked at the Douglas Aircraft Plant near Oklahoma City, building airplanes. In December of that year she married William Marshall, a high school classmate, after he returned from military service in Europe. They settled in Bonham, Texas, and raised four daughters—Linda, Joy, Mary Ann, and Billie Gail. Nina worked in a doctor's office for twenty-six years before they retired in 1988. After the death of Mr. Marshall, Nina married Theo Garrett, a long-time friend. Always an avid reader, Nina loves to study genealogy and write family stories. As a member of "Telling Our Stories," at Austin College in Sherman, Texas, she has attained several awards. She entered a contest of "Telling Our Stories" with her first published story about her family traveling to Arizona and California in 1934. She was awarded $100 for her entry.

Leon Hale is a Houston newspaperman and novelist, the author of eleven books. He retired in 2014 after a sixty-four-year career as a columnist with *The Houston Post*, and since 1985, the *Houston Chronicle*, for whom he continues to blog. He has received the Lon Tinkle Award from the Texas Institute of Letters as well as awards for fiction and non-fiction from that organization, the Headliners Foundation, United Press International, the Associated Press and others. A graduate of Texas Tech, Hale fought in World War II as an aerial gunner on fifty combat missions. He is married and has two children, one stepson and three grandchildren. He divides his time between Houston and Washington County, Texas. Most of his books are available from the Texas Book Consortium http://www.tamupress.com/Catalog/ProductSearch.aspx?search=Leon+Hale.

Carol Hanson was born and raised in Dallas, Texas—a child of August and Mary Helen Stanglin. She has four brothers and one sister; two of her brothers, Phil and David, accompanied her on the Sesquicentennial Wagon Train in 1986. Carol received her Masters of Library & Information Sciences from North Texas State University (now University of North Texas) in Denton in 1979. She has been a librarian at Dallas Public Library, Zula B. Wylie Library in Cedar Hill, and a branch library in Grand Prairie. On June 17, 1989, she married Pete Hanson in Cedar Hill, Texas, where they still live, and they have a son, Erik. Carol joined the Texas Folklore Society in 1985, after being a member of the Dallas corral of the Westerners' organization and being encouraged to attend a TFS meeting. Carol attended in 1985 with Ruth Lambert, and has been hooked ever since. Almost anything concerned with history interests her, which explains her long-time dabbling with her family's genealogy and being considered the family historian.

Kay Bailey Hutchison is a former U.S. Senator, and was elected to Senate leadership, becoming the fourth-highest ranking Republican Senator. She also served as Texas State Treasurer and as a Member of the Texas House of Representatives. Senator Hutchison has written three acclaimed history books: *American Heroines, Leading Ladies,* and *Unflinching Courage.* She currently serves as a senior counsel at Bracewell & Giuliani. The Dallas City Council named the Dallas Convention Center for her in 2013. She grew up in La Marque, Texas, and graduated from the University of Texas and the University of Texas School of Law.

Elmer Kelton was a native of Crane, Texas. He grew up on the McElroy Ranch, and later attended the University of Texas at Austin, where he eventually became a Distinguished Alumni, the highest award given by the Texas Exes. He was farm and ranch writer-editor for the *San Angelo Standard-Times* and later editor of *Sheep and Goat Raiser Magazine,* and associate editor of *Livestock Weekly.* He served two years in the U.S. Army, including combat infantry service in Europe. He met his wife Ann, a native of Austria, while serving there. Author of over forty novels, he won the Western Heritage Award from the National Cowboy Hall of Fame, several

Spur awards from Western Writers of America, the Lon Tinkle Award from the Texas Institute of Letters, the Lone Star Award for lifetime achievement from the Larry McMurtry Center for Art and Humanities at Midwestern State University, and honorary doctorates from Hardin-Simmons University and Texas Tech University.

Mary Koock was for many years the proprietor of a restaurant and catering service at her home, "Green Pastures," in Austin. She traveled throughout Texas gathering recipes ranging from down-home cooking to high-class affairs, and from regional favorites to ethnic specialties. Scattered among these are the author's anecdotes from her vast and varied encounters with the famous and influential. Her *The Texas Cookbook* is a portrait of good food and good company. It goes beyond wonderful recipes and invites us to share the hospitality of leading Texans of the 1960s. It is a Texas we'll never know again, peopled by larger-than-life personalities and embellished with a lifestyle of grace and fun.

Wanda Landrey, a descendant of one of the pioneering boarding house families, searched the Big Thicket to find survivors of the boarding house era and to collect their stories and recipes. Leon Hale noted, "Wanda Landrey causes me to remember a special day, long ago, when I ate sweet potato pie at the Bragg Hotel in the Big Thicket. This book makes me hungry, not just for the boarding house dishes Wanda describes, but also for a time in Texas culture that is gone forever." Landrey is an historian, writer, and researcher who lectures on the culture of the Big Thicket region of Texas, and holds B.A. and M.A. degrees in history from Lamar University. She lives in Beaumont, Texas. Her previous publications include *Outlaws in the Big Thicket*.

Gary and Laura Lavergne met in the halls of Church Point High School in the heart of Cajun Country, Louisiana. Today they live in Cedar Park, Texas, and both work in the Office of Admissions at the University of Texas. Education and writing have always been a large part of their lives, including the publication of four university press books written by Gary and edited by Laura: *A Sniper in the Tower: The*

Charles Whitman Murders, Bad Boy from Rosebud: The Murderous Life of Kenneth Allen McDuff; Worse Than Death: The Dallas Nightclub Murders and the Texas Multiple Murder Law; and, *Heman Marion Sweatt, Thurgood Marshall, and the Long Road To Justice,* which won the Writers League of Texas Award for non-fiction, the Coral Horton Tullis Award from Texas State Historical Association, and the Carr P. Collins Award from the Texas Institute of Letters. They are the parents of three Longhorns and one Aggie. They have one granddaughter. Every Sunday they all eat Cajun food—because it's good.

James Ward Lee has been a member of the Texas Folklore Society since 1958. He served as President in 1967–68 and was named a Fellow of the Society in 2006. He is a member of the Texas Institute of Letters and the Texas Literary Hall of Fame. An Emeritus Professor of English at the University of North Texas, Lee is author of many articles and several books, the most recent being a collection of essays, *Adventures with a Texas Humanist,* in 2006, and *A Texas Jubilee: Thirteen Stories from the Lone Star State* in 2013. He lives in Fort Worth.

Marilyn Colegrove Manning was raised in Texas by Yankee parents, and she says there were always little differences between her and her peers. Still that's what makes for interesting conversations. She says they all grew up in a brand new town, Lake Jackson, where crime was unheard of and their policeman rode a horse. Graduating from Brazosport High School and then Southwestern University, her path went from teaching in the public schools to getting a Masters in Counseling at the University of Houston. Then their family, consisting of her, Vic Manning, and their two sons Allen and Victor, took off for London for almost three years where they all learned how to be British for a while. They did a stint in Cleveland, Ohio, and then went back to Houston, where she decided that private practice in psychotherapy was for her. And she's still at it!

Archie McDonald was a "teacher, author, lecturer, and Nacogdoches' own personal historian." He received his B.S. from Lamar

University, an M.A. from Rice University, and a Ph.D. from Louisiana State University. His wife, Judy, was Nacogdoches' mayor. He was a professor at Stephen F. Austin State University for forty-eight years, where he was a Regents' Professor and Distinguished Alumni Professor. He published articles and books regularly; served as President of Texas State Historical Association and Chairman of the Texas Committee of Humanities; was Executive Officer of the Texas State Library and served on the Texas Historical Commission; and, received the J.P. Bryan Leadership in Education Award, among others. He was Executive Director of the East Texas Historical Association and editor of the journal from 1971 to 2008. He was also an editor of the *New Handbook of Texas* and *The Journal of Confederate History*. Ab Abernethy writes: "proud to say, Archie . . . looked and dressed better than anybody else on campus. He was immaculate from sole to crown and wore his hats as if they were specially made for him."

Jane Clements Monday holds a B.S. degree in education with concentration in history and government from the University of Texas at Austin. Her publications are *From Slave to Statesman, the Legacy of Joshua Houston* (with Patricia Smith Prather), winner of the Austin Writers League's Violet Crown Award, the San Antonio Preservation Award, and the Ottis Lock Award for Best Book by the East Texas Historical Association; *Voices from the Wild Horse Desert* (with Betty Bailey Colley), winner of the San Antonio Preservation Award; *Tales of the Wild Horse Desert* (with Betty Colley); *Petra's Legacy* (with Frances B. Vick), winner of the TSHA Coral B. Tullis Award for the Best Book on Texas History, and the San Antonio Preservation Award; *The Master Showmen of King Ranch* (with Betty Colley), winner of the San Antonio Preservation Award; and, *Letters to Alice* (with Frances B. Vick). She has been mayor of Huntsville, Texas; Texas State University System Boards of Regents; The University of Texas Exes President; Texas' Public Commissioner, Southern Association of College and Schools; Distinguished Alumnus, University of Texas at Austin; Member of the Texas Philosophical Society and the Texas Institute of Letters. She lives with her husband, Charles W. Monday, M.D., in Huntsville, Texas.

Darlyn Alford Neubauer is the first-born daughter of Dovie Labraces Lee and Quebe Alford, and niece of Evelyn Lee Haynie, all from the San Angelo area. Her mother and father married in San Angelo on July 4th, 1935. Her father became a Conoco employee, where he remained for forty-seven years, and thus she became an "Oilfield Child." They lived in Iraan, Texas, at her birth, moving to McCamey in 1944 where she started school, Santa Rita in 1947, and Todd Field in 1952; she graduated from Ozona High in 1956. North Texas State was her choice of college from 1956 to 1960, where she obtained her "Mrs." degree in December 1950, marrying Robert E. Neubauer and received her B.S. in Education in January 1960. They ventured to Miami, Florida, for a few years as teachers, eventually ending up in Dallas, Texas. She retired in 2004 and remained in the Dallas area, where she stays active with substitute teaching, friendships and hobbies. She is an avid Red Hat Lady, with the royal title of Queen Road Runner. She enjoys almost any sport (especially hockey), loves to travel anywhere at any time, and loves her family and friends. She is very honored as well as thrilled to have her aunt's recipe in the folklore cookbook, and she is sure her aunt will be as soon as the news reaches Heaven. Her aunt was a very interesting character—an active strong Republican who built her own ranch house in the Oklahoma Hills, and loved Minnie Pearl as well as any other music; she had several restaurants in San Angelo through the times that Ernest Tubb drove a beer truck in the 1930s to support himself. Ernest would make her restaurant his last stop, pull out his guitar, and a "jam session" and dinners would continue late into the evenings.

The Norse Smørgasbord has been held each fall since 1949 at Our Savior's Lutheran Church in the Norse Historic District. Since the community was predominately Norwegian, the most colorful of Norwegian peasant costumes, the Hardanger, was chosen as the official dress for workers at the feast. The Smørgasbord has become an annual tradition that has been widely recognized both near and far. Proceeds benefit a variety of worthy causes. The Smørgasbord is mainly advertised by word of mouth and it is sold out every year. The food is prepared by recipes passed down from generation to generation, and each new generation learns the details. The Smør-gasbord spans two nights, with two serving hours each night, at 6:30 and 7:30 p.m. Seating is limited to 120 persons each serving hour. You can read about the Norse Smørgasbord at http://oursaviorsnorse .org/smorgasbord.html

George Owens is a clinical systems analyst for Trinity Mother Fran-ces Healthcare System in Tyler. He divides his off-time between duties with the Texas State Guard Medical Brigade, cooking, writ-ing, drawing, and dreaming of retirement with his wife Carol. A life-long interest in the history of Texas, particularly the latter half of the nineteenth century, has provided material for a number of stories stemming mainly from the experiences of Robert Wilson Booth, who came to Texas after the Civil War and witnessed the final advance of civilization through the Southwest.

Barbara Davis Pybas lives on a ranch in Cooke County bordering the Red River where she has been for the last sixty-five years. She was romanced into coming to Texas by a handsome ex-Marine she met at Oklahoma A&M College in 1947. Real pioneers, they moved to Warrens Bend bottom on Red River, the site of the U.S. Army training base, Camp Howze, from 1942 to 1946. All improvements had been removed. There was not a house, a barn, fence, or well left. The former owners were allowed to buy it back from the Govern-ment. Jordan Ed and Barbara Davis Pybas established their home in a jungle in a tent. Ultimately, they expanded to 2000 acres and a 400-head cow herd. She has six professional children (not ranchers), eleven exceptional grandchildren and six great-grands who consider the working ranch a Bed and Breakfast. Barbara is a member of the Cooke County Historical Commission, the Texas Folklore Society, and Texas State Historical Association. She has been a presenter at annual TFS meetings with articles included in their publications. She has served on the board of the Cooke County Morton Museum and the Sivells Bend United Methodist Church; she is also a former board member of the Sivells Bend ISD P-K through 8 grades, a country school located twenty-five miles from Gainesville. She grew up in southwest Oklahoma, the short grass country. Some of her published books are *Cooperton Valley to Cooke County, High Flying Times,* and, *How it Was, Stories by J. E. Pybas.*

Peggy A. Redshaw, a native of central Illinois, is a Professor of Biology at Austin College. She holds the B.S. in Biology from Quincy University and a Ph.D. from Illinois State University. Since 1990, she and Dr. Jerry Lincecum have directed "Telling Our Stories," a humanities project at Austin College that aids older adults in writing their autobiographies and family stories. Peggy is a long-time member of the Texas Folklore Society, has given many presentations at their annual meetings, and has published several papers in the Society's annual publications.

Joyce Gibson Roach is an author, historian, folklorist, rancher, and naturalist. She is a Fellow of Texas State Historical Association, past-President and Fellow of the Texas Folklore Society, an elected member of the Texas Institute of Letters and the Philosophical Society of Texas, past-President of the National Horned Lizard Conservation Society, an Honoree in the National Cowgirl Hall of Fame, a founder of the Center for Western Cross Timbers Studies (which is dedicated to documenting, recording, educating, and informing about the Western Cross Timbers and the Southern Plains through a website and small workshops at Crosswinds, the family ranch), and Executive Director of Old Town Keller Foundation. Most notably, she is from Jack County and has never gotten over it, nor is she trying.

Erin Marissa Russell, a new member of the Texas Folklore Society, is a senior English major at Texas Woman's University. She works at the TWU Write Site and serves as editor-in-chief of the campus literary and arts journal, *The Daedalian,* as well as works with Brookhaven College's student newspaper, *The Courier.* She was a student of Dr. Phyllis Bridges in her Shakespeare class, then had the pleasure of taking her Folklore class. Erin also helped with design for *Marking New Trails: An Informal History of the Texas Woman's*

University, which Dr. Bridges authored. Upon graduation, Erin will continue research for a novel based on a Texas legend.

Jean Granberry Schnitz was born in Spur, Texas, on October 11, 1931. She graduated from Raymondville High School in 1948, and from Texas College of Arts and Industries (now Texas A&M University) in Kingsville in 1952. She and Lew Schnitz were married in 1953. They have three sons and four grandchildren. A retired legal secretary, she lives near Boerne. Jean served two separate terms on the Texas A&I Alumni Board. She has served on boards for several United Methodist Churches, and on the board of the Wesley Community Center in Robstown, Texas. She was President of the Nueces County Legal Secretaries Association in Corpus Christi. Since 1990, she has presented eleven papers to the Texas Folklore Society. Jean became a Director on the Board of the Texas Folklore Society in 2002, was elected Vice-President for 2005–2006, and President at the 91st annual meeting in San Antonio, Texas in 2007. She was a participant in the Texas Folklife Festival in San Antonio for her 31st year in 2012.

Craig Stripling is a fifth-generation Nacogdoches County, Texas, native. While he's a lawyer by trade, his likes are old-timey "saddling" horses, old pocketknives, hunting and cooking venison, and hearing and reading good old stories about good old times.

Ellen Temple is an independent publisher and writer, a philanthropist, and a conservationist. A graduate of the University of Texas at Austin with a B.A. degree with honors, she served as a UT Board of Regents, she is a Distinguished Alumna, and she received the Pro Bene Meritis Award from the College of Liberal Arts. She also received an M.A. degree from Stephen F. Austin State University. She was Board President of the Lady Bird Johnson Wildflower Center, the Board Chair of Humanities Texas, Board President of Angelina College, and is a former President of The Philosophical Society of Texas. She established the Liz Carpenter Award for Research in the History of Women at the Texas State Historical

Association, and the Ellen Clarke Temple Award in the Study of Women in History at the Center for Women's & Gender Studies at the University of Texas at Austin. She is married to Buddy Temple and they have four children, John, Whitney, Susie and Hannah, and six grandchildren.

Frances Brannen Vick is retired director of the University of North Texas Press and, before that, president of E-Heart Press. F. E. Abernethy edited its first book, *Built in Texas.* She holds B.A. and M.A. degrees in English from the University of Texas at Austin and Stephen F. Austin State University, respectively, and a Doctor of Humane Letters (*honoris causa*) from the University of North Texas. She received the Pro Bene Meritis award from the UT College of Liberal Arts. In retirement, she has co-authored *Petra's Legacy,* which won the Coral Horton Tullis Award for the best book on Texas history; was editor of *Literary Dallas;* and, co-authored *Letters to Alice: Birth of the Kleberg-King Ranch Dynasty.* She has written chapters for *Texas Women Writers, The Family Saga, Celebrating 100 Years, Texas Women on the Cattle Trails, Notes from Texas Writers* and recently *Her Texas.* She is a past-president of the Texas Institute of Letters, the Texas State Historical Association, The Philosophical Society of Texas, and is a Fellow of the Texas Folklore Society and the Texas State Historical Association. She and Ross Vick, Jr. have three children—Karen, Ross III and Pat—and six grandchildren and seven great-grandchildren.

Nelda Grohman Vick is from the German community of Rockne, Texas. She is a lifetime member of the Texas Folklore Society and a lifetime member of St Anne's Society, as well as a member of the Auxiliary of Daughters of Foreign Wars. She enjoys gardening and cooking.

Patrick Brannen Vick, is a seventh-generation Texan and is active in the Texas Folklore Society, of which he is a lifetime member as well as a current Board member. He is also a lifetime member of the Texas State Historical Association. He is President of the

Vick Family Foundation, a founding partner in Saron Partners (a holding company that includes investments, timber, and land in East Texas), and is a member of the Texas Forestry Association. He holds a B.A. degree in history from St. Edwards University in Austin, is a former member of the Longhorn Foundation and the Littlefield Society, and is a lifetime and founding member of the University of Texas Club. He is a former member of Trueheart, a performing group with his brother Ross and sister Karen, and still is actively recording.

Lucy Fischer-West grew up in El Paso, daughter of a Mexican mother and a German father. Her memoir, *Child of Many Rivers: Journeys to and from the Rio Grande*, was published in 2005 by Texas Tech University Press; it received a Border Regional Library Association Southwest Book Award, a WILLA Literary Finalist Award from Women Writing the West, and a Violet Crown special Citation from the Writer's League of Texas. Her essays have appeared in *BorderSenses*, *Password*, and four Texas Folklore Society publications: *The Family Saga*, *Both Sides of the Border*, *Celebrating 100 years of the Texas Folklore Society*, and *Cowboys, Cops, Killers and Ghosts*. She is featured in *The Best of Texas Folklore* Volume 2 from Writer's AudioShop, *Literary El Paso*, and *Grace and Gumption: The Women of El Paso*. A career educator, she was a finalist for the Mary Jon and J.P. Bryan Leadership in Education Award. She currently teaches world history at Cathedral High School and in 2014 was named Teacher of the Year of the El Paso Diocese. She is past-President of the Texas Folklore Society.

John W. Wilson was born November 2, 1920, near the town of Navasota in the Grimes County cattle and cotton country of East Texas. After graduating from high school in 1938, he worked as a bookkeeper in a local bank and as sports writer and editor of the local weekly newspaper. His first short story, "Us Goin' to Town," published in 1940 by *Southwest Review*, led to the publication in 1948 of his first (and only) novel, *High John the Conqueror*, by Macmillan Company. His writing career and his education were interrupted from 1943–1946 by service with the First Marine Division in the South Pacific, Okinawa and North China; and again on recall to active duty 1951–1952 in the Korean conflict. He worked from 1953–1985 for Texas Instruments Incorporated and its predecessor company, Geophysical Service, Inc., in public relations, advertising, and employee communications. Since retirement he has worked on a re-issue of *High John the Conqueror* (with an Afterword by James Ward Lee) in 1998 by Texas Christian University Press; *Engineering the World*, a 75th anniversary history of Texas Instruments; and, most recently, *Tales from Texas Past*, a collection of short stories originally published during the 1940s and 1950s, and, together with commentaries on their historic or folkloric settings, republished as a Kindle e-book in 2013. He currently resides in a retirement community in Dallas.

J. W. "Dub" Wood spent his professional career as a Petroleum Engineer, writing numerous engineering reports and editing thousands of additional geologic and engineering reports. As a hobby he likes to cook and create his own recipes, which are often simpler versions of other original recipes found in the 200-plus cookbooks in his personal cookbook library.

Jane Roberts Wood lives with her husband, Dub, (Judson W. Wood), in Argyle, Texas, with its vistas of meadows and Dutch-banded cattle, and the place where they enjoy their family and friends. Her favorite destinations are London and the drive around the Ring of Kerry in Ireland. She is currently at work on a short story called "I Know You Really Miss Her." Her previously published novels include The Train to Estelline trilogy—*The Train to Estelline, A Place Called Sweet Shrub,* and *Dance A Little Longer*—followed by *Grace, Roseborough,* and a collection of stories called *Seven Stories.*

INDEX

A

Abarca, Hugo, 351
Abarca, Meredith, 346, 347–351, 358
Abernethy, Ab, 8, 36, 39
Abernethy, Francis Edward, 36, 45
Abernethy, Hazel, 8, 39
Acosta, Maria Aurora, 61–69
Alaska Crippled Children's
    Association, 231
Allison, Sharon, 5
Ambrosia (variation), 186
Ambrosia, 184–185
American Indian recipes, 232
Andrews, Jean, 1, 288, 289–295,
    358–359
Angelina National Forest, 41
Anthony, Susan B., 35
Appell, Sherry Holland
    Dougherty, 272
Art of German Cooking, The, 232
Asian culture, 229
Atlanta Journal, 183
Attoyac Cemetery Homecoming and
    Dinner on the Ground, 51–52
Aunt Jemima, 238
Ausburn, Shirley, 142, 147

B

Baked Rice, 307
Banner Ice-cream factory, 320
Baptist traditions, 230
Baptist Vatican at Waco, 38
barbecue sauce, **Sam's Famous
    Barbecue Sauce, 18**
bar-b-ques, 301–302
Barbour, Judy, 241
BARS ranch, 330
Barton, Ann, 241

Bauman, Jon, 152
Baylor University, 38
Bean Tamales, 73
beans
    Bean Tamales, 73
    **Beans, According to J. Frank
        Dobie, 239**
    Julia's Beans, 272
    Old Settlers Beans, 153–154
**Beans, According to J. Frank
    Dobie, 239**
Bear Meat, 23–24
Bedichek, Roy, 305
Bedichek dinners, 305–311
beef
    Beef Tea, 21–22
    **Boiled and Pickled Cow's
        Tongue, 249**
    **Carne Guisada (Por Lew
        Schnitz), 84–85**
    **Corned Beef Hash and
        Eggs, 26**
    Frito Pie, 292
    German Hash, 248
    **New York Café Beef Enchiladas,
        108–109**
    Pan-Fried Steak, 31
    Recipe for Jerky, 241
    Roast a la Baboo, 271
    **Spanish Hamburger Casserole,
        77–82**
    Tamales, 69–72
    White House Hash, 311
beef jerky, 238, 339–340
    Recipe for Jerky, 241
Beef Tea, 21–22
Bennell, Julie, 231
berry picking, 5, 89, 176, 320–321
Bessmay Hotel recipes, 26–29
Best Devil's Food Cake, 167